Reprints of Economic Classics

ORIGIN

OF THE

NEW SYSTEM OF MANUFACTURE

COMMONLY CALLED

POWER-LOOM WEAVING

Z5·40p

**Books are to be returned on or before
the last date below**

LIBREX —

ORIGIN

OF THE

NEW SYSTEM OF MANUFACTURE

COMMONLY CALLED

POWER-LOOM WEAVING

FULLY EXPLAINED

IN A

NARRATIVE

CONTAINING

WILLIAM RADCLIFFE'S

STRUGGLES THROUGH LIFE

WRITTEN BY HIMSELF

[1828]

AUGUSTUS M. KELLEY • PUBLISHERS

CLIFTON *1974*

First Edition 1828

(*Stockport*: *Printed and Sold by* James Lomax,
Advertiser - Office. *Also Sold by* Messrs. Longman &
Co., *Paternoster - Row, London*; and by the Booksellers
*in Manchester, Ashton-under-Line, Bolton, Blackburn,
Chorley, Preston, Oldham, Wigan, Carlisle, Glasgow,
and Macclesfield*, 1828)

Reprinted 1974 by

Augustus M. Kelley Publishers

Clifton New Jersey 07012

Library of Congress Cataloging in Publication Data

Radcliffe, William, 1760-1841.
    Origin of the new system of manufacture
commonly called power-loom weaving.

    (Reprints of economic classics)
    Reprint of the 1828 ed. printed by J. Lomax,
Stockport.
    1. Weaving. 2. Radcliffe, William, 1760-1841.
I. Title.
TS1490.R26 1974   677'.02824'0924 [B] 68-30541
ISBN 0-678-00877-9

PRINTED IN THE UNITED STATES OF AMERICA
by SENTRY PRESS, NEW YORK, N. Y. 10013
Bound by A. HOROWITZ & SON, CLIFTON, N. J.

ORIGIN

OF THE

THE NEW SYSTEM OF MANUFACTURE,

COMMONLY CALLED

"POWER-LOOM WEAVING,"

AND THE PURPOSES
FOR WHICH THIS SYSTEM WAS INVENTED AND BROUGHT INTO USE,

FULLY EXPLAINED

IN A

NARRATIVE,

CONTAINING

WILLIAM RADCLIFFE'S STRUGGLES THROUGH LIFE

TO REMOVE THE CAUSE

WHICH HAS BROUGHT THIS COUNTRY TO ITS PRESENT CRISIS.

WRITTEN BY HIMSELF.

"It is a manifest instance of the great national advantages in trade this nation enjoys, that it hath not been ruined long ago by the consequences of our own ill management."
Essay on Trade, reprinted in Edinburgh, 1756.

"Trade has always been the best support of all nations, and the principle cause of the wisest." *Lord Chesterfield's Speech in Dublin, October* 8, 1745.

"Mr Locke in his considerations, page 86, asserts it to be an *undoubted truth,* "that he (i. e. the Landholder) is more concerned in trade, and ought to take *more care* that it be well managed than even the merchant himself; for he will certainly find, that when a decay has carried away one part of our own money out of the Kingdom, and the other kept in merchants or tradesmen's hands, that no laws he can make, nor any little arts of shifting property among ourselves, will bring it back to h m again; but his rents will fall, and his income every day lessen, till general industry and frugality, joined to a *well-ordered trade,* shall restore to the kingdom the riches and wealth it had formerly."

STOCKPORT:
PRINTED AND SOLD BY JAMES LOMAX, ADVERTISER-OFFICE.

ALSO SOLD BY MESSRS LONGMAN AND CO., PATERNOSTER-ROW, LONDON ; AND BY THE BOOKSELLERS IN MANCHESTER, ASHTON-UNDER-LINE, BOLTON, BLACKBURN, CHORLEY, PRESTON, OLDHAM, WIGAN, CARLISLE, GLASGOW, AND MACCLESFIELD.

1828.

DEDICATION.

TO THE WEAVERS, MANUFACTURERS, AND OTHERS, OF THE COTTON DISTRICTS.

Fellow Countrymen,

I here present you with some details of the " Struggles through Life" of one of yourselves, of " AN OLD MANUFACTURER," well known to many of you. They are thrown together without regard to method, according as I had documents at hand, or that memory supplied me with matter. I think you will agree with me that it is best it should be so, rather than attempt to connect or polish, and sacrifice thus my sincere. however, rudely expressed, sentiments, to a bootless search after graces of language or style, which would embarrass my meaning, and not correspond to the warmth of my feelings.

After an active life of years spent amongst you in the greatest harmony of private friendship ; after long and zealous endeavours to correct and improve what appeared to me defective in the Cotton Manufacture and the Laws which regulate it ; after having been united in that object with some of the most eminent of the trade, here, in Scotland, and the Metropolis, I have reflected that a few notices relating thereto might be interesting ; at all events, I offer them as my mite towards contributing some account of the cotton,—that immense manufacture,—which is still a desideratum even on the very soil of that country which it might have enriched the most.

I am, Fellow-Countrymen,

Your Friend and Well-wisher,

WILLIAM RADCLIFFE,

Stockport, May 3rd, 1828,

INTRODUCTION.

THE period has at length arrived when I am at liberty to report the progress I made in Parliament nine years ago, on the great national question respecting the great evil of exporting our cotton yarns, a debt I have long owed to the weavers, manufacturers, bleachers, printers, dyers, finishers, merchants, and bankers interested in the cotton trade, who so handsomely supported me by their memorial to the Prince Regent and petitions to the Honourable the House of Commons in the years 1816-17, in my application to government. But as few persons are aware of the just claims I had to take a lead in this important question, and as I may perhaps by some be thought a busybody in the business, I think myself called upon to shew the grounds on which I took so prominent a part at the period to which I allude. In performing this duty I shall at the same time give an outline of the origin and progress of the new system of manufacturing, best known under the name of *power loom weaving*, and of the cause that occasioned its introduction, in order that the motives which induced me to sink an independent fortune in perfecting this system for practical use, may be fully and correctly appreciated.

With a view to enable the public to judge whether the cotton manufacture at that time required the
aid of this new system or not, it will be necessary to
go back to the state of things prior to its first
introduction, as well as to the gloomy aspect that
lay before us at that period, which was the cause of
the trade requiring additional aid from machinery,
if it could be found. But could I have foreseen that
after the new system had shewn itself equal to work
up the surplus produce of our spindles, that the
export of cotton yarns would have been continued,
I believe I never should have made the attempt ; I
acted simply on the opinion generally expressed by
spinners, manufacturers, bleachers, printers, dyers,
and more especially by that of the merchants who
exported finished goods to the continent. Having
the means and confidence within myself that I could
find out this system so absolutely necessary to keep
so lucrative a trade in the nation, I went to work
(with the patronage and assurance hereafter mentioned) as if the protection of the manufactures and
commerce of our country had for a time been offi-
cially committed to my care ; and I confidently
appeal to every candid man who may read the following narrative, whether placing himself in my
situation at the time I commenced, he would not
have acted in the same manner.

In the performance of what I now undertake
(with my limited education) I flatter myself the
reader will readily grant me his indulgence, as regards
language and style, for as the poet says,

" He whose sole object is the people's good
Cares not to shine, so he is understood."

The narrative I am now about to publish, was
written in the years 1819 to 1822 inclusive, having
been addressed in successive letters to a monthly
club, the members of which were power-loom manu-

facturers; which club *I had formed* in 1811, with a view of conveying to the trade such practical improvements as daily experience brought out, either in the system itself, or in the teaching and management of the hands. Our works at all times were open to every member when he had any difficulty to overcome; and whenever a master spinner, instead of selling his yarns for export, had a wish to manufacture them by our patent hand-looms or by power-looms, we were equally open to him,—if he even wanted hands to set him going, we furnished him with the best we had, so long as he might require them; for this purpose we always kept one or two hands more than our business required. This liberality operated greatly against our private interests, but I shall by and by shew that I considered it no more than my duty, a national remuneration having been promised me from such high authority.

If to the changes connected with national wealth and manufactures recorded in history, and to the energies of our own nation for many centuries past, were added a true history of the rise and progress of the cotton trade both at home and abroad, and the effects it has produced by its continued improvements during the last fifty years, it would be of more value as a guide to the statesman who has to frame laws for the government of his country, than all the jargon of political economists. Food, raiment and shelter, form the only wants in life. No nation ever flourished if confined to the production of the first, and through every age of the world that people which excelled in the production of the second stands pre-eminent in history. All that has been recorded of former ages on this subject can only relate to the old system of fabricating raiment by the labour of the hands, a species of industry that has at length given way before the magical power of machinery, which subjects wool, linen, silk and cotton to illimitable production by mechanical agency that consumes no bread. Of these cotton has attained a decided pre-eminence over every other substance, whether animal or vegetable, and by the magnitude of its manufacture, must now justly rank as the staple trade of this kingdom. By a necessary consequence the fluctuations of this gigantic manufacture naturally tend to raise or depress not merely every other species of manufacture, but even the whole property of the kingdom which is at all times more or less affected by the prosperity or depression of the cotton trade.

It is to be regretted, that amongst the various publications which deluge this country, no authentic detail has yet been given of a trade, which, while it produces abundant wealth to one class of persons who have embarked in it, has brought total ruin to another class by whose personal labour they have been enriched—for from such detail alone can the statesman derive that knowledge whereby he might frame protecting laws congenial with existing circumstances. It is unhappily now too late to enquire whether the remarkable change effected by the cotton trade in our manufacturing population is for the better or otherwise; it nevertheless is consolatory to know that the evils of the present system are not absolutely irremediable, and that it only requires that they should be properly understood by those to whom the welfare of the State is confided, to enable them to give appropriate protection to a manufacture of such acknowledged importance, and the very numerous population whose existence depend on its prosperity. In the reign of Elizabeth, spinning, one of the most ancient arts of social life, was rendered obligatory on every parish. One of the earliest Acts of Parliament for regulating our poor, enjoined all overseers to employ those who received relief, in spinning, for which purpose they are authorized to purchase wool and flax out of monies raised by a rate on the parishioners. The quantity of yarn, especially woollen, produced under this regulation was immense—but in place of following up the system of industry so *judiciously* introduced, and *weaving* the yarn so spun—the Flemings were permitted to export the greater part to Flanders, from whence it was returned to this country in the shape of cloth. The whole of the productive labour on the weaving, and other processes of the finished manufacture, and the commerce emanating from it, were thus lost to the country. Time, however, opened the eyes of our statesmen, who having at length discovered the value of the English fleece, by wise restrictions, and salutary encouragement, for many years held a monopoly of what, until the cotton trade arose, was justly considered the most valuable and extensive of any manufacture yet known in society. Possessing a raw material of surpassing quality, it was the natural and obvious policy of the state not to suffer so inestimable a product to pass into the hands of the foreigners, until it had received the last effort of human ingenuity and labour, fitting it for consumption. On this principle successive laws were passed, prohibiting the export of the wool, whether in the fleece or in yarn, or in fact, in any other state than that of manufactured cloth or stuff, under penalties of peculiar rigour and severity. The policy of manufacturing our yarns into woollen cloth, does not appear to have been fully understood until the reign of William and Mary. That Prince and Princess were accompanied from Holland by persons of sound judgment, who convinced the people of this country that their interests, as regarded commercial polity, had been grossly misunderstood. It is indeed true, that but little progress was made in the restrictive system during that reign; but it laid the solid foundation of that system—the little that was done, was found to work so well, that it was followed up by every parliament until the commencement of the reign of George the Third, at which period the restrictive system was finally established. It was at this period, (and I beg the reader to bear it in mind) that spinning by machinery commenced, and with this began the competition between hand labour and mechanical operations, impelled in the first instance by water power and subsequently by that of the steam engine. Spinning machinery, as was inevitable, has long since extinguished the old system of hand-spinning. The industrious spinsters were finally deprived of their domestic and useful occupation, and the hand wheels which had found a place in every cottage and farm-house, thenceforth became useless.

But for the reason before mentioned, I must not attempt to write the history so much wanted, I will proceed to narrate such parts as concern myself, and rest content with occasionally recording some particulars that may hereafter be of use to the historian.

NARRATIVE.

As some persons may have the curiosity to ask from whence the narrator of his own struggles through life proceeds, I will in the first place answer that question by a brief sketch of my pedigree, beyond which, (and for the authority of this sketch) I refer to the records in the college of arms.

My great great grandfather, George Radcliffe, Esq., of Mellor Hall, and owner of nearly all the township of Mellor, with great part of Whitle Hamlet, &c., was slain in the Churchgate of Stockport, in 1644, in a contest with the Roundheads, as recorded in the Stockport register. The principal part of his estates was seized by the Cromwellites, leaving only to his family a few small farms, on one of which, Podmore, my father, was born. The principal estates being gone from the family, my father resorted to the common but never-failing resource for subsistence at that period, viz.—the loom for men, and the cards and hand-wheel for women and boys. He married a spinster, (in my etymology of the word) and my mother taught me (while too young to weave) to earn my bread by carding and spinning cotton, winding linen or cotton weft for my father and elder brothers at the loom, until I became of sufficient age and strength for my father to put me into a loom. After the practical experience of a few years, any young man who was industrious and careful, might then from his earnings as a weaver, lay by sufficient to set him up as a manufacturer, and though but few of the great body of weavers had the courage to embark in the attempt, I was one of those few. Availing myself of the improvements that came out while I was in my teens, by the time I was married, (at the age of 24, in 1785,) with my little savings, and a practical knowledge of every process from the cotton-bag to the piece of cloth, such as carding by hand or by the engine, spinning by the hand-wheel or jenny, winding, warping, sizing, looming the web, and weaving either by hand or fly-shuttle, I was ready to commence business for myself; and by the year 1789, I was well established, and employed many hands both in spinning and weaving, as a master manufacturer.

From 1789 to 1794, my chief business was the sale of muslin warps, sized and ready for the loom, (being the first who sold cotton twist in that state, chiefly to Mr Oldknow, the father of the muslin trade in our country.) Some warps I sent to Glasgow and Paisley. I also manufactured a few muslins myself, and had a warehouse in Manchester for my general business. In the spring of the year 1794, two gentlemen, one from Berlin, the other from Copenhagen, occasionally bought a few muslins from me. In the summer they called upon me in Mellor, when finding I also sold cotton yarns, they were very pressing to buy from me, either in the cop, hank, or warp, to send over to the Continent to manufacture themselves.—This offer I declined, (with inward disdain,) resolving not to sell to a foreigner in any shape, except as in the woollen trade, ready for cutting up by the milliner, mantua-maker, or tailor. Nor at that time did I suppose it legal to export yarns, and in fact, urged this as my objection. To this they answered by informing me that it was not unlawful, as they were at that time buying yarns in Manchester, which they shipped off at Hull, without any impediment. But although at the time I should have been glad of an order from any English or Scotch manufacturer, at a lower price than they offered to give me, I declined their offer of purchasing yarn from me. From this period to 1800, though I never did sell either those gentlemen, or any other foreigner, a pound of yarn, yet I saw with inward grief this most impolitic and undermining traffic of selling our raw material to continental customers, instead of piece-goods, increasing every year. The consequences became at length so glaring, that the manufacturers, bleachers, dyers, printers, and merchants, alarmed at the future prospects of our trade, called a public meeting in Manchester, on the 22nd April, 1800, when amongst other resolutions they unanimously passed the following:—" Resolved, that the exportation of cotton " twist is highly injurious to the manufactures of " this country, and unless some means are speedily " adopted to restrict the exportation under certain " regulations, will ultimately end in the destruction " of the cotton manufacture of the kingdom."— Another meeting was called on the 29th, when after passing strong resolutions to the same purport, a committee was formed of the following gentlemen to follow up their views in this business, viz.—

THOMAS RICHARDSON, Esq.
PETER CROMPTON, Ero.
———— SILVESTER, Esq.
LEIGH PHILIPS, Esq.
———— GARDINER, Esq.
JAMES OLIVANT, Esq.
THOMAS SLATER, Esq.
ROGER HOLLAND, Esq.
WILLIAM LEAF, Esq.
JAMES DERBYSHIRE, Esq.
THOMAS DARWELL, Esq.
RICHARD RUSHFORTH, Esq.
JAMES WARDLE, Esq.
ROBERT PARKER, Esq.

NATHANIEL GOULD, Esq.
JOHN PARKER, Esq.
THOMAS POTTER, Esq.
JOHN RAILTON, Esq.
CHARLES HORSFALL, Esq.
BOLD COOK, Esq.
———— LOCK, Esq.
LAWRENCE PEEL, Esq.
ROBERT PEEL, Jun., Esq.
SAMUEL SMITH, Esq.
———— KERSLEY, Esq.
JAMES HIBBERT, Esq.
JOSEPH SEDDON, Esq.
THOMAS AINSWORTH, Esq.

12

SAMUEL TAYLOR, Esq.
JOHN HEYWOOD, Esq.
H. FARRINGTON, Esq.
WILLIAM STARKEY, Esq.
JOHN TETLOW, Esq.

THOMAS BELCHER, Esq.
JAMES HALL, Esq.
AND
THOMAS SCHOLES, Esq.

Amongst other proceedings of this committee, they stated their case to government in a memorial to the lords of the treasury, signed by the first houses in the trade. But what most immediately concerns myself, was their secretary addressing a letter to the manufacturers of Stockport and its vicinity, to solicit their aid in following up the question during that Session of Parliament. On receipt of this letter a meeting was held at the Castle Inn, to take the subject of it into consideration, and which was attended by all the trade in Stockport and the neighbourhood. The letter being read, the subject was fully and deliberately discussed in all its bearings. The parties present were unanimous in wishing to co-operate with the Manchester gentlemen if the object could be effected without injuring the spinners who had sunk so much property in mills and machinery. It was at that time impossible to get more weavers than were then employed, although many descriptions of goods, printing cambrics in particular (which I was the first to make under that name) were in such demand that any quantity might be sold. In this discussion, on comparing notes, we found there was not a village within thirty miles of Manchester, on the Cheshire and Derbyshire side, in which some of us were not putting out cotton warps, and taking in goods, employing all the weavers of woollen and linen goods who were declining those fabrics as the cotton trade increased; in short, we employed every person in cotton weaving who could be induced to learn the trade. But want of *population*, want of *hands*, and want of *looms*, set us fast on the subject upon which we were then assembled. In this forlorn situation, I remarked that from practical experience I had for some time past been of opinion, that with the same hands now employed in weaving, we might, by a division of labour and the invention of some plan or other in a straight forward process, something like the carding, &c., introduced by Sir Richard Arkwright in spinning, instead of the present mode of warping, sizing, dressing, &c., by which they would be able to produce more work than we then got from them ; and as young hands would be more easily taught, we might ere long be able to consume all the surplus yarns at that time spun for export. Having confidence in what I stated, I pledged myself to the meeting that I would devote my best attention to these improvements, on *condition* that if I succeeded, the gentlemen present would pledge themselves on some future occasion to join the Manchester gentlemen in following up the question to a prohibition of the export of cotton twist, and this pledge they all gave. Here then is the *origin* and *foundation* of the new system of warping, sizing, dressing, drying, winding on to the beam, drawing and twisting-in, spinning pin cops for the shuttle, inventing shuttles to receive them, (all original), and, to complete the whole, a new loom (half the size of the old ones) taking its cloth up by every motion of the lathe, which loom was solely intended for every cottager in the United Kingdom, who depends on the labour of the loom to work up the surplus yarns. And I beg every person interested in the benefits that have resulted from it, or in the losses it has and may occasion, so long as the pledge is unredeemed, will bear this in mind, that but for the occasion which called this meeting at the Castle Inn, and the mutual pledge then given, in all probability the new system had never been known. As this meeting took place in the evening, a further pledge was given me in the following toast, in bumpers of generous wine, viz.—" *The shuttle of the United Kingdom, and may it very soon consume ALL the produce of the British spindle."*

If it is objected that this pledge is only that of a single town or district, and cannot be binding upon the other districts of the trade, I grant the objection is well founded, but if in the course of my narrative I succeed in proving that with not more than five to ten exceptions of spinners for export (to whom out of delicacy the pledge was not asked for,) that all the leading spinners, manufacturers, &c. in England and Scotland, and the few from Ireland who visited us during the period of our probation, fully and heartily coincided in my ulterior views, pledging themselves that when the new system was sufficiently established, to convince the trade of its capability to work up the surplus yarns, (which was the case) I think every impartial man will allow that I am justified in saying that the trade stands pledged to come forward and assist me in my ulterior object, as well as to support me in my applications for national remuneration for the fortune I sunk in establishing the system.

About nine months prior to this meeting in Stockport, my concern having been so extended, (and residing at my works, 14 miles from Manchester, in which town I also had a warehouse), I had taken a Mr Ross into partnership, in order to be relieved from attending the sales and correspondence. But having since our connection, brought this part of our business to a new mart just then established in Stockport, called the Muslin Hall, we both attended the meeting before mentioned, and on our way home in the evening we had a conversation on the subject of a new process of manufacture.—Mr Ross theoretically differed in opinion from me, as to restrictions on trade, and though he could see nothing of my ultimate motive, yet he cordially agreed with me, that if we could devise some plan to make printing cambrics in quantity, there could be no risk of its doing well for the concern, and here the *seeds of the new system* lay slumbering (but not forgotten for a day) for more than twelve months.

At Midsummer, 1801, on taking stock very accurately, we found we had upwards of £11,000 in our concern ; I had also a landed estate in Mellor, in which was comprehended Podmore, where my father was born, with a rent roll, and good tenants of upwards of £350 per annum, charged with about £1,800 on mortgage. Mr Ross's father was a merchant and magistrate in Montrose, and rich, and my partner being an only son, could at any time lend us a few thousands, which he afterwards did to the amount of £6,000, including the £2,500 paid down on the formation of our partnership.—With this real capital—an unlimited credit, (£5,000 with our bankers amongst the rest), an excellent trade, and every prospect of its continuing so for a time, we came to the conclusion of purchasing the premises in the Hillgate, from Mr Oldknow and Mr Arkwright, then standing empty, which I never should have thought of for a moment, but from what had passed at the Castle Inn, for the sole purpose of filling them with looms, &c., on some new plan, and just so much spinning machinery as would supply the looms with weft. But beyond the common warping, sizing, weaving, &c., all was a chaos before me ; yet so confident was I, that with such assistance as I could call in, we should succeed, that before I began I laid a trifling wager with my partner, that in two years from the time I commenced, I produced 500 pieces of 7-8th's and 9-8th's printing cambrics, all wove in the building in one week by some *new process*, which I won easily. And as the price for weaving alone when we began was 17s per piece, and had never been below 16s at any time, we thought we were justified in what we were doing, even if little improvement

could be found. And if the goods made abroad
from the annually increasing export of twist, and
their prohibitions of our goods in consequence, had
not gradually reduced this price of weaving from
17s (with a profit of 10 to 20 per cent. to the master,)
to 4s to the weaver (and no profit to the master!)
we should have been handsomely rewarded by
our trade. But to return from this digression, we
concluded our contract about Michaelmas with
Messrs. Oldknow and Arkwright, for the premises above mentioned; and I brought my family
to Stockport in the latter end of Dec. 1801. I must
here observe that we had at that time a large concern
in Mellor, that with its various branches for putting
out work, employing upwards of 1000 weavers,
widely spread over the borders of three counties, in
a vast variety of plain and fancy goods, * all of
which had been raised (like a gathering snow ball)
from a single spindle, or single loom by myself, and
was then upon such a system as apparently might
go on without my personal attention. Hence when
I sat down in Stockport, and gave the sole management of the old concern to my partner, (at such a
critical time as the political change in the states of
Europe created) that my attention might not be
drawn from the new system I was going to commence.
Events proved that this was no small sacrifice to
myself, my partner, and my family; when in the
prime of life (40) I took away the main spring that
had raised and conducted this concern to its present
pitch of independence, with the fairest prospects of
future success. And what was a source of the greatest
consolation to me at the time, was, that in forming

* Suited to the taste of the merchants who frequented the fairs
of Leipzic, &c., in cavalcade, like a caravan in Arabia, from the
various provinces of Greece, Russia, Tartary, &c., up to the north of
China, which trade we have now lost by furnishing the intermediate
States with the *raw material,* from which their goods were made.

this small, though independent capital, in ten or twelve years, with a large family of young children, under many local disadvantages, such as distance from market, small streams of water for turning machinery, &c., I can truly say that it had not been got by "grinding the face of the poor;" for my greatest pride was to see them comfortable; and in every transaction with them, my equals and superiors, " I did by each, as I would they should have done to me," and I challenge enquiry in the circle I moved in, that no fact can be found to contradict what I have said; and I give the same challenge as to any deviation from this principle to the present day. These remarks to some may seem uncalled for, but should they come before two or three persons I have in my eye, *they* will understand what I mean. While in self-defence I am driven into this disagreeable subject of speaking of myself, it may not be amiss to state how I stood in public estimation before I left Mellor, and afterwards since I came to Stockport.

During my last ten years in Mellor, it was well known that I was the most active person in the township in all public improvements, amongst which repairing and diverting roads might be said to be my hobby. I was, unsolicited, made a trustee on three distinct commissions; on one of them I contracted to make about two miles, half a mile of which was a new line altogether, over a most intricate valley, requiring an elevated stone bridge over a small brook. I finished the whole just before I left, entirely on what is now called Mc Adam's plan, and the best he ever showed has not surpassed it; this I did not undertake for profit, the funds were low, and if I had not done it, it might have remained to this day as it was. Had I remained in Mellor, the magistrates in the High Peak Hundred had fixed upon me as the person they intended to recommend

18

to the Lord Lieutenant as a magistrate for that division on my retiring from business, which I intended when I took a partner.

In less than four years from my coming to Stockport, I had been a commissioner of the property tax, and regularly took my seat at the board. The Fourth Class of Volunteers being called for in 1803, while Buonaparte lay at Boulogne and was expected to cross the channel at every tide, I was persuaded to come out with them, and by a large majority of the principal inhabitants of the town, was appointed Captain Commandant over two companies, amounting to about 180 men. To the duties of this office I attended as long as the occasion required. In 1804, I was appointed (while on my visit in Glasgow) to be Mayor for the year ensuing, and Lord and Lady Bulkeley, as a mark of their opinion of me as a disinterested public man, presented me with a gold chain for the occasion, no chain having been worn by my predecessors. From the specimen I had shewn in Mellor of road making, on the first opportunity that occurred after I came to Stockport, I was appointed a commissioner on the Buxton and Manchester Road. As this happened at the time I began to be embarrassed by the great sums sunk in establishing the new system, I, beginning to doubt my qualification, did not take my seat at the board. Just after I had gone through the Gazette, on the parish going to Parliament for an Act to re-build St. Mary's Church, I was named in the bill as a trustee, and regularly attended the board for years; and those who are satisfied that the organ and ring of bells are more consistent with this noble structure, than a box of whistles, and a light peal of bells, fit only for a chapel of ease or a village, are indebted to me for what they possess.

To return from this unpleasant digression, as the new system is now fully introduced into the

trade, and will go on at all hazards, whether for good
or evil—the former to a certainty, (after the pledge
is redeemed) beyond any precedent, but without
this I fear it will do much harm to that class, *the
poor weavers and their masters, whom it was intended
to serve!* However, as I am only accountable to my
country, on the *conditions* on which I undertook it,
and not doubting but that the eyes of the trade will
be sufficiently opened, (by events that are coming)
to bring them forward as with one voice to redeem
their pledge, I will now detail facts as they occurred,
which will shew to whom the country is indebted
for its introduction, and the reasons, which, in my
opinion, called for it, and if it is at present, or ever
should, become like a mine of great value to individuals or the nation, I can assure them it was not
stumbled upon by accident, or the result of a first
thought, nor from any view of popularity or private
interest; it was only come at from the absolute
necessity of it at the time, in a national point of
view, to protect our " ships, colonies, and commerce,"
and our nation from that ruin predicted by the late
Mr John Entwistle if the export of twist was continued!—and this prediction coming from not only
the greatest merchant in Manchester, but decidedly
the most industrious and clever tradesman in the
town, urged me at all hazards to undertake it, especially as the spinners made this the only condition
on which they would consent to a prohibitory law
similar to that of the woollen trade, viz. " *if some
system could be found to consume it all at home,*" and
although many had tried, and others were attempting, to find this philosopher's stone, without the
slightest success, yet I believe it existed, but at what
depth no one knew, nor what labour, anxiety, perseverance, or *expence* it would require to come at it
with effect, no one could tell. However, remembering my pledge, and confident that the system was

to be found, I shut myself up (as it were) in the mill on the 2nd Jan. 1802, and with joiners, turners, filers, &c. &c. set to work; my first step was some looms in the common way in every respect, which I knew would produce the cloth so much wanted, and in some degree cover our weekly expences.

Before the end of the month I began to divide the labour of the weavers, employing one room to dress the whole web, in a small frame for the purpose, ready for the looms in another room, so that the young weaver had nothing to learn but to weave ; and we found this a great improvement, for besides the advantage of learning a young weaver in a few days, we found that by weaving the web as it were back again, the weft was driven up by the reed the way the brushes had laid the fibres down with the paste, so that we could make good cloth in the upper rooms with the dressed yarn quite dry, which could not be done in the old way of dressing, when the weft was drove up against the points of the fibres, which shewed us the *reason* why all weavers are *obliged* to work in *damp cellars*, and must weave up their dressing, about a yard long, before the yarn becomes dry, or it spoils.

This accomplished, I told my men I must have some motion attached to either traddles or the lathe, by machinery, that would take up the cloth as it was wove, so that the shed might always be of the same dimensions, and of course the blow of the lathe always moving the same distance, would make the cloth more even than could possibly be done in the old way, except by very skilful and careful weavers.

Amongst my old weavers I had a very respectable elderly man, residing in Bredbury, who with his family had worked for me many years, of the name of Thos. Johnson. He had a son whom I knew to be more ingenious about his loom, than fond of close working. One day about this period, the

father bringing in their work, I had a conversation
with him respecting his son, whom I engaged to take
into our work, and employ in a line most agreeable
to his taste. He came, and I told him what I
had told the other men from the first, viz. that
before we had done, we must complete a system
similar to the carding and drawing in the spinning
line, but the first thing he must attend to was the
motion I have before described, for taking up the
cloth as it was wove. For this, as in every step
afterwards, he suggested many plans before I would
be at the expence of trying any one ; for having been
a practical weaver, I flattered myself to be a judge
of what *might do*, and *what would not*, and to this I
attribute our success in the end, as I never allowed
our mechanics to go to work on any plan that, when
tried, was not an improvement upon what had gone
before.

This motion to the loom being at length accomplished to our satisfaction, I set Johnson to plan for
the warping and dressing, suggesting several ideas
myself. His uncommon genius led him to propose
many things to me, but I pointed out objections to
them all, and set him to work again. His mind was
so teased with difficulties, that he began to relieve
it by drinking for several days together, (to which he
was too much addicted) but for this I never upbraided
him, or deducted his wages for the time, knowing that
we were approaching our object ; at length we brought
out the present plan, only that the undressed yarn
was all on one side, and the brush to be applied was
first by hand, then by a cylinder, and lastly the
crank motion. At last we set to work, but the difficulties, expence, and loss in the warping part
were immense, such as in turning back when a
thread broke, laying the threads of full bobbins,
which run easy, even with other threads, from
bobbins nearly empty, that had more friction,

&c.—to keep the diameter of yarn on each end the beam equal, &c., were such as no one will credit, now he sees the system complete. Then, again, with all these imperfections in this process, and when the beams were put in the machine all on one side, the yarn crowded in the brushes, and while piecing up a thread, the paste in the yarn not dressed, all going dry, and the hands all being to be taught, &c., we got into such a dilemma, that *every man I had about me* gave up all as lost!—In this situation, Edmund Partington, my foreman over all; Thomas Johnson, my conjuror, (as he was called in the works, his room being locked up;) Daniel Wild, foreman of mechanics; and Samuel Wild, foreman of weavers;—the four men I had to execute my plans, held a private consultation together, when they each came to the conclusion which I have before stated,—that all was lost!!!—and deputed Edmund Partington and Thomas Johnson, to wait upon me to inform me of such conclusion, with their advice to give up spending more money in so fruitless an attempt.

I listened to all they had to say, as to the difficulties which to them at the time were insurmountable, but relieved their minds considerably by examining their difficulties in detail, and at length, in some measure, convinced them that they consisted chiefly in the prejudice and inexperience of the hands. Although, if viewed in the gross, they might appear insurmountable; yet when encountered severally, I told them they would all be got over. I then requested them to point out that part of the system which they thought the most insurmountable, and that if I got over that difficulty, they would engage to get over the minor ones.—To this they all agreed.—When in less than an hour, *with my own hands*, I shewed them that the particular part of the machinery which they wished to throw aside, would not only answer, but become an essential part of the system:—this raised their spirits, and induced them to persevere in the good cause, as we called it, (remembering my pledge,) and we soon got to see our way more clearly, but it was only by dividing the warp, say half the dry beams on one side, and half on the other, so as to have the yarn thin in the brushés, that this *noiseless* simple DRESSING-MACHINE, which, when the pledge is redeemed, might annually redeem *twenty-five millions sterling*, of our national debt, or lodge it in the purse of John Bull, to be ready when called for, which is the same thing, became complete. But the difficulties and expence attending it, simple as it now appears, can only be appreciated by those who witnessed or experienced them at the time.

We had now been nearly two years at work, all our hands, warpers, dressers, weavers, &c. (3 to 400,) had been hired at weekly wages, and owing to the great fall in the price of weaving, I think from 17s. to 10s. 6d., in a very short time, (besides our usual liberal profits as manufacturers, cut up by foreign cheap labour on the twist they had from us,) it appeared, on making an estimate, that we found we had been sinking £70 weekly, for many weeks, before we could get our hands upon piece-work. But we had too deeply embarked to think of retreating ; and had I desisted at this trying point, there would not have been a power-loom at work this day in the kingdom, if we may credit what several gentlemen, who had visited us at various periods of our probation, have since said, when they saw us fairly afloat, and sailing away on the *system now working*, they were all unanimous in this remark :—"Well, Radcliffe, this does you credit, as there is not a man in the kingdom would have got over the difficulties you have done, except yourself."—In the number of these gentlemen, were Sir Robert Peel, Bart., M. P.; the late John Horrocks, Esq. M. P.; Kirkman Finlay, Esq. M. P.; and the late Robert Parker, Esq.

By this time (Jan. 1804) we had taken out three patents, two for the taking-up of the cloth by the motion of the lathe, and the other for the new mode of warping and dressing with the dry yarn all on one side; and as we had accomplished this great improvement by dividing the yarn as before mentioned, and found it so very satisfactory and complete, I was advised by Sir Robert Peel to secure it by another patent, assigning as his reason for this advice, that there might be no ground for disputing my right to any part of the system when any application might be made to Government to purchase the whole for the use of the trade at large. On his first visit, (when we were dressing the webs by hand in one room, and weaving them in another) I told Sir Robert what I expected to accomplish before I had done with it. After expressing great doubts of my success, Sir Robert added, "that if I should succeed and bring out a system by "which the surplus yarns might be worked up in this "country, Government ought to give me a million "of money!" Under this advice I took out a fourth patent; but before I proceed further, I must describe the principle and grounds on which I took out all our patents, with a view to show that our laws as regard patents might be improved.

In Dec. 1802, when I was preparing for the first patent, my partner returned from the Continent, where he had been since July, with a great assortment of the fine fancy goods I have before described. He had visited the fairs of Frankfort on the Maine, and Leipsic, in order to dispose of these goods, and to form connections for the great stock we had on

hand, and weekly accumulation from 1000 weavers. *
On his return from Frankfort and Leipsic, where he
had been already unsuccessful in his endeavours to
effect sales, Mr Ross called at Berlin on a manufacturer of cotton goods, who was also spinning a little,
to whom he had a letter of introduction. Mr Ross
found this gentleman intently poring over the
Repertory of Arts (just received from London), containing the specification of Anthony Bowden's
machine for *batting cotton*, from the specification and
drawing of which he had constructed one, and was
then setting it to work. The reader may judge how
I was shocked at the idea of taking out patents
which precluded all my neighbours for 14 years from
using my inventions, while *our rivals* at Berlin and
every part of the Continent might fall to work upon

* This accumulation came suddenly upon us in consequence of
the peace just concluded; for although our old customers still came
over as usual, they now came to purchase the raw material instead of
manufactured goods.—Hence we were caught in the way our farmers
are at this time (1822) with their heavy stocks of corn.—Our stock at
that time, in the hands of the weavers, in the grey state, at the
bleachers', in the finished state in the Muslin¦Hall, and in London,
could not be less than £40,000; and although these goods were not
made to order, yet we had as certain a market for them as any farmer
in the kingdom, in the year 1820, had for his wheat when laying down
his land in the autumn of that year, for the harvest of 1821.—We
made the best retreat we could with the loss of £10,000 ;—lessening the
number of our weavers, as any of them could get work elsewhere, and
reducing the wages of those that remained. I hope our farmers will be
able to stand foreign competition in producing food, better than we did
in that of raiment!—Practical men, with a little of the old school in
them, will appreciate these brief remarks.—Political economists of the
modern school, (while they legislate *solely* for the interest of the foreign
loom, and foreign plough,) will say we over-traded, speculated, &c.;
which is all very true, as regards the interest of our rivals abroad, but
not so as regards the " ships, colonies, and commerce" of our country.—The farmer, when his *own market* is glutted with foreign corn,
brought here *solely* through the influence of the exporters of cotton-
twist, (a raw material, according to a Special Act of Parliament,) are
also told they grow too much! They ought to throw their inferior soils
out of cultivation, &c. How long such a metaphysical doctrine as this
can sway a nation like ours, time only can decide ! ! !

them immediately, with impunity! To provide
against this, I consulted our solicitor, Mr Dale,
and the remedy he suggested was to get an Act of
Parliament to lodge the specification under seal for
14 years. On this I advised with Mr John Peel, of
Burton, requesting him to confer with his brother,
Sir Robert Peel, on the subject; but Mr John Peel
dissuaded me from this, by reason of the trouble and
expence that would attend it. I again consulted Mr
Dale. when he suggested that I should take it out
in the name of one of our men, and we fixed upon
Thomas Johnson who had shewn such extraordinary
talent in executing my designs, the patent right
being nevertheless to be secured to us as if taken
out in my name. This plan I adopted, taking out
the patents in the name of Thomas Johnson, afterwards paying him a consideration of £50. (as per
deed), besides the two guineas per week wages,
which he had from nearly the first of his coming
to us.

When taking out the different patents, I waited
on Mr Wyat, the Editor of the Repertory of Arts,
and prevailed upon him not to publish any of my
specifications, at the same time giving him my
reasons for so doing.—By these precautions, I kept
them secret to the end, for though many foreigners
searched at the petty bag office, they had no clue to
any name besides that of Radcliffe or Ross, and it
is only by the name of the patentee that any search
can be made; my motive for all this was solely to
prevent our rivals abroad getting for a *shilling* what
had cost us a *fortune;* for all the trade know that I
was liberal to the extreme in shewing every thing to
my neighbours, or natives of the United Kingdom,
(my eye, like the needle to the pole, always fixed to
the mutual pledge)—one instance of this liberality I
will record. When Mr Higginbotham and Mr Horrocks of our town, were first engaged in making

their power loom. They both called upon me one day, and stated that their only difficulty lay in the imperfect mode attending every plan, either in England or Scotland, of taking up the cloth regularly as it was woven. This conversation took place as we were walking in the garden. I told them if they would go with me into our mill, I thought I could remove this difficulty; they went with me into a room we called the horse-walk, where I shewed them our plan of taking up the cloth in our hand-loom, as before mentioned, by the motion of the lathe. Mr Horrocks, on his knee, examined it carefully, and when he rose up, thanked me kindly, saying he was now satisfied. On returning home he applied it to his loom, and this movement formed the *only* new point in *his patent*. A reference to the two respective looms, and the date and specifications of the two patents, will confirm my assertion on the question; and I record it without fear of contradiction. This movement made Mr Horrocks' loom so complete, that when he had taken out his patent, Mr John Peel, of Burton, engaged all his looms from him, and as he wished Mr Horrocks to make his warping and dressing machines also, Mr Peel agreed with me for the patent right, and paid us £200. down on our signing his licence, which had been drawn up by his own solicitor; and as Mr Peel was privy to the intention of his brother, Sir Robert, respecting the application to Government, a condition was inserted, that we were to return the £200. when the sale to the public was effected.

Mr Horrocks, about the same time, bargained with me also for liberty to make dressing machines for others, with some improvements, as he called them, of his own, for which he was to pay me £20. a machine for all he set up; and besides some payments we received, we proved on his estate for about £170. for premiums under this contract. Mr H.

and my neighbours will know *why* I record these particulars ! ! !

After we had taken out our last patent in the spring of 1804, for the improvement before mentioned, we went on, not only to our own satisfaction, but to that of all the principal persons in the trade who visited us, and I may say the first houses in England and Scotland did so ; and amongst those who expressed a desire to introduce our plan into their works, I will mention a few who either got their machinery from us or made it themselves, paying us the patent right, viz. Sir Robert Peel's House, at Tamworth— Messrs. Jno. Peel and Co., Burton—Messrs. Strutts, Derby—Messrs. Daintry, Ryle, & Co., Macclesfield— Messrs. Watson & Co., Preston—Messrs. Holland, Dixon, & Co., Bolton—and many others, no one directly or indirectly *ever questioning* the entire originality of *every* part of the whole system. In order to shew the intelligent manufacturers of Scotland, who have always taken such a lead in this gigantic *cotton trade*, that there was now a system completed, whereby the surplus yarn might be worked up in the United Kingdom, instead of exporting it to our foreign commercial rivals, I went down to Glasgow in the autumn of 1804, Mr Richard Ainsworth, of Halliwell, and Mr John Railton accompanying me, having, on this visit, arranged with Mr John Monteith to give our system a trial. On my return home, I sent T. Johnson down with a set complete of warping and dressing machinery, the beams filled with twist ready for dressing, &c. There was, as usual, some prejudice to contend with ; but instead of patiently shewing how to work the system as he had left it with us, Johnson's taste for improving led him to leave Mr Monteith before he had shewn the hands how to work it, by which he nearly upset every thing we had attempted. Of this unfortunate result we had sufficient evidence from his proceedings at Mr Sheriff's, in Glasgow, (to whom he had gone without my knowledge,) and at Messrs. Watson and Co's., in Preston, where I had ordered him to stay a while on his return, at which concerns he had had his full scope of trying all the schemes, or whims, I had rejected, as before mentioned. After much labour, and an expence of many thousands, our system, *so simple in itself*, was rendered so complex at these concerns, that neither himself nor any other could understand or work them, (here lies the cause, why, to this day, Glasgow is not able to make a piece of shirting that can stand a comparison with those of our neighbourhood.) These facts sufficiently confirm my statements, if any thing more is wanted, as to whom the country is solely indebted for the new system.

I think it unnecessary to say more, in order to make out my claim to the invention of this new system, as well as to the taking-up of the cloth as it is woven, either in the hand or power loom, by the motion of the lathe; or to the patriotic motives *(though I say it)* which led me to enter upon the undertaking, and to persevere to its final accomplishment under the losses occasioned by the sudden and great fall in the price of weaving, and the cloth when wove.

The want of two papers, which I had mislaid, prevented me from stating in regular course the unexpected, voluntary, and prompt manner in which my views were taken up and acted upon, *(unfortunately rather prematurely*, he not having first consulted Sir Robt. Peel) by the greatest manufacturer of the age, who, had his life been spared to have followed up this question, would have been, as a commercial Statesman, of inestimable value to his country. In the autumn of 1802, long before our system was complete, the late Mr Horrocks, of Preston, came over with Mr Bateman, of Manchester, they spent

some hours in our works, when I explained to Mr
Horrocks what had passed between Sir Robert Peel
and me, and my ulterior object, viz. to bring out a
system whereby the surplus yarns, produced for
exportation, might be worked up at home with advantage, and at once extinguish the unnatural competition that we had ourselves created in the markets
abroad. I was particular in shewing them our small
neat hand-looms, with the simple motion, attaching
the lathe to the cloth beam, which, by only two
small wheels, regularly takes up the cloth. I
further stated, that though at that time I was obliged
to bring such a number of boys and girls into the
factory to work the looms, yet, when the hands had
been taught to work them, it was my intention to
disperse all these looms into the cottages of the
weavers throughout the country, in lots, proportioned
to the number of children in the families, delivering
them the warps dressed and prepared ready for
weaving off the beam, and their weft in *cops* ready
for the shuttle, without previous winding, &c.
These gentlemen expressed their entire satisfaction
with my views on this subject, Mr Horrocks adding,
"I see your system will answer, and you only want
time to teach your hands to work it." This was all
that passed between us, (except some remarks Mr
Horrocks made to Mr Bateman, the great iron-mas-
ter, as to the extensive demand this new system
would create for articles in his line,) ※ until the

* 1827—A firm in Lancashire, a few years ago, built a mill
expressly for this new system of manufacture, of course including room
and power for spinning the yarns necessary. On looking through their
mill, I put the following question to the active partner,—"How many
tons of iron, in round numbers, do you suppose you will require for the
building, steam-engine, shafting, and machinery, to complete the
whole?" He answered, "200 tons at least." When complete it will con-
tain about 500 looms, and taking the mill as one hundredth part of
the trade, in which I am under the mark, 20,000 tons have already
been taken by this trade, with bricks, timber, &c. &c. &c. in proportion, for manufacturing only.

March following, when I received a letter from Mr
Horrocks, inviting me to come down to Preston and
spend a day or two with him at Penwortham Lodge.
On my arrival, to my great surprise, I found him
preparing to bring the question immediately before
Parliament, in consequence of the great encouragement he had received from Lord Sidmouth, then
Chancellor of the Exchequer, in some interviews which
he had had with his lordship on the subject. There
was at the same time, with Mr Horrocks a Mr Walker,
from London, who was preparing statements which
he afterwards published in a pamphlet, on the exportation of cotton yarn, shewing, in a national
point of view, the absolute necessity of some legislative measure to stop the growing evil.

Mr Horrocks brought this measure before the
House of Commons on the 14th of March, 1803, in
the following open and candid manner:—

" As the cotton trade of this country is now
become an object of the utmost importance, and a
great difference of opinion exists in the trade, as to
the propriety or impropriety of exporting cotton
twist, I think it my duty to inform the house, that
I intend to submit to its consideration certain pro-
positions, which I conceive not only conducive to
the general interests of the trade itself, but also of
advantage to the revenue. From the discussion
which will naturally arise when the question comes
before the House, and the minutes thereof are entered
upon the journals, its proceedings will convince
those who may be *hereafter concerned, whose opinions
were most correct;* I am anxious that those interested
in the object I have in view, may not be taken by
surprise, but that gentlemen should have time to
consult their constituents ; therefore, for the present,
I shall content myself with moving that an account
be laid before this House of the quantity of *cotton
wool* exported from this country between the years

1790 and 1802, distinguishing the quantity each
year, and to what parts exported."

A similar motion was then made as to *cotton
twist.*

These motions were seconded by Mr W. Dundas,
and the accounts required ordered accordingly.

This short, but business-like, speech to the
House, gave such alarm to the few individuals whose
interest had already become, as they erroneously
supposed, identified with our opponents abroad,
that in order to " nip this question in the bud," as
they had succeeded in doing in 1800, they again
delegated certain persons to obtain an interview
with the minister ; and an interview was granted, at
which, by acting well up to their professed and
established maxim, of keeping Government in the
dark, these parties a second time succeeded in laying the question " on the shelf." The information
that leads me to make these invidious remarks I
received from two authorities, first from Lord Sidmouth himself, who told me in the year following,
in the presence of the late Mr Egerton, what had at
that interview been related to him, and from which
he considered the exports of twist too trifling for
ministers to act upon ; my other authority was one of
the individuals delegated, and who was also present
at that meeting. From this gentleman I learnt that
their spokesman had deluded the minister with
misrepresentations so gross, in order to effect the
purpose they were sent upon, that his ears " burnt
with shame!" * He added, that on returning to
their hotel, the party were highly amused in recapi-
tulating the manner in which they had succeeded
in blinding the minister, and preventing those

* This is not my language, I only record it in the words it was
conveyed to me, and as a true history of the cotton trade, and the cause
of its rapid decline ever since the peace of Amiens, cannot be known
unless this important fact be given ; and as probably I am the only per-

minutes on the journal of the House from being further acted upon, which, if done, to use their own
words, "would not have left them a leg to stand
upon." The death of Mr Horrocks occurring shortly
after, no one was left who had sufficient courage to
undeceive the minister !

Notwithstanding this repulse, my neighbours
had still to redeem their pledge, which they under-

son living to whom it was told, I think it my duty here to state it, as a
reference for the historian.—But even here I should shrink from such
an invidious task, were it not for the consequences this malversation
has already, and will yet occasion.

It has already (besides great loss to themselves) created a dark
political cloud, that now hangs in frightful aspect over the United Kingdom, and its West India Colonies, which ere long will break down
upon our heads with such a tremendous crash, as history gives us no
example, unless the cause which is every day filling this cloud with
almost geometrical progression, be speedily removed, and which can
only be done by the nation redeeming the pledge so often given to me
by the trade. Ninety-nine out of every hundred in the trade, are ready
to come forward, if they durst, but they are so entangled, and so de-
pendant on *foreign influence*, that they dare not!—every manufacturer who requires any credit for his cotton or twist, and every bleacher,
calico-printer, dyer, &c., will understand what I mean. In this forlorn situation, I will presume to hoist the signal of our immortal Nelson,
and say, " England expects every man to do his duty ;"—I therefore,
with humble deference, call upon the landed and shipping interest,
with the whole " nation of shopkeepers" to come forward and redeem
this pledge, which the trade wishes, above all things to do, but no one
in it dare shew the way !

My conscience tells me I have hitherto done my duty to the
best of my humble abilities and power, and I am still ready to go on,
reckless of consequences, and unbiassed by any private interest, save
that of any other individual in the State, but as one of them I have a
great private interest in following up this question ; for if we succeed,
I shall be able to leave an invaluable legacy to my family, viz. a staple
trade that will always support my successors with common management
and care, so long as children are born naked, and raiment wears out.
But if through faintheartedness, for there is no other impediment in
our way, we do not succeed * * * * * * ! I dare not give language
to my predictions, for fear I should be laughed at, as my colleagues in
the years 1800 and 1803 were, when they predicted " that the
export of cotton yarns would eventually ruin the trade in manufactured
goods."

took with spirit, and without being called upon made a bold effort during the session of 1804. While I was in London, in the middle of March this year, taking out my last patent, the Castle Inn gentlemen, *in cordial union with the operative weavers*, called a public meeting, when the following proceedings (as stated in one of the documents alluded to) took place :—

At a meeting of the manufacturers and weavers, and other persons concerned in the trade, held at the house of Mr John Wild, Stockport, on Friday the 16th instant, the following resolutions were unanimously agreed to :—

1st, That the unrestricted exportation of cotton yarns is the principal cause of the extreme depression under which the trade, in piece-goods, now labours.

2nd, That it behoves not only the manufacturers, weavers, bleachers, dyers, printers, and all others immediately interested in the making of piece-goods, but even the spinners themselves (who must ultimately be ruined by whatever is fatal to the other branches *) to come forward, and by every legal means in their power endeavour to put a stop to this ruinous traffic.

3rd, That an humble petition be presented to the Honourable House of Commons, praying that Hon. House to take such measures as to its wisdom may seem meet for removing the evil complained of.

4th, That a subscription be immediately entered into, for defraying the expences of such petition.

> JOHN BENTLEY, President.
> WILLIAM BRADSHAW, Secretary.

March, 1804.

This step I considered the more flattering, as it was, like that of Mr Horrocks', in the preceding year, taken without my interposition or even knowledge ; the first notice I had of it was in a letter from a person present at one of their meetings, informing me that a petition, numerously signed (I think upwards of ten thousand) and was nearly

---

* Nov. 1827—The spinners for export at this time can best tell whether this prediction was well founded !

ready to be sent up. Meeting, however, with un-foreseen difficulties in their proceedings, as I fully stated in a pamphlet I published ten years ago, and, as a body, despairing of being able to redeem their pledge to me, one of them, Mr Sykes, of Edgeley, sent his son Edmund to say, that if it would be acceptable to me, the gentlemen would raise a sub-scription amongst themselves to present me with a service of plate, as a token of their respect, and as a small acknowledgment for the great things I had done for the town and the trade. Flattering as this intimation was, yet, after returning my sincere thanks for such liberal intentions, I requested the gentlemen would drop the idea, as the only return that could give me real pleasure, was the final accomplishment of the important object we all had in view.

During the years 1804-5, anxious, if possible, that Stockport might be unanimous on the great question whenever it should come forward again, and knowing the great weight the name of my neighbour, Mr P. Marsland, had in Manchester, Glasgow, London, &c., wherever the cotton trade was mentioned ; and knowing that his name stood on the list of those who signed their names in favour of the foreign loom, against the Manchester gentlemen in 1800, as well as against Mr Horrocks in 1803 ; and observing that by this time he began to see that the true interest of *every spinner* lay in having *his* yarns manufactured in our own country, by any means, rather than exporting them, I was much gratified one day when he called upon me, to learn that he was making warping and dressing machines, and power-looms, all upon new plans, and had already taken out a patent for his loom ; and when his warping and dressing machines should be complete, he was going to obtain patents for them also.

Having nothing of *self* about *me*, where the commerce of our country was at stake, and having shewn him our plans, I invited Mr M. to call again at any time, and that if any part of our system would be of service to complete his own, he should be welcome to it on his own terms. He called several times and examined every part, but said his own would be far better when complete. At length Mr M. invited me down to see his plans and give my opinion of them; I accordingly went, and after a careful inspection, told him frankly my opinion, that they would not answer.

When we first began in 1802 to contrive and scheme for our new system, and when we had fixed on our plans, I enquired for some person in the neighbourhood who could undertake to make the looms, &c., &c., and contract to fill each room with machinery for this system. Out of several that applied, I fixed upon Mr Charles Axon, who, by the period I am speaking of, had made us 2 or 300 looms, such as I have before described, with 20 to 30 dressing machines, and the preparing or warping machines requisite for them, many of which were re-made several times over, as further improvements suggested themselves. At this time, and when Mr Marsland was quite perplexed with the difficulties of his new plans that were to surpass every thing, and spending thousands on theories that were impracticable, * I had a conversation with him at the time he had just lost his principal foreman by a sudden and melancholy death. Mr Marsland consulted me on the general

* Except in his loom, and for the purpose of shewing that it is not necessary that a man who takes out a patent should, in the literal sense of the word, be actually the inventor of every new part described in the specification; for if he suggest to another what he is in want of, and is at the trouble and expense to make it, and try the experiment, the equitable spirit (as I will term it) of the patent law gives him an exclusive right for a given time to all the benefits arising from such invention. Mr Marsland, with his loom, is a case in point,

character and capability of Mr Axon to fill the place of his late foreman. From my own knowledge, I was able, conscientiously, to give such a character of Mr A. that Mr M. engaged him immediately.

For some weeks or months after, while Mr Axon was finishing with us and commencing with Mr Marsland, we had frequent opportunities of consulting together on the progress Mr M. was making in the weaving department, Mr A. knowing my reasons for being anxious for Mr Marsland's success. After

---

for while deeply engaged in search of the philosopher's stone, before mentioned, he availed himself of the aid of Mr Watt, Jun., of Birmingham, to assist him in forming his loom, who, finding out what Mr Marsland was in want of, suggested to him a certain motion which they technically called a horse head, to give a greater effect to the blow of the lathe. Mr Marsland attaching this motion to Dr Cartwright's loom in the way Mr Watt directed, the loom worked pretty well, and Mr Marsland took out his patent for it. And further, to shew that the greatest genius in the kingdom was called into play during this general search for some new system to work up the surplus twist, I must also record that a little previous to this loom, Mr Marsland had formed an idea that some new mode of sizing the warps would accomplish every thing the trade required. Hence, he called in the aid of Mr Lawson, (the gentleman who set up and superintended the coining machinery in the mint with so much credit to himself, and the house in Birmingham which he represented) and on suggesting to him his wants, Mr Lawson at first sight invented and made him a vessel for the purpose, and being set to work by steam, as Mr Lawson directed, answered so well that Mr Marsland (as he had an undoubted right to do) took out his patent for this system. This patent sizing was hailed through the trade as a plan that would supersede all others, so much so that Mr Finlay, of Glasgow, who had visited us several times during our probation, and always went away fully satisfied that ours, amongst the hundred schemes then afloat, would, in the end, be the best, had his confidence so much shaken by the great things he heard of this patent sizing, that before he made up his mind what plan to adopt himself, he resolved to pay Stockport another visit. He, therefore, came up and brought his managing partner, Mr Buchanan, with him. In passing through Manchester he saw many of his old friends, to whom he related the object of his journey; one of them, Mr Atkinson, of Bank Hall, Pendleton, engaged these gentlemen to dine with him on their return, where he had a few of Mr Finlay's friends to meet them. Over their wine, Mr Atkinson asked Mr Finlay if they had seen the two plans so much spoken of, and were satisfied as to which of them they would.

some very nice management on the part of Mr Axon,
he succeeded at last in prevailing on Mr M. to
re-model his establishment on our system of warping
and dressing, which being done, his machinery was
put to work with complete success, so that I considered the grand point at which I had been aiming
at for two years to be at last accomplished.

After three years of intense application and
study, during which time I never went to bed without having some difficulties to ruminate upon, either
in the mechanical part of the system, or the prejudice
of the hands I had to work it, with my spirits soar-
ing above them all, after a few minutes' study on
my pillow in the morning, I was at my post with
the bell, which called them to work, and by persevering in this plan, and rendering my personal
assistance to every weak hand, until I had got their work
in good order, and shewn them how to keep it so,
raising their spirits with soft words, and sometimes
a joke or something that would bring up a smile,—in
short, by being familiar with all of them, and doing
to every one as I could have wished they should
have done to me, had our situations been reversed,
we got through the difficulties I have before men-

adopt ? Mr Finlay replied that they had spent half the day with Mr
Marsland, who had shewn them his sizing, and explained the advantages
that would accrue to the weaver, so clearly, that they had left him
under a conviction that Mr Marsland was right in his conclusion, that
the new mode of sizing was every thing the trade required. The other
half day they had spent with Mr Radcliffe, from whom they had been
equally convinced, that sizing was not only unnecessary, but that it
was very injurious to the warps, &c. Therefore, finding the two great
Doctors differ so much, they were returning as wise as they came ! and
so the subject ended with a hearty laugh. My object in recording
these anecdotes, (which I had from Mr Watt, Mr Lawson, and Mr
Finlay, themselves) is to shew the rising generation, engaged in this
new system of manufacture, how universally it was wanted at the time,
and that it formed the leading topic of conversation amongst all classes
in the trade.

tioned ; the system became complete, and my pledge
at the Castle Inn fully redeemed ; but instead of the
trade coming forward to redeem their pledge, the
following part of my narrative will shew that I was
doomed to be repaid in a different way than I had
anticipated.

It had come to my knowledge, that the late Mr
Horrocks had experienced the most severe run upon
his credit, that the combined strength of Manchester
and Liverpool could bring against him, for the motion
he had made, as before stated ; but his strength was
beyond their reach. I will leave the reader to draw
his own conclusion after he has read what follows,
whether the foreign influence then established in
Manchester, and which, if the pledge was redeemed,
would immediately be upset, had not something to
do in the narrowing of my credit, one *strong instance*
was told me, but I do not like to mention names.

However painful it may be to my feelings to
speak again of myself and my former affairs, yet, as my
name is so indissolubly united with the warping
and dressing machinery, which, for ease and simpli-
city, are allowed to surpass any other inventions in
the cotton manufacture, I consider it a duty I owe
to my character, as well as to a large family, that I
should now state some few facts on this subject, in
order that a certain class of men, who, like the ass
in the fable, take great delight in giving any old
lion a kick when he is down, may, for the future, be
more cautious when my name is in question, as well
as some others, who, from envy or worse motives,
have an equal pleasure in keeping reports in circulation, that tend to nibble away character which
misfortune never could touch, even under the
strictest examination that creditors, with hostile and
prejudiced feelings, could institute. These prejudices
were, and could only be, hatched in pot-houses and
other low places of resort, during the nine days'

wonder, (which no one, acquainted with our immense expence, wondered at, when it had taken place,) yet, the party I allude to, though no fact existed on which they could ground further enquiry before the Commissioners, pursued me with a most vindictive spirit, even up to a petition to the Lord Chancellor against my certificate, as if I had really concealed a large sum of money to set me up again in business. Besides, the temporary, though happily transitory, pain these wicked inuendoes inflict upon an honest man's heart, were I now to remain silent, the reports I allude to are calculated to give a fraudulent tinge to tradition that might attend the name of Radcliffe to posterity, in conjunction with the fact of his having been the inventor of this invaluable machine.

It was in 1806 that our finances began to be straitened by the great loss on the goods made weekly by a thousand weavers in the country, who were generally allowed to be the most select body of weavers in the trade. Although, for two or three years, I had seen their trade going to the continent with the fine yarns exported, as clearly as we see winter approaching as the days grow shorter, yet, I could not bring my mind to abandon these unfortunate persons until I could find them some other master. For this purpose I opened negociations with flattering prospects of success—first, with Messrs. Fieldens, of Blackburn ; next, with Messrs. Horrocks and Co., of Preston ; afterwards, with Mr John Pooley, Manchester ; and lastly, with Messrs. Bury, Middleton, and Rooth, of Stockport. In the end, I succeeded with the two last concerns, but not until some months after our partnership expired and was dissolved ; but during the two years we were waiting for an opportunity to do it, owing to the gradual decline on the value of goods, (similar to what has since taken place in 1810, and 1814-15) we lost five to seven thousand pounds in each year, by continuing these weavers for what might be termed charity, in the same manner that great capitals have been reduced, and moderate ones lost, during that and the two other periods I have mentioned.

Notwithstanding these heavy losses, added to the great sums we had sunk in establishing our new system, though embarrassed in finances, my position was such that I could not see the least cause to doubt getting through them very soon. In proof of my confidence on this point, I may state, that on the first of July, 1806, the partnership between Mr Ross and myself having expired, and having then two concerns in Stockport, I proposed to Mr Ross that he should take one,—that in Adlington-square, well filled with weaving machinery,—taking to myself the other, that of Hillgate, and patent rights, with all its incumbrances, the greatest of which, as it afterwards proved, was the shock connected with the out-door business, which proposal was accepted. On taking stock and valuing the patents, which had already brought us in upwards of one thousand four hundred pounds in premiums, at a certain sum, there appeared as the share of Mr Ross, which he took in the machinery, &c., in the square £1,100. or thereabouts, and we separated on the same friendly terms we had met and spent seven years together.

The partnership being thus dissolved, I proceeded in my business with a double prospect of success ; first, by the real business I was doing weekly, of 6 to 700 pieces per week, of printing * cambrics,

* So called from a fabric that I was the first to name and make, by perhaps twelve months, having commenced in 1797 with my old weavers in the country, and though we put out work in Macclesfield, Congleton, Mottram-in-Longdendale, in Cheshire, and all parts of the hill countries of Derbyshire, within the distance of a day's journey. from Mellor, as well as the circuit round Stockport ; yet, so scarce were the weavers that would condescend to work this article at 16 or 18 shillings per piece, that at no period of the four or five years preceding the commencement of our new system, could we ever get 200 pieces per week of them woven in all the places I have mentioned.

mostly woven in the factory, and the other part in weaving-families in the neighbourhood, on the small looms I had furnished to them, delivering them dressed warps on the beam, and pin-cops for the weft. This system had now become practicable, and was so greatly approved of by the weavers, that, had I weathered the *calm*, which soon after came upon my credit, I might, in a short time, have had all my looms in the dwellings of the operative weavers on the plan I had been driving at from the first, and from the superior advantage of machine dressing. The evenness produced by this mode of preparation, and the working in my loom, not only rendered these goods of ready sale, but gave me a weekly profit of 90 to £100., which, along with the second branch of income that formed my double prospect, viz. the premiums of licenses under patent rights beginning to pour in from the first houses in the trade, to the amount of £1,500. in the eight months from the first of July, 1806, to March, 1807, when my vessel became quite becalmed. To prevent this, I had for some time felt myself justified in raising means by every proper method in my power, mortgaging my Mellor estate, and also my patents, and the Hillgate premises. And although I afterwards accepted of a loan of £5,000., freely granted by four gentlemen, yet, the whole came short of my wants, for the whisper was gone abroad that I must stop ; and although my vessel was calculated to weather any storm with her weekly income and fair play, yet, her progress was arrested by the dead calm that paralysed her movements.

With our bankers, we, for years, had a credit of 5 to £6,000., but this was coolly whispered down, in the short space I speak of, from 6,000 to about 100 pounds. A contraction of the cotton credit, followed with the cotton dealers, my transactions with whom during 16 years, had been unlimited in point of amount of credit and period of payment. As my acceptances ran off, my credit was contracted, not only with the cotton dealers, but with many wealthy spinners, of whom I may truly say that my purchases from them for 16 years had largely contributed to their realising that wealth ; yet, these were the very men whose whispers were most audible, as they successively got out. Had they either kept their opinions in their own breasts, or spoken well of the *bridge* that *had carried them safe over!* the ground they left would have been as firm for the few who came voluntarily into their places, as it had been for them. In this way all my heaviest old creditors were paid off, except a few, and nearly all of these were paid 15 to 18 shillings in the pound. After paying off all those claimants, whose confidence had been shaken, to the amount of £20,000. in about eight months, and to within about £2,000. of the claims of *this class* of creditors, I was obliged, on the 6th of March, 1807, to come to a pause, and consult the four gentlemen who had so liberally advanced me £5,000., which had been applied in payment of the other creditors before mentioned. Their own credits were also granted to me without limit, during the whole time, (independent of the loan) and those new debts formed the bulk of the comparatively *small amount* which I owed at the period of my stoppage.

I shall, perhaps, be thought a little prolix on this part of my struggle through life, but, I think it proper to state, not only such facts as may be necessary to clear my character from the imputations I allude to, but, also to caution people against judging from appearances, of the motives and actions of men who may become unfortunate, without giving themselves the trouble to enquire into all the circumstances on which alone can be formed a correct judgment. I shall, therefore, concisely narrate the material proceedings that took place from the time

I am speaking of, up to October following, when a
Commission of Bankrupt was taken out against me,
as they will show, by example, a fair struggle between
the principles of the old school in trade, which were
to do, by an honest man in distress, as they would be
done unto, viz. forbearing and rendering assistance.
That a concern like mine, with a profit of three to four
thousand a-year from regular trade and premiums
for patent rights, instead of acting on principles so
diametrically opposite, that might seem to have
governed the new school, whose plans, coming into
collision with those of my four liberal and disinterested friends, upset all they had done. Happily,
I was taken at this time by the hand, by, I may
say, a stranger, who, unsolicited and almost unknown to me, made himself acquainted with the
minute particulars of the circumstances that led to
my shipwreck, and my character as interwoven with
it. Finding that I had ruined myself by leaving
Mellor, as before related, from a motive, that, in his
opinion, did me the greatest credit, viz. to establish a
system for the purposes so often mentioned, and, having succeeded in doing this to his entire satisfaction,
he resolved that I should not want a friend to set me on
my legs again. This excellent man was the late Chas.
Frederick Brandt, Esquire, of Manchester, whom I
shall again have occasion to mention. But I will
first explain what I allude to by the current reports
circulated against me. While my affairs were under
investigation, Mr Oldknow, my assignee, told me
he had heard certain reports, which, though he did
not believe them, yet, they had been mentioned to
him in such a way, that he felt it his duty to require
some explanation. These reports were—that in my
journies of late to London, instead of appropriating
large sums of money, which occasionally must pass
through my hands in the regular course of business,
to pay my creditors, I had been laying up a future

provision for my family, and that I had, either by purchasing annuities or some other appropriation of my property, succeeded in securing an income of from 6 to £800. a-year to my children ! !

It is scarcely necessary to repeat my answer, after the declaration I now make, (and I make it because the reports are credited by many people to this day) viz. that on the 6th of March, 1807, all the money I or my family possessed was about two guineas, and, from that day to the present time, not one shilling, directly or indirectly, of my former fortune, which I had when I came to Stockport, or of the money of my creditors, has, or ever will, come into our hands, and with the exception of one guinea a-year, which I had then paid to the Travellers' Society for six years, I had never laid out one shilling for such provision. But, say the persons who still credit the reports, if this was the fact, how was it that you supported yourself and family for a considerable time before you commenced business again ? and by what means were you enabled to commence on so respectable a scale? To set these questions for ever at rest, and clear my family from the reproach that might otherwise go down with them to future generations, I will answer those questions after I have shewn how I was discharged from the remnants of my old concern. And in detailing the facts I shall add strength to the subject on which I am now writing.

The commission being opened, I met my creditors in the usual manner. The last meeting was in Dec. 1817, and my certificate was signed by the Lord Chancellor on the 8th of Feb. following. This certificate I never looked upon as a discharge from the comparative small sums I owed when I failed, nor do I to this day, entertaining as I am justified in doing, a well-founded hope that the trade will

assist me in applying to Government for that remuneration which may enable me to pay off all those
remnants.

The facts in answer to the questions above
stated are simply these ;—that in the early part of
the struggle before-mentioned, (from March to Oct.)
Mr Brandt put £30. into my hands as a present to
my family ; this, with a similar sum, a free gift from
another quarter, and some assistance from my son,
who had a situation with a salary that enabled him
to provide us with the little extras we wanted,
furnished us with the necessaries of life until my
certificate was finally obtained. On the completion
of this document, I had the agreeable surprise of
being informed by Mr Brandt, that he had had
several conversations with Mr Wm. Jones, the banker,
respecting me, and particularly as to the mode to be
adopted for setting me up again, that I might perfect my system as a model for the trade, and a
living to my family ; and that their conclusion was
that they would each lend me £500., (without any
preference in case of future misfortune) if I could
get two other friends to do the same, which was
soon accomplished.

The loan of £2,000. being completed, Mr Brandt
and Mr Jones called on the late Mr Duckworth to
give him instructions for the necessary bonds. In
due time, Mr Brandt informed me that they were
ready, and that I might call on Messrs. Duckworth,
Chippendal, and Co., to sign them. I give these
minutiæ of the transaction, in order that I may
record also the liberality of the late Mr Duckworth
on this occasion. When I had signed the bonds, I
asked that gentleman, to whom I was a perfect
stranger, how much I was indebted to him? before
he replied, he asked one of the clerks the amount of
the stamps, which being given, Mr D. said that was
the sum I had to pay,—I, of course, rejoined,—but

what am I indebted to you for consultations, drafts, engrossing, &c. ? To which Mr D. "replied nothing ! I consider myself handsomely rewarded by the pleasure I have had in making out the bonds and papers, for this is the most generous and liberal transaction that has come before me since I was in business."

I am not so vain as to attribute all this to my character for integrity in the eyes of Mr Brandt and Mr Jones solely ; no, it was to the having succeeded in the new system, so as to promise the working-up of the surplus yarns in future, that biassed them so greatly in my favour. I regret that our communications on this important point were all verbal, and I believe the only trace left of their sentiments will be the letter I wrote to Mr Jones, at Mr Brandt's request, after he informed me of their conclusion. Though I have not a copy, I recollect distinctly that in thanking him for it, and the handsome manner in which it had been done, alluding to what had passed between them, as related to me by Mr Brandt, I, on public grounds, expressed my sanguine hopes that he, Mr Jones, would, ere long, see the benefit that would result to his town and country from the legislative measures that might soon be brought about without injuring the spinner, which had hitherto been the only bar to a prohibition.

In order to throw a little more light on one branch of this new system of manufacture, I shall state some particulars that have come before me respecting the motives which originated the power-loom, and as they accord so exactly with what I have already described, as to my motives for bringing out the warping and dressing for any loom,—the unison of the two inventions, in my opinion, deserves particular attention. From what follows, it will appear that Government, when called upon, are ready to do their duty, and, for this, have already given their pledge to the contract, and a sufficient sum of money as an earnest of their sincerity. I consider, therefore, that the trade, and the *landed interest in particular*, are under the strongest obligation, immediately to call for an investigation of this important subject, in order to prevent the *evils* and RUIN that must otherwise occur.

In the spring of 1808, I received a letter from Mr Serjeant, Solicitor, in Manchester, requesting me to call upon him, which I did, when Mr S. informed me that he had been requested by Dr Cartwright, the inventor of the power-loom, (and who was then before Parliament for a remuneration for the expense he had been at in bringing it to bear) to send up witnesses to be examined before a committee, then about to sit, on the merits of that invention, in a *national point of view*, and to what extent the general application of it to our manufactures in general would entitle him to national remuneration. Mr Serjeant said he had already consulted several gentlemen in Manchester on the subject, and some from Bolton. After a long conversation, I consented to go before the committee, along with a Mr Joseph Taylor, and we were the only witnesses sent up or examined. Mr Joseph Taylor, to prove Dr Cartwright the inventor, having been his engineer at the time he invented it, (the same as Thos. Johnson and others were to me in the warping and dressing, and hand-loom) and myself to give an opinion as to its national utility. My evidence before this committee is already printed in a pamphlet I published in 1811, to which I refer, (see page 31) but as very few may possess it I will here reprint it, as, in my opinion, it forms a material link in the chain of my narrative.

Being called before a committee of the House of Commons on the 4th of April, 1808, to speak to the probable merit or advantage that might accrue to the cotton trade from the general adoption of Dr Cartwright's power-loom, after several questions were put to me and answered, the committee thought the subject I began to speak upon, when I alluded to the evils arising to the cotton trade from the exportation of cotton yarns, of such weight and consequence, in a national point of view, that they requested I would take a day or two to write down my ideas, and present them to the next meeting; they adjourned to the 7th, when I laid before them as follows:—

" This subject is so comprehensive, I cannot speak to it fully without enlarging a little upon the history of the cotton trade for about fifteen years past; in which I will point out to your honourable committee certain evils which have insensibly crept into this late flourishing, but now distressed, branch of our British manufacture.

" During a period of about nine years, say from 1793 to 1802, the machinery for spinning cotton yarns, with the ingenuity, practical knowledge, and persevering industry of the persons concerned in this branch, became so perfect as to enable the spinners to produce more yarns than could at that time possibly be made into cloth by all the weavers Great Britain could collect for the purpose. The demand for cotton goods was equal during this period to take off the whole produce of the spindle, could weavers have been found to have made it into cloth; but this being impossible, the spinners began to export the surplus to the manufacturers abroad, say to France, Germany, Switzerland, Prussia, Russia, Holland, Spain, &c., countries possessing hundreds of thousands of weavers formerly employed in weaving linens, silks, stuffs, &c., whose labour might be had at half the price such labour was paid for in this country. The consequence of this has been, that these foreign manufacturers began to furnish their neighbours with such cotton cloths as heretofore they could only obtain from this country ; hence, by degrees, the British manufacturers and the East India Company nearly lost all their trade for piece-goods to those countries before-mentioned, which is the *sole cause* of all the distress you now hear of in the cotton trade. This distress has been foreseen all the while, as a memorial, presented by the merchants and manufacturers in Manchester to the Lords of the Treasury or Board of Trade, in the year 1800, will shew, and to which I beg leave (with due deference) to refer your honourable committee. The present distressing effects from this cause have been also foreseen by the weavers themselves in the towns and neighbourhoods of Bolton and Stockport. Those weavers, in the year 1804, drew up a petition, praying for a tax on twist exported, or a prohibition altogether, which was signed by more than 11,000 weavers, and would have been presented to your honourable house, had they not been persuaded that some other measures might probably produce a remedy without parliamentary interference.

" To that part of your question, Whether I think the general adoption of the loom by power will operate to the prejudice of the weavers in the old way? I answer, No. In the first place, their situation for the last twelve or eighteen months has been such that it cannot be made worse, as during this time, generally speaking, they have neither been able to, pay rents or buy themselves clothes; all their earnings have barely been sufficient to keep them alive ; and those who have families to support, are obliged to work from sixteen to eighteen hours in the day to do this. In the next place, their distressed situation has prepared them for any measures the legislature in its wisdom may direct, provided those measures have a tendency to bring back their trade by degrees, and yet, as soon as circumstances will admit of, to the state in which it was about fifteen years ago ; that is, that there shall be no surplus twist or yarns to be exported, but that all the cotton yarns spun in Great Britain shall also be made into cloth in the United Kingdom. This is what I call the true interest of this country; and I have no doubt that ere long the legislature, master spinners, and manufacturers will see it in this light; and as to the weavers, I think I know them well, and can almost answer for it, that they will individually and as a body submit to, and go hand and heart into, any measure adopted as a remedy to the cause of all their distress.

" This invention of Dr Cartwright's, coupled with some other improvements that have lately been discovered for preparing and dressing the cotton twist ready for the loom, either by hand or by power, are particularly calculated to remedy this evil speedily, by working up these surplus yarns ; and that which will be chiefly wove in the power-loom will be into fabrics that will not interfere with the cotton goods heretofore made by our weavers, but, as I before stated to you in answer to your former questions, vast quantities of strong stout cotton goods for shirtings, sheetings, &c. will be made in them, and not only answer as a substitute for the linens heretofore imported from Russia and Germany, for the consumption of this country and her colonies, but will come much cheaper, and answer all the purposes of family use as well as linens ; this is proved already to a considerable extent, during the three or four years these goods have been known in the trade. The description of cotton goods I am here speaking of have also of late been very much approved of and sought after by the Americans, which they have bought for their consumption in lieu of Russian and German linens ; and I can see *no bounds* to the *vast quantity* of business this country has it in her power to command in this line, *provided she is true to herself.*

" Of late years, the Germans have manufactured a variety of stout cotton goods from the twist they buy from this county, (which twist,

to say the best, has not for the last three or four years brought more-
than prime cost to the spinners on the average, and in many instances
very little more than the spinners have paid for the cotton), *these goods
they have regularly sent down the Rhine into Holland, where they
have been shipped off to America.* THIS IS EVIDENTLY TAKING THE
BREAD, DUE TO OUR WEAVERS HERE, AND GIVING IT TO THE
WEAVERS ON THE CONTINENT.

" As I know many of the spinners who are now ready to appropriate a part of their mills to weaving by machinery on Dr Cartwright's
principle, when a fair demand for stout piece goods springs up ; this at
once points out the way in which a complete cure of all these evils may
be effected in a few years ; for as any spinner appropriates a part of his
mill to weaving, it operates in a two-fold degree, in lessening the surplus of yarns to be exported.

" When something in this way is acted upon *(and not till then)*
with *unity, spirit,* and *vigor,* the trade of piece goods will immediately
revive, and by degrees markets will not only open again for British
cotton cloth in an *unparalleled* degree, but also for the cotton goods
imported by the East India Company, who have suffered very greatly
by the foreigners making from our twist similar goods to what they were
used to purchase at the India sales, which have answered their purpose
abroad as a substitute for India *cotton goods.*

" Hence I infer that this invention of Dr Cartwright's is so
important to the future prosperity of the cotton trade in general, to
work up the surplus twist, rather than export it, that were it suppressed,
or its application no further extended, the cotton trade in this country
will ere long be chiefly confined to spinning, and the weavers on the
continent in the end be the sole manufacturers for the consumption of
the continent of Europe and her dependencies." *

* 1827—The soundness of this argument has been very fairly
called in question, as, without some reason assigned, its truth, in the
most favourable light in which we can view it, is very paradoxical.
My principle reason at that time for stating it, was that the great
mill-owners and spinners for export, (as before stated) would not
consent to a prohibition, unless we could find out some plan to work up
the surplus twist at home, in which case *their opposition was to cease ;*
and as I knew the weavers would lose their trade if the export continued, I concluded my evidence by the inference above stated, and as
this is the only statement in a pamphlet of forty-five pages, which I
published in 1811, the truth of which has ever been called in question,
I am thus particular in shewing the grounds on which I stated it, but
if any thing more is required to clear up this paradox, MR HUME, in
the House of Commons, on Friday the 5th of May, 1826, (as reported
in the *Edinburgh Advertiser* of the 9th of that month) has said
sufficient :—" He was also sorry for the infatuation of the distressed manu-

My object for introducing this, as a further reference to the historian, is to relate what the Doctor said to me on reading over this evidence on the morning of the day I was going to present it to the committee. When he saw the drift of my evidence, the Dr exclaimed, " this is very extraordinary ! as it brings to my recollection a general conversation that first brought the idea of a power-loom to my mind." "This conversation," the Dr added, " took place at a public table in Buxton," (or Matlock, I forget which, where he was with his family in the season, before he commenced operations for inventing the power-loom, and, but for which conversation he should not have thought of it)—the subject in discussion was Sir Richard Arkwright's new system of spinning cotton yarn. The world, as I may term it, had for several years previous to this period (now 40 to 50 years ago) been divided in opinion as to whether the system would answer or not, but by this time its success had become established beyond all doubt, and this being admitted by every gentleman at the table, some one turned the conversation to the evil it would ultimately create in depriving not only the cottagers who earned their bread by the hand-wheel, but also the small farmers of the means they had hitherto possessed, in long winters and the absence of agricultural employment, of making up their rents, as they had always done, from hand-carding, hand-spinning, &c. Their attention was at that time particularly called to look at it in this point of view, from the riotous destruction of several

---

facturers of Blackburn and other places, who thought, that by destroying power-looms they could better their own situation ; though it was abundantly clear, and fully proved by evidence before a Committee of that House, that but for those very power-looms, an important branch of manufacture would have been driven from the country."

small mills in Lancashire by the above class of people, then under the greatest alarm for the loss of their trade and the ruin of the *spinsters!*

" Another gentleman" (says the Dr) " suggested a query,—whether, after the term of Sir Richard Arkwright's patent was run out, this system of spinning would not be carried too far, and more yarns spun than could possibly be wove in this country, in which case an export to the continent would infallibly follow, and our weavers in the end suffer greatly from such a competition. This suggestion, with the remarks that followed upon it, the Dr added, made such an impression on his mind while he remained, that on his way home he could scarcely think of any thing but the contriving of a loom to work up the surplus yarns that might thus be ultimately produced.

When he reached his abode in Nottingham, he put a turning-lathe, which he had for his private amusement, with other tools, in order, and with the assistance of Jos. Taylor, before-mentioned, brought out his loom. Dr Cartwright, although possessed of a very handsome paternal fortune, eventually embarrassed himself by his various efforts in Glasgow, Manchester, &c. to bring it into use. However, the committee, upon the evidence of myself and Joseph Taylor only, gave him (as I understood) £10,000. for his invention, although his patent had run out for I believe 16 years, and the loom for many years gone into disuse ; and so it would have remained to this day, but for my plan of warping, dressing, &c., which, though never intended for such an union, yet, it is worthy of notice, and should never be forgotten, that each branch of this new system owes its origin to the same cause, and whatever distress may come upon the country, while the raw material is permitted to be exported, no blame can attach to

this united system ; on the contrary, the very name of
its cloth has given millions of pieces to the old
weavers to work, which, when finished with what is
known in the trade as bleachers' weft, and *stamped
as power-loom cloth*, have gone to all parts of the
world as such, or the weavers would never have
recovered from the distress they were thrown into
after the peace of 1814-15. But this will not last !
the bleachers' weft will not stand the test of the
wash-tub : foreigners will in future give their orders
for twist, and make what they want themselves ! and
I tremble when I contemplate the deep distress our
weavers are doomed, ere long, to encounter. So
long, indeed, as the trade in fine muslins, such as
book, mull, jaconet, cambric, stripes, check, and all
the vast variety of fancy goods, heretofore the staple
articles of Paisley, Glasgow, Bolton, Preston, Stockport, Ashton-under-line, &c., as well as the ginghams,
quiltings, dimities, and a variety of other descriptions of cotton goods, and fine goods made from the
mixture of cotton yarns with silk or wool, none of
which the new system of manufacture has hitherto
attempted. I say, so long as the weavers in these
descriptions of goods are equally distressed, if not
more so, by low wages and want of work, as those
who have been heretofore employed in such goods as
the power and hand-loom, under the new system,
now make. Surely there must be some other cause
for their distress, than the interference of the new
system, which, in fact, has never yet interfered
directly with them at all. If it should be said that
it has indirectly injured them by driving the plain
weavers into the fine and fancy articles, and thereby
over-charged this market with a super-abundance
of hands, I deny the fact, and am prepared to prove
a contrary effect, as many hands in the finer description of plain goods have gone to common calicoes,

which, when finished and stamped as before-described, have been shipped as power-loom cloth. Hence, I fearlessly repeat, that, but for this new system, the distress from whence emanated the blanket expedition in 1817, the great Peterloo meeting in 1819, and the rebellion in Scotland in 1820, would have had no relief—but, as I before observed, this will not last !

While relating what passed between Dr Cartwright and the party at Buxton, I touched upon the riotous proceedings of the Lancashire hands in destroying carding mills, &c. for fear of the trade of the spinsters being taken away by the introduction of machinery ; * but their opposition was of short duration, as a great demand immediately sprung up for weavers, either lads or lasses, while the mothers and younger children with their hand-wheels, found plenty of employment in winding the weft. The hands, turned adrift from hand cards and the spinning wheel, soon found full employ in the loom on machine yarn, with three to four-fold more wages

---

* To shew that the spinsters had gallant friends at the time (1799) I will relate an extraordinary occurrence I was witness to in our church (Mellor) one Sunday morning during these troubles. The minister, then 80 years of age, when he came to what should have been the middle of his sermon, introduced the subject of these riotous proceedings, then going on in Lancashire and threatening to visit our neighbourhood. But while giving good and salutary advice to his congregation not to join in such proceedings, he was interrupted by a respectable yeoman, the churchwarden, who, rising up in his seat opposite the pulpit, said in an audible voice, Mr * * * * * " it will become you better to follow your text than to ramble away about such temporal affairs." Here, before the churchwarden could finish his speech, he was also interrupted by the venerable minister, who, although he was always a very mild and good-tempered gentleman, yet, this unprecedented interruption (as he termed it) completely upset him—he came down from the pulpit into the aisle, when, after giving the gallant yeoman a warm lecture at the door of his pew (which the agitation of his nerves prevented him from opening) the devotious of the morning were ended, the minister being so irritated, as not to be able to return to his former situation.

than they had been able to earn in their own trade ;
and it was from the demand thus created for labour
on the yarns so spun, and not by the profits of
machine spinning, that the high price of labour, and
the profits to the manufacturers, bleachers, printers,
dyers, finishers, &c., and, though last not least,
the old English merchants, with their cent. per cent.
on all these labours and profits united, proceeded,
and brought into our country the vast additional
wealth that carried us through a war as unprecedented in expence as it terminated in glory.

From this important source was Mr Pitt chiefly
enabled to raise taxes sufficient to pay the interest
of the debt and the increasing expences of the war.
As the landed and agricultural purses were filled
even to the brim by every article produced from the
soil, or the farm yard being raised in price in proportion to the advanced labour and profit above-
mentioned. This source held out even when the
income from manufactures and commerce had gone
to the continent with the raw material, cotton yarns ;
but unless this new system checks its decline, it cannot hold out much longer! Hence, I protest against
the produce of our spindles going abroad in the raw
state, unless the shippers will send with every cargo
a proportionate amount of consols; for I contend
that the raw material, ✻ on which so much of our manufactures & commerce were then founded, were equally
pledged to remain " as they were" at the breaking
out of the French war, as the very soil of our islands,

* So long as the exporters of cotton yarn suffer the following,
with many other Acts of Parliament, to remain on the statute-book
unrepealed, I shall persist in calling yarns a raw material, whether they
be made of wool, silk, linen, or cotton. The three Acts I refer to, as
well as every dictionary I have consulted on the word manufacture,
fully bear me out in this term :—12 Charles 2nd, chap. 18 ; 2 William
and Mary, chap. 9, s. 2 ; 28 Geo. 3rd, chap. 38, s. 9.

the raw material on which alone the landed interest can raise their quota of the annual taxes. And further, I will fearlessly add, that had Mr Pitt lived until 1816, when the misrepresentations I have before stated were brought to light, viz. that instead of a trifling export, and even that trifle, only the refuse, such as our weavers would not work! was, in fact, the best of our twist, and if perchance any of the inferior sort happened to go abroad with the good, it was often sent back to us!! which our poor weavers in Lancashire and Glasgow, to my knowledge, have been glad to get hold of and *work without a murmur!!!* Hence, I say, that had Mr Pitt lived to have had these facts laid before him, the cringing cant of the person or party that should have dared to have said to him, as they have since said to his successors, (who knew nothing of the malversations I speak of) with too much effect, " *It is too late, there is so much property sunk, &c.*" would have been answered according to their deserts—they would immediately have been sent " to the right about "— the great pilot would have stopped this *vile traffic,* and the weavers, &c. in Great Britain would have been restored to their legitimate trade, when the surplus yarns would have found an inexhaustible market in Ireland, and given full employment to hundreds of thousands (I had almost said millions) of its industrious poor, who are now gradually sinking into hopeless ruin, by the introduction of cotton goods into every linen draper's shop *at home or abroad,* in successful competition with their linens; thereby not only driving one portion of its cloth out of the market altogether for want of demand, but reducing the price of that which remains so low, as to give nothing like a remuneration to their flax-grower, spinner, and weaver; or their manufacturer, bleacher, and merchant, who follow in their train. There would have been no want of means in Ireland to have manufactured our surplus yarns, for our spinners and exporters of yarns, when cut off from the continent, would have been equally active in London to have raised loans for the Irish, in order to make them good and safe customers, as they have been for the Russian, Prussian, and other governments, who have taken their loans—the chief object they had in view in taking them, was to enable them to assist their merchants and manufacturers in purchasing the raw materials from us on the best terms!—witness the provisos, &c. of the commercial bank in St Petersburgh, established on the receipt of their first loan.

It is said the land is pledged to pay the interest of our national debt—be it so—but when the produce of their lands reverts back to its old price, and there are no hand-wheels in the small farm houses, to enable the industrious to eke out their rents, as they did 50 years ago, I can not see how the land will be able to pay the interest of the debt, even as it stood prior to the American war ; and if my doubts are well founded, how is it possible for the land to pay the interest of the vast loans that were raised on the commerce created by the manufactures, &c. before-described, when these manufactures, and the commerce inseparable from them, are handed over to the continent of Europe.

While on this subject, it may not be irrelevant to record what I have been witness to, as to the manner in which the cotton manufacture operated in raising the price of land in the districts in which this trade first planted itself. The extent of country in which the machine yarns were immediately adopted for the fabrication of every description of clothing, from the strong fustian to the finest book-muslin and cotton-lace, and their mixtures with wool, silk, and linen, may be divided into four districts, viz. 1st, Manchester, with thirty to fifty

miles in every direction round it. 2nd, Glasgow
the same, but extending to Perth, Aberdeen, and
through a great part of the Highlands. 3rd, Nottingham, taking in Derby, Warwick, Lichfield, &c.
And the 4th, Carlisle, branching out in every direction, so as to meet the Manchester and Glasgow divisions. These divisions I will suppose to be sub-divided
into from one to two thousand sub-divisions, and to
illustrate my argument by example, I will state facts
as they occurred to myself:—In one of those sub-
divisions (which will equally apply to any other) a
small district on the edge of Derbyshire, (Mellor)
fourteen miles from Manchester, I, as before-stated,
was born, and from early infancy employed in the
various branches of manufacture already enumerated.

In the year 1770, the land in our township was
occupied by between fifty to sixty farmers; rents, to
the best of my recollection, did not exceed 10s. per
statute acre, and out of these fifty or sixty farmers,
there were only six or seven who raised their rents
directly from the produce of their farms; all the rest
got their rent partly in some branch of trade, such
as spinning and weaving woollen, linen, or cotton.
The cottagers were employed entirely in this manner,
except for a few weeks in the harvest. Being one
of those cottagers, and intimately acquainted with
all the rest, as well as every farmer, I am the
better able to relate particularly how the change
from the old system of hand-labour to the new one
of machinery operated in raising the price of land
in the sub-division I am speaking of. Cottage rents
at that time, with convenient loom-shop and a small
garden attached, were from one and a-half to two
guineas per annum. The father of a family would
earn from eight shillings to half a guinea at his
loom, and his sons, if he had one, two, or three along
side of him, six or eight shillings each per week;
but the great sheet anchor of all cottages and small

farms, was the labour attached to the hand-wheel, and when it is considered that it required six to eight hands to prepare and spin yarn, of any of the three materials I have mentioned, sufficient for the consumption of one weaver,—this shews clearly the inexhaustible source there was for labour for every person from the age of seven to eighty years (who retained their sight and could move their hands) to earn their bread, say one to three shillings per week without going to the parish. The better class of cottagers and even small farmers also helped to earn what might aid in making up their rents, and supporting their families respectably. The price of land, rent of cottages, and prices of provisions, were all upon an equitable level with the earnings of this class of the people, which forms the sinews and strength of any nation ; but particularly ours, for notwithstanding the high sounding words at county and other higher meetings, that agriculture is the prop and support of the nation, I fearlessly maintain, and will prove, that but for our nation surpassing all others in our manufactures and commerce, the land of this kingdom would have been of no more value than the lands on the banks of the Wolga, the Neva, the Don, the Vistula, the Danube, the Rhine, the Elbe, the Scheld, the Meuse, the Rhone, the Loire, the Garonne, and the Seine were before the inhabitants of the sovereignties, through which those rivers flow, got our raw materials, cotton yarns, to furnish them with the means of productive labour, on which a very dangerous rivalship to our "ships, colonies, and commerce," is more than commenced !

Having stated the condition of the small farmers and cottagers to be in that state of ease which may be thought to comprehend " wealth, peace, and god- liness," in that sense in which our progenitors so wisely introduced it into our excellent liturgy, I will give a brief sketch of the facts as they passed daily before me, at the period I allude to, which will apply generally to every other sub-division of the manufacturing districts, and to most of them on a much larger scale.

From the year 1770 to 1788 a complete change had gradually been effected in the spinning of yarns, —that of wool had disappeared altogether, and that of linen was also nearly gone,—cotton, cotton, cotton, was become the almost universal material for employment, the hand-wheels, with the exception of one establishment ❋ were all thrown into lumber-rooms, the yarn was all spun on common jennies, the carding for all numbers, up to 40 hanks in the pound, was done on carding engines; but the finer numbers of 60 to 80 were still carded by hand, it being a general opinion at that time that machine-carding would never answer for fine numbers. In weaving no great alteration had taken place during these 18 years, save the introduction of the fly-shuttle, a change in the woollen looms to fustians and calico, and the linen nearly gone, except the

❋ This was a family of the name of Tomlinson, on one of the small farms in Mellor, called Bull-hill ; it consisted of four or five orphan sisters, the youngest of which was upwards of 40. They had a complete spinnery, consisting of two pair of cards, and five hand-wheels, by which they earned more than paid the rent of their farm, on which they kept three cows, one horse, and always ploughed a field, this farm was also celebrated for its cheese, poultry, eggs, &c. These spinsters entered their solemn protest against any innovation upon their trade, and the property they had embarked in it, either by Sir Richard Arkwright or any other person, and declared they would never surrender a right that had descended to them through their pre-decessors from the earliest period of time, and till now had never been disputed. They disapproved of the riotous proceedings before-men-tioned, and expressed a strong confidence that Government, when they heard of these machines, would stop them as they ought to do, but so far as they were concerned, they came to the following noble resolution : —that until these machines were ordered by Government to cease working, to the *ruin* of all his majesty's loyal and dutiful *spinsters* in his dominions, they would oppose them with all their wealth, power, few fabrics in which there was a mixture of cotton. To the best of my recollection there was no increase of looms during this period,—but rather a decrease. Although our family and some others in the neighbourhood during the latter half of the time, earned from three to four fold-wages to what the same families had heretofore done, yet, upon the whole, the district was not much benefited by the change ; for what was gained by some families who had the advantage of machinery, might, in a great measure, be said to be lost to the others, who had been compelled to throw their old cards and hand-wheels aside as lumber.

One of the formidable consequences of this change now began to make its appearance, the poor's rate, which previous to this change had only been known in a comparatively nominal way by an annual meeting at Easter to appoint a new overseer, and the old one to make up his accounts which nobody thought it worth while to look into, as they only contained the expenses of his journey to a petty sessions at a distance, and a few cases of very old persons, 70 to 90 years of age, (whose eyes or hands failed them) having had a weekly allowance. Relief to persons who could not get employment, or bastardy, were alike unknown on their books,—this I state partly traditionally, and partly from many

---

and industry, with the aid of their legitimate cards and hand-wheels. They did so, and have fought nobly under this resolution for nearly half a century, no one ever giving way to the right or left, except three or four of them who have died in the combat ! but the one or two who are left in the field of battle I understand are still carrying on the combat, as I saw some of their yarns just brought from this celebrated spinnery on the same farm by a respectable manufacturer in our town, only a few weeks ago, (1822) but were I not opposed by an old saying we have, " that while there is life there is hope," I should be inclined to express a doubt of their ultimate success, however just may be their cause.

years under my own observance. There was no
material advance in the rent of land or cottages
during this period, but in the articles of butcher's
meat, butter, cheese, and sundry necessaries of life,
there had been some increase of price. *

The next fifteen years, viz. from 1788 to 1803,
which fifteen years I will call the golden age of this
great trade, which has been ever since in a gradual
decline.

I have already stated that up to the year 1788,
no great advantage had been realised in my neighbourhood by the change in the mode of spinning, as
what had been gained by the few, was, in a great

---

* With two or three short exceptions, such as that occasioned
by Buonaparte marching his armies through the countries where our
rivals had been at full work for years, filling all foreign markets with
goods made from our yarns. But the day that General left Paris for
Moscow, our legitimate trade gradually revived, and was fully restored
to us for a time ; † for as every weaver through the whole line of his
march, was taken from his loom into that army, General Ludd, in our
districts, lost one of his followers, who deserted him and ran home to
his loom, where he met with full work and good quarters, and the poor
general and his lady being left without one follower, were never heard
of again until Buonaparte was sent off to St Helena! when the whole
continent with their low rents for cottages, low price of provisions, and
consequently low price of labour, were again at full liberty to resume
(as they had a right to do, so long as we allowed it,) that deadly
rivalship, which, in less than six months, brought our poor weavers
down from their legitimate wages of 15 to 30 shillings per week,
according to their skill and dexterity, to the level of their rivals on the
continent,—say three to six shillings per week,—but as our poor
weavers could not exist on this small pittance, they again took the
field under the standard of radical reform !—when that campaign ended
in the noted blanket expedition.

† With the exception of the fine goods made in Paisley, &c.
this branch felt but little of the revival I speak of, owing to their
deadly rivals fabricating these goods on fine yarns sent by this country,
in the southern parts of Europe, where they were not much disturbed
by this march to Moscow. Hence, these goods could not advance
much in price, and the weavers, of course, got but little advance on
their wages.

measure, lost by the many ; the reason of which was, we all aimed at spinning, and spinning only, which, of itself, without a manufacture attached to it, *never did* nor *ever will* enrich any nation, or render it contented and happy; for if the wealth of our nation emanated from this source, the present period would be the happiest our country ever experienced. But view it now—with the eye of an Adam Smith, if such an eye is left, and no one will hesitate to say that the latter would be infinitely more lucrative to the nation than the former, *if it could once have fair play*.

In Bolton, Blackburn, Manchester, Stockport, Oldham, &c., the water-twist and common jenny yarns had been introduced to a great extent for calicoes, in addition to their old fustian and other fabrics, and a great manufacture was carried on, and a commerce corresponding with it, though a tremendous shock convulsed the trade in the year 1788, from the failure of Livesey, Hargreaves, & Co., and some others in the trade. These failures were occasioned by an over supply sent to France after the commercial treaty, and to other parts of the continent before the fashion of the consumers could have had sufficient time to change from silks, stuffs, and linens, to cotton fabrics. Yet, this shock was but of very short duration in lessening the demand for weavers, for, if my recollection does not fail me, it did not generally lower the price of their labour ; but, however this might be, the shock blew over with the year. The over supply on the continent had been sold for what it would fetch, tempting, as it were, the taste and fashion of the consumers to adopt them, which, from the intrinsic merit of the articles, succeeded, and the unlimited demand for the future was the consequence.

I have already observed that water-twist and common jenny yarns had been freely used in Bolton, &c., for some years prior to 1788 ; but it was the introduction of mule yarns about this time, along with the other yarns, all assimilating together and producing every description of clothing, from the finest book muslin, lace, stocking, &c., to the heaviest fustian, that gave such a preponderating wealth through the loom, and the sale which while securing to us "ships, colonies, and commerce," could not fail at the same time to raise the produce of the soil on which this vast wealth, in trebled "wages for labour, and profits upon that labour," were in daily circulation to an amount in proportion to the increased wages and profits. But to return to my own division, and to shew the immediate effects produced when all hands went to work *on machine yarns*, I shall confine myself to the families in my own neighbourhood. These families, up to the time I have been speaking of, whether as cottagers or small farmers, had supported themselves by the different occupations I have mentioned in spinning and manufacturing, as their progenitors from the earliest institutions of society had done before them. But the mule-twist now coming into vogue, for the warp, as well as weft, added to the water-twist and common jenny yarns, with an increasing demand for every fabric the loom could produce, put all hands in request of every age and description. The fabrics made from wool or linen vanished, while the old loom-shops being insufficient, every lumber-room, even old barns, cart-houses, and outbuildings of any description were repaired, windows broke through the old blank walls, and all fitted up for loom-shops. This source of making room being at length exhausted, new weavers' cottages with loom-shops rose up in every direction ; all immediately filled, and when in full work the weekly circulation of money as the price of labour only rose to five times the amount ever before experienced in this sub-division, every family bringing home weekly 40, 60, 80, 100, or even 120 shillings per week ! ! ! It may be easily conceived that this sudden increase of the circulating medium, would in a few years not only shew itself in affording all the necessaries and comforts of life these families might require, but also be felt by those who, abstractedly speaking, might be considered disinterested spectators ; but, in reality, they were not so, for all felt it, and that in the most agreeable way too ; for this money in its peregrinations left something in the pockets of every stone-mason, carpenter, slater, plasterer, glazier, joiner, &c. as well as the corn dealer, cheese-monger, butcher, and shopkeepers of every description. The farmers participated as much as any class by the prices they obtained for their corn, butter, eggs, fowls, with every other article the soil or farm-yard could produce, all of which advanced at length to nearly three times the former price. Nor was the portion of this wealth inconsiderable that found its way into the coffers of the Cheshire squires who had estates in this sub-division, the rents of their farms being doubled, and in many instances trebled. These landlords have been censured for raising their rents at this period, and subsequently still higher ; but when it is considered, that with this vast increase of money circulating every week amongst the various classes I have mentioned, with such an increased demand and advance in price for every article the soil can produce, it is quite natural to suppose that many would be on the look out to catch any farm where the lease was running out, and to offer advance of rent to secure a preference. This being well known to the old tenant it was not less natural that he should offer (as he could well afford) a handsome advance to have his lease renewed, which, in most instances,

was accepted, the old tenant having a preference
generally, even at a lower rent than a stranger would
have given. If every manufacturer or merchant (for
it is to this class I am alluding) will now only fancy
himself to have been one of these land-owners at
that time, and lay his hand upon his heart and say what
he would have done under the circumstances I have
been stating, I think there is not *one* of these theoretical
censors that would be found to cast a second stone.

To return to the operative weavers *on machine
yarns*, both as cottagers and small farmers, even with
three times their former rents, they might be truly said
to be placed in a higher state of " wealth, peace, and
godliness," by the great demand for, and high price
of, their labour, than they had ever before experienced. Their dwellings and small gardens clean
and neat,—all the family well clad,—the men with
each a watch in his pocket, and the women dressed
to their own fancy,—*the church crowded to excess
every Sunday*,—every house well furnished with a clock
in elegant mahogany or fancy case,—handsome tea
services in Staffordshire ware, with silver or plated
sugar-tongs and spoons,—Birmingham, Potteries,
and Sheffield wares for necessary use and ornament,
wherever a corner cupboard or shelf could be placed
to *shew them off*,—many cottage families had their
cow, paying so much for the summer's grass, and
about a statute acre of land laid out for them in
some croft or corner, which they dressed up as a
meadow for hay in the winter. As before observed,
I was intimately acquainted with the families I am
speaking of in my youth, and though they were then
in my employ, yet, when they brought in their work,
a sort of familiarity continued to exist between us,
which, *in those days*, was the case between all *masters
and men ;* and out of these familiarities I can state a
few anecdotes as they occurred, that I think will fully
redeem the pledge given before,—that the *plough*

was wholly indebted to the *shuttle* for the means
which enabled the former to contribute so largely
to the Property Tax,—and I think I can prove this
to such a demonstration, that all the modern theorists
on political economy will not attempt to refute ;
inasmuch as the facts I now relate apply to the present state of things, which will bring the most learned
in political economy back to his A. B. C. As every
measure recommended to the statesman for allevia-
ting the distress of the agriculturists of the United
Kingdom to answer the end intended, must be
grounded on things *as they are*, the world being
thrown almost into chaos by the baneful powers of
our machinery, while unprotected ! that has already,
or will very soon, turn millions of people into the
streets and lanes to get their bread as they can, if
not prevented by the remedy we seek. To understand what led to these simple anecdotes that are to
prove so much ; it is necessary to inform the reader
that I always attended Manchester Market on Tues-
days, bringing from the bank my cash for the wages
of the week. Next morning, soon after six, I entered
the warehouse to serve the weavers, of whom there
were generally ten to twenty waiting behind the
counter, on which I placed the money to count into
the drawer before I began business, when one of
them exclaimed, "Eh ! mester, what a seet o' money
yo han theer, I wonder weer yo'n get it ?" "From
London," I answered. At other times, to similar
questions, my answer would be Frankfort, Paris,
Amsterdam, Moscow, &c., always alluding to the
quarter where my goods were gone. At one time
they were very much astonished, (it was about the
year 1801,) we were then paying seven hundred
pounds per week in wages alone, and the bundle of
Abraham Newland's, in passing into the drawer,
attracted their extraordinary attention, and the old
question being put by one of them, I replied, "You

will be very much obliged to me when I tell you I have brought this from Leipsic for you, and our friends there have got it from Bucharia, a rich trading country, lying north of Persia and Hindostan:" alluding to a conversation I had lately had with a merchant from Leipsic, who, while making a large purchase from me, had told me from whence many of their best customers came, in the style, he added, " of the Arabian caravans, *laden with money to purchase these goods at their fairs.*" They all joined in expressing their obligations and thanks, but still wondered how this could be done.

As a daily observer, I am sorry to say that many great men of the first rank, who, I again repeat, stand high at county meetings on agricultural distress, and higher meetings still, seem to be as ignorant of the source of our wealth as the country weavers I have been speaking of. These gentlemen, while reaping the harvest from the commercial seed, sown by their forefathers from the time of William & Mary, to the middle of the reign of George the third, must have lost sight of the true history of their country, which uniformly attributes the strength or weakness of our nation at different periods for centuries past, to the healthy or sickly state of our commerce alone, which commerce (I cannot too often repeat it) emanates entirely from our loom; hence, if our landowners wish their plough to flourish, it behoves them to act in the way Ld. Chesterfield and the immortal Locke have pointed out to them for food and raiment, I again repeat, form the only necessary wants of the population of the world ! for as our *old* London merchants, who poured their rich cornu-copias in such golden streams upon our islands, could never have raised themselves to the princely rank they held (till of late) by adventuring the former, the produce of our little speck of cold soil,—it must have been as the merchant in the comedy of the West Indian says—by " *shipping the cloth.*"

In the introduction to this narrative, I mentioned that I was *now* at liberty to publish the progress we made in Parliament in the sessions of 1817, towards redeeming that pledge I have so often spoken of. But as so much time has elapsed, and the sentiments of our opponents are *so much altered* by the ruinous effects of this traffic, during this period, I do not think it necessary to do more than to publish a few documents, as a specimen of our proceedings, and to shew the impression these proceedings made upon the Cabinet itself! and the promising situation this question was placed in at the close of that session. For although for seventeen years, foreign influence, by their agents (under the rose) had been throwing dust in the eyes of every member of that Cabinet, as well as every M. P. of influence, prompting them to place every obstacle in our way—which obstacles had been represented to all of them as insurmountable mountains. Yet, when the writer of this narrative had the honour to be introduced to the Chancellor of the Exchequer, for only seven or eight minutes, on the simple statement of a few facts, these mountains vanished like the dew of a summer's morning, and nothing but small mole-hills remained!—The Chancellor, as far as he could go, went over them at a step, by voluntarily granting us all we were seeking for, which, to use a homely expression, these foreign agents had been at their *wits-end* to prevent, viz., a committee up stairs, and his approbation, if *we could accomplish it*, of forming this committee of members not personally interested in *this traffic.* It did not occur to me at the time,

* Here, and here *only*, and in *this very question too*, lies the *heart-root*, from whence has sprung up all that general cry for radical reform, from the time this traffic commenced to this day!—And if the landed interest have any desire to get rid of it, they have only to pursue the principle laid down by Lord Chesterfield and Locke, when they may with great ease remove this cause. Then, and not till then, I can assure them, will the effect cease.

that I was here touching upon a very delicate subject, and one we had studiously avoided in all our proceedings. I am no reformer, or advocate for any change in Parliament, save that of the House acting a little more firmly up to its *own rules*, as was the case up to 20 or 30 years ago. I will mention a precedent I had in my mind at the time I had this interview with the Minister, and my instructions from the trade in Bolton, and I may add from the greatest and most loyal men in that town and neighbourhood, was not to give my consent to any other, in order to avoid that foreign influence which hitherto had baffled every effort they had made to procure an impartial hearing. The precedent I allude to, occurred when a bill was before the house for supplying the town of Manchester with water, which had the approbation of Sir Oswald Moseley, the Lord of the Manor, who had then a seat in the House. A very strong opposition was raised in that town against its and the opposers of the bill put their case into the hands of Sir Robert Peel, then also a member of the House. But before that honourable House came to its final decision on this hard contested bill, both these members were *ordered to withdraw*, as it was presumed each of them might possibly have some individual interest in the results of that question.— I think it necessary to record this part of my proceedings, though very briefly, in order that the trade in Bolton may be aware that I acted to the best of my humble abilities up to their instructions.

The reader will bear in mind, that the former part of this narrative was penned many years ago in a series of letters to a certain society, some of the members of which might be supposed to be as well informed as myself, as to the cause of the declining state of the trade in 1800, that led to the public proceedings in that year:—therefore I did not think it necessary to go into detail in those letters, nor if

I had, was I then in possession of sufficient documents, to shew the general feelings of all classes in the trade at that time. But having since been favoured with a few printed papers by one of the gentlemen whose names I have given, as forming the committee in Manchester, and to whom I think he acted as secretary,—who, without any previous inquiry from me, after paying me a few compliments for the spirited stand I had lately made against the influence so often mentioned, and urging me to persevere, put these papers into my hand, saying they were the only ones he could find out of a voluminous heap he possessed at the time the question was agitated; all the rest he feared had been lost, but as the few left might be of some service hereafter, he begged leave to place them under my care.

For the last 27 years, in the midst of all the troubles our manufacturing districts have been doomed to experience, although at three distinct periods they went on to open rebellion! yet, in the midst of them I have always contended that in no instance did these disturbances proceed from sedition or dissatisfaction to Government, but solely from the deepest distress, —yea, *that degree of distress*, which is most clearly defined in the old saying we have, " *that hunger will go through a stone wall!*" proceeding from some other cause. These troubles, like every thing else, had a beginning, and that the cause of them may be clearly understood, it is necessary to trace them up to the source from whence such torrents of misery have deluged the empire,—like a canker-worm in the root of every branch in which the loom, the sail, and the plough are interested, *down to this day !* It is well known that the seeds from whence these troubles have sprung up first began to vegetate amongst the weavers in Lancashire, in the latter end of 1799 and the beginning of 1800, changing the aspect of the manufacturing districts from that of wealth, peace,

and godliness, to that of complaints against the masters,—murmers against the ministry,—and a general
cry for peace! which cry was put into their mouths
by certain foreigners and their agents in Manchester,
to whose traffic in the raw material the war was a
great impediment, as it took *their* weavers from the
loom to fill up *their* armies, by which the consumption of yarn was very much reduced. This cry, and the
murmurs accompanying it, led Government to seek
for and afterwards to conclude the peace of Amiens. *

However, the few papers I am thus introducing,
will shew that that cry only proceeded from the
superficial part of the operatives, such as are easily
carried away by subtle and designing men, when they
fancy they have an interest in so doing ; for in these
papers we find the sensible and thinking part of
the weavers, in cordial co-operation with their
employers, (after a little bickering and mutual explanation) discovered *another cause*, which, in itself,
was more than sufficient to account for all the distress
that led to these murmurs, &c. but the papers shall
speak for themselves.

The Association of Weavers, &c. &c.—To the Public.

"The present existing laws that should protect weavers, &c.
from imposition, being trampled under foot, for want of a union
amongst them, they have come to a determination to support each
other in their just and legal rights, and to apply to the legislature of the
country for such further regulations, as it may in its wisdom deem fit
to make, when the real state of the cotton manufactory shall have been
laid before it.—The members of this association have no other object
in view but the mutual interest of both employers and employed—
well knowing that to combine their interest together is the only
method to expect success ; being sensible that the fair trader is exposed
to difficulties through injurious practices that have crept into the
cotton manufactory, and to study his interest is to study their own ;
for if a fair chance is given to him, theirs of course will follow.—

* This being acknowledged by ministers, I record it as a fact

These being their sentiments, they flatter themselves with the support of men of this description, earnestly desiring them to give the situation of weavers, &c. their candid consideration, how very necessary of life has increased in price, whilst the price of labour has undergone a continual decrease ; this being the case, it becomes a duty incumbent on both parties to search out the cause, and, if possible, remove it, that the effects may cease. And ye who are our enemies, do you not blush to hear these facts repeated—Great Britain holding the reins of universal commerce, is it not shameful that her sons should be thus imposed on ?—are you afraid that we should approach Government, and there tell the truth ?—that ye use the mean artifice of stigmatizing us with the name of Jacobins, that ye raise your rumours of plots, riots, &c.

"We disdain your calumny, and look upon you with that contempt you merit. To the public we address ourselves—rioting, or any illegal behaviour, we detest, and are firmly attached to our King and Country, and to promote their prosperity shall ever be the object most dear to our hearts—How unjustly do those calumniate us who assert, that our meetings are calculated to sacrifice the independence of our country : it is the reverse ; for should the clarion ever sound—"To arms ! England is in danger !"—we know what is our duty, and what is our interest ; and not only ours, but the duty and interest of every individual, to rally round Government, and strike the daring foe prostrate at our feet. These being our genuine sentiments, is there any thing to fear by us meeting together ?—We shall neither interfere with church nor state, but strictly confine ourselves to a private grievance, which we wish to lay before Government, and it will remain to be determined by it, whether or not our case merits redress ; but having that confidence in Government, which ought to be universal, we believe that when our real situation is laid before the legislature, some method will be devised to ameliorate our condition.

" There are some so ignorant of the very laws they pretend to administer, that they would willingly confound our meetings with those which are only calculated to undermine Government ; it is wonderful that they are not ashamed to expose their ignorance to the public view—but, that their ignorance may not infect you, we will take the liberty to state, that it never was the intention of Government to infringe upon the right of meeting together to lay any matter of this kind before them.

" On the contrary, the late laws on meetings appear to us to be only intended as a bridle to that wild democratical fury that leads nations into the vortex of anarchy, confusion, and bloodshed : if, then, the laws of your country guarantee to you the right of meeting together to consider of a private grievance of this kind, are you so foolish to be deterred in your proceedings by the misrepresentations of ignorant and designing men, who do more hurt to the Government than good ? Government does not stand in need of a blind attachment, for the more it is considered the more it is admired ; and the friends who are attached to it from understanding are the only real ones to be found.

" It is the interest of every occupation to step forward and support us; even the landed property feels the want of regulation in the cotton manufactory; and to convince the landed interest that this is the case, we will point out the situation of those employed in it :—they are continually subject to reductions in their wages, which never find their level; draw the analogy any distant time back, and what we assert will be found true ;—but to be more particular, we will suppose a man to be married in the year 1792 ; he at that period received twenty-two shillings for forty-four yards of cloth ; we will follow him year after year, his family keeps increasing, together with the price of every necessary of life, whilst his wages for labour decrease—let us look at him in the year 1799, and we shall perhaps find him surrounded with five or six small children, and, lo! instead of forty-four yards, they have increased the length to sixty, and give him only eleven shillings for it ; and, to make ill worse, he must work it with finer weft! —No wonder that poor-rates increase, when people are situated in this manner—a little reflection will shew how matters of this kind affect the landed interest.

" It is in vain to talk of bad trade if goods are actually not wanted, they cannot be sold at any price ; if wanted, two-pence or three-pence per yard will not stop the buyer; and whether does it appear more reasonable that two-pence or three-pence per yard should be laid on the consumer, or taken from the labourer ? a single two-pence per yard would increase the wages from eleven to twenty-one shillings, three-pence to twenty-six shillings ; consider how little it would affect the one, and how important to the other. How imprest with gratitude must that man be with five or six small children, when informed that Government had devised certain measures, that where he now received only eleven shillings, he might receive above twenty shillings for his work.

" Ye whose hardened hearts are dead to those humane feelings which should always adorn the human mind, may say it is impracticable : and are we yet to continue suffering on your barely asserting this ?—No : we are determined that those who are appointed by the constitution of our country to redress our grievances, shall have our real state laid before them ; and it must be their wisdom that must determine this point, and with their determination we shall always think it our duty to comply. A peaceful demeanour shall always guide all our actions, and we trust a candid public will give the subject a mature consideration, and afford us that support we merit.

" It was resolved unanimously, that this address should be printed and distributed in the Towns, in the name of the General Committee, assembled at Bolton, on Monday the 13th of May, 1799.

"JOHN SEDDON, President.

Bolton and adjoining Country.
JOSEPH SHUFFLEBOTTOM,
JAMES DRAPER,
JOHN ROPER,
JOHN LOMAX,
RICHARD NEEDHAM,
WILLIAM HASLAM.

Manchester and Salford.
ADAM RIGBY,
JAMES WILD,
RALPH PARTINGTON.

Stockport.
JOHN ROWBOTTOM,
EDMUND PARTINGTON.

Oldham.
JOHN RATTCLIFF,
STANLEY BRINNAND.

Wigan.
JOHN ROBINSON,
WILLIAM PEMBERTON

Warrington.
WILLIAM HARRISON,
JOHN DORBA.

Blackburn.
RICHARD FAIRHURST,
JOHN ASPIN.

Chorley.
JAMES GREENHALGH,
THOMAS HARTLEY.

Newton.
GEORGE HOUGHTON,
RICHARD PENNINGTON.

Bury.
RICHARD MEADOWCROFT,
JOHN SCHOFIELD.

Whitefield.
JOHN BUCKLEY.

Chowbent.
ROBERT TAYLOR.

New Chapel, near Leigh.
JOHN WILKINSON.

" This Committee earnestly desire, that Weavers in general will step forward and give their support, and others who are interested in the welfare of the cause, are desired to come forward as they have nothing to fear.

"JAMES HOLCROFT, SECRETARY."

Association of Weavers.

" The Public are respectfully informed that the subscription on account of the Weavers' association is postponed till something farther shall have been developed upon the subject, for which purpose if the manufacturers should think proper to condescend so far as to call a meeting, the committee of the association will send a deputation to wait upon them to make such communications upon the subject as will inform them of the particular objects in view; they do not consider themselves in opposition to the masters—on the contrary, they entertain the same sentiments that certain prejudicial practices prevail, that incommode the regular progress of trade ; and that such practices may be put a stop to, is the grand end the members of this association have in view, not from any power of their own, but by appealing to government ; they find such practices press very severely upon them, and they know they have a right to apply for redress—for should it be the practice of monopolizing the *raw material* or *exporting it raw and half wrought*, or should it be found to be certain practices that have crept in amongst employers ;—or on the other hand, the employed, (or all combined together,) they ought if possible to be removed ; for there is no sacrifice on the part of the association, but it will be freely made to put trade on a better foundation. The fore-mentioned practices are very alarming to the association, *particularly the exportation of the raw and half wrought material;* it appears to us that this practice if continued *will ultimately ruin the manufactory here.* We feel the effects of foreigners finishing what is half done here; and shall the spirit of ingenuity be cramped in this country, whilst they deliberately get machinery of their own, which they are straining every nerve to accomplish, holding out allurements to our artisans clandestinely to leave the country that gave them birth; every possible means are made use of by our enemies both external and internal to attain their desirable object to the ruin of the cotton manufactory. We are aware of opposition in this matter; there may be large capitals employed in this ruinous business, but it will avail little, when the fate of myriads is at stake; the opulent expect that government should guarantee to them the peaceable enjoyment of their property, the poor have the same claims upon it and expect the same, which property is the full value of their labour, and if any practices prevail that infringe upon it—humanity and justice declare they ought to be removed: with respect to the injurious practices that may prevail amongst the employers and employed; it is the wish of the association that they should be put a stop to, and nothing shall be wanting on their part to accomplish what they conceive to be necessary for the protection of trade, and they humbly desire the manufacturers to give what has been advanced, their most serious consideration, for we believe, that if regulations could take place by mutual consent, it would be a mutual benefit to both parties. We know it would be a folly to say masters must give wages, without having the means in their power to do it consistent with their own interest, and what in fact never entered our thoughts. Calumny may insinuate that we are led by such chimerical imaginations, but calumny here, as in other cases, misrepresent us, the fact is, the means being put into the hands of the employers, is a day of rejoicing for the employed, and that the cause that deprives them of the means may be removed is the sincere desire of the members who compose the association, who, in gratitude, return their thanks to those who have already subscribed, and they hope to act worthy of the support given.

"By order of the committtee of delegates from Manchester, Stockport, Oldham, Ashton, Preston, Blackburn, Wigan, Warrington, Newton, Chorley, Bury, Whitefield, Rippendon, &c.

"*Assembled at Bolton, on Saturday the 20th day of June,* 1799.

"JOHN SEDDON, President.
"THOS. BENTLEY, Vice-President.
"JAMES HOLCROFT, Secretary."

*A second Address to the Inhabitants of Manchester and
its Vicinity, on the Exportation of Cotton Twist.*

"FRIENDS AND FELLOW TOWNSMEN,

" Since the publication of my first address on the Exportation
of Cotton Twist, a writer, under the specious name of " *Candour*," has
appeared, and endeavoured to prove, by what he calls a few *simple
facts*, that the exporter of twist is engaged in a *legal, honourable,* and
praise-worthy trade. That the trade is *legal,* no one is disposed to
deny ; or why should we be under the necessity of applying to Parliament for redress ? But how it can be called *honourable* or *praise-
worthy,* I have yet to learn.

" The greatest admirers of our excellent laws must admit, that
legal, honourable, and *praise-worthy,* are not always synonymous
terms. For instance, the man who informs against his neighbour, is
engaged in a *legal,* but not an *honourable* act. The speculator, who
buys large quantities of grain, and thereby raises the price of it, is
legally, but neither *honourably* nor *praise-worthily* employed. To
spin and ' give bread to thousands,' is certainly very *honourable* and
praise-worthy ; but to export twist, and deprive tens of thousands of
the means of procuring a subsistence, deserves a very different name.

" The arguments of this writer for continuing to export, because ' twist is of double the value of raw cotton,' will hold equally
good for checking the exportation and encouraging our own manufactures, many of which are of five times the value of the raw material.

" If neighbouring Powers will not look on and see us engaged
in other branches of our trade, because they must wish to have their
own subjects employed : what reason have we to suppose, that they
will let us quietly enjoy our spinning ? Have they all sworn never to
interfere with our spinners ? Or can they be persuaded that this is the
only part of our trade that is not a profitable one ?

" I must own, that I am not convinced by any arguments I have
yet heard, that a prohibition of our cotton manufactures would be the
necessary consequence of our not supplying the Continental nations
with twist ; or that the exporting twist can possibly encourage the manufacturing part of our trade. The people who buy the greater part
of our exported twist, have already prohibited the use of our manufactured goods. The British merchant and manufacturer can therefore
have nothing further to dread from their resentment. Nor do I learn,
that the woollen trade has at all suffered by the unsuccessful applications that have been made from the Continent, to houses in this town,
for woollen yarn.

" ' Wool,' says " *Candour*," ' is the *exclusive* produce of our own
island ; and cotton, the *general* produce of (I may almost say) all the
world.'—Is this a *simple fact ?* If it be, it is strange that other nations, when concluding a treaty with us, do not bind us to keep up a

certain number of sheep, and stipulate with us not to eat mutton more than so many times in a season, lest our stock of sheep should be lessened.

" 'The spinners are a numerous body, and it is much easier to excite discontent and riot, than to allay them.' Is this the language of " *Candour ?* " I would advise this writer, if he does, as he threatens, take up his pen again, to avoid such intemperate appeals, lest the manufacturers should cry with a voice so loud, that the sound shall reverberate through every garret and cellar, from one extremity of the county to the other. *

" ' Are not the spinners necessary to the manufacturers, and are not their operations and interests identified?' This question is not so clearly expressed as could be wished, but with verbal criticism we have nothing to do, being engaged in a business of much greater moment. If the writer means to ask, whether their operations and interests be not reciprocal ? I reply,—by no means. Without spinners the manufacturers could not carry on their trade, it is true ; but without manufacturers in this kingdom, the spinners may flourish for a time. Their interests are no more the same, than those of the machine-maker and the spinner. As the maker of spinning frames might by exporting them be in a flourishing state, while the spinner was every day growing worse in his circumstances ; so also may the spinner be growing rich by the exportation of twist, while the manufacturer is starving.

" ' Competition,' adds this writer, ' is the life and spirit of trade, and best promotes its essential interests. What have we not gained by a generous competition with each other ? and why should we fear a fair competition with the nations on the Continent?' Competition in trade may be advantageous to a certain extent, and yet ruinous if carried beyond it. Let us suppose, for instance, that fifty attornies (or fifty persons in any other profession or trade) in Manchester, had, by vying with each other, not only engrossed all the business of Manchester, but that of the neighbouring towns for twenty miles round : — Would they be able to maintain the advantages they had gained, if five hundred more came to practise in these places, equal to them in abilities and industry, and able to live considerably cheaper ? Or would a colony, which had by great cultivation maintained twenty families comfortably, produce, by any exertions, enough to support two hundred ?

" His next remark is—' Let not the Manchester manufacturer, therefore, fear the *ruin of his trade ;* I am a Manchester manufacturer, and not an exporter of cotton twist.' Is the writer not a *spinner* as well as a manufacturer ? But even granting that he is not—what does this observation amount to ?—only, that it is his simple opinion that

_____

* This prediction was fully verified by the Luddites, Radicals, Blanket Expedition, Peterloo Meeting, Rebellion in Scotland, 1820; and even to the latter riots in Manchester, Blackburn, &c., in 1826.

our trade is not in danger; and that he is not infallible, is already evident by his remarks on sheep's wool.

"As the spinners, by their letters, remarks, &c., seem to think themselves able to bring forward so many arguments in support of the policy of continuing to export twist, they surely will not object to a parliamentary investigation of the business; which is all that is wanted by

"A MANCHESTER TRADESMAN."

"April 29, 1800."

A third Address to the Inhabitants of Manchester and its Vicinity on the Exportation of Cotton Twist.

"FRIENDS AND FELLOW TOWNSMEN,

"My opponents multiply so fast, that they seem like the Hydra of old, to be renewed after every attack. No sooner has 'Candour' been laid low, than a 'Mercator' and a 'Cotton Spinner' start forth, and as if all the powers on earth were not sufficient to support a tottering cause, 'Mercury' is called from heaven to their assistance. Surely we must be either very dull of apprehension, or these writers not very happy in their explanation of the subject, and yet they seem to think every one who runs may read it.

"Of the 'Cotton Spinner' I shall only observe, that his powers appear not equal to the weight of machinery he attempts to move. His words are multiplied without adding any force to his arguments.

"The writer, who assumes the name of Mercury, the god of thieves, did not, I hope, mean to reflect upon any part of our trade. His only reason for taking this character must be, that he might indulge himself in all the flights of fancy. One while talk of gold and gingerbread for the amusement of the 'junior branches of families,' another personify Commerce, and shackle and physic her, to make the unlearned stare with astonishment. Such arts are well enough suited to the character assumed, and while we hear only of gold gingerbread, we recal our boyish days, and relish the language; but the other flights of his imagination are so daring, that his arguments are all lost in clouds and smoke, and soar far above the ken of vulgar eyes.

"The writer most deserving of notice is 'Mercator,' * who, from the length of his observations, seems the most likely to make the worse appear the better part. But, however, my friends, let us not be carried away too hastily, and conclude a person infallible, because he has gone over various parts of Europe, and says with Merrick's traveller, in his fable of the Cameleon :

* A German, who is also supposed to have wrote, or dictated some papers signed CANDOUR. This gentleman has always been considered as the founder of the Foreign Sovereign Junta in Manchester, of whom I shall hereafter have occasion to speak freely.

' Sirs, if my judgment you'll allow,
' I've seen—and sure I ought to know.

" But let us weigh the arguments he has advanced coolly, before
we give implicit credit to them.

" As it would be a presumptuous attempt for a plain tradesman to
combat so many learned men, I shall endeavour, as is no uncommon
practice in the political world, to set my opponents against each other;
and to shew, that, in their arguments, they are not only at variance
with each other, but frequently with themselves.

" To begin with sheep's wool:—

" ' Wool is the *exclusive* produce of our island.'—CANDOUR.

" ' Fine cloth is made altogether of Spanish wool.—English wool cannot
even be so mixed with Spanish wool as to enter into the composition without
spoiling and degrading, in some degree, the fabric of the cloth.'—ADAM SMITH,
quoted by MERCATOR.

" How ingenious the same people may be represented in one instance, and how stupid and dull in another, to serve a writer's purpose.

" ' They (some of the Continental nations) have besides every other requisite for the establishment and carrying on of *cotton factories*—Mechanics of
every description, *not inferior in skill to any other nation*, and in point of
patient accuracy *superior*, as I think, to *many*; and a great population, which
supplies them with an abundance of hands at an easy rate.'—MERCATOR.

" ' All that we can do, and *all that we have to do*, is to give full scope
to our powers and ingenuity, in order to maintain the *superiority of our manufactures*, which in times of peace will *always ensure* them a preference.'—
MERCATOR.

" Since, then, it is so very easy a thing for us to excel the continental nations in manufacturing, and so very difficult to maintain our superiority in spinning, those who wish well to our trade, will rejoice that
we are petitioning Parliament to protect our manufactures. We cannot, it is evident, be spinners for any length of time with so many
difficulties to encounter.

" ' The cotton business abroad cannot be materially hurt for any length
of time by the want of a supply of twist from England. Indeed, I do not believe, that any political measure can be devised to stop its progress.'—MERCATOR.

" Cheering as the prospect was in the last sentence, this must
cast a damp upon the mind of every manufacturer and merchant in the
trade.

" ' I confess myself surprised to see it (the question concerning the exportation of twist) again taken up, and, at a moment, too, when there is so far
from cause of complaint on the state of our trade, that it is allowed to be
*flourishing, extending in every branch of it, and every hand acknowledged
to be employed.*'—MERCURY.

" ' The *temporary depression of some branches of the cotton manufacture* is not owing to the exportation of twist, but to causes which affect
alike every manufacturing town in the kingdom.'—MERCATOR, and RESOLU-
TIONS of the SPINNERS.

" Thus is our trade represented either has flourishing or depressed,
which ever best suits the writer's purpose.

"Mercator has favoured you with some quotations from the celebrated work of Dr Adam Smith. This author being considered almost infallible in what relates to trade, I will likewise give you a quotation from him. It is to be found in the *midst* of those, which Mercator has made use of, but was *unintentionally*, I dare say, overlooked by him.

"'The violence of these regulations, therefore, seems to have affected neither the quantity nor the quality of the annual produce of wool, so much as it might have been expected to do (though I think it probable that it may have affected the latter a good deal more than the former,); and the interest of the growers of wool, though it must have been hurt in some degree, seems, upon the whole, to have been much less hurt than could well have been imagined.'

"'These considerations, however, will not justify the absolute prohibition of the exportation of wool, but they will justify the *imposition of a considerable tax upon that exportation*.'

"Here we see this writer, whose favourite hypothesis is, that all trade should be free; and who in support of it had gone so far as to doubt the propriety of limiting even public houses, is obliged to confess, that the growers of wool had not suffered so much as might be expected by prohibiting the exportation of it. His arguments, which have been partially quoted with so much confidence by the spinners and exporters, when fairly examined, correspond exactly with the sentiments expressed in the resolutions passed at the meeting of the merchants, &c., held the 29th of April.

"In most of the papers from the spinners, some threat is thrown out respecting emigration. Government has not much to fear on this head from any of those concerned in the cotton trade. Were any thing to be apprehended, the merchant and manufacturer are surely much more likely to emigrate than the spinner, whose capital is in part vested in buildings and machinery.

"MERCATOR has informed us, that none of the low numbers of water twist are exported; the other writers say only a few. May we not then, fairly infer from hence, that the exportation of twist is the principal, if not the sole cause of the depression of some parts of our trade? For contrary to the assertion of MERCATOR, the heavy articles are at this moment the most in demand.

"A MANCHESTER TRADESMAN."

"*May* 6, 1800."

[Manchester, printed by C. Wheeler and Son; and sold by Messrs I. W. and W. CLARKE, booksellers, in the Market-place.]

Remarks on the Exportation of Cotton Twist.

"The attention of the public having been much engaged by the contradictory opinions entertained respecting the exportation of cotton yarn, a bye-stander, who is neither a spinner nor exporter, has deliberately made enquiry into the nature and extent of this busi‑ ness, with a wish to discover how far the manufactures of Great Britain are likely to be injured by the continuance of such exportation; and after the most careful researches, he is of opinion that the facts are of such a nature as to speak very unequivocally for themselves, and that the merits of the argument may easily be understood by every disin‑ terested person, who wishes for information, and has the welfare and prosperity of the country at heart.

"It being admitted that very large quantities of twist of the best quality are annually exported, it is very proper to enquire whether this is a business of a *long* standing, or of a *recent* date, and whether it increases, or is in a declining state.—To these queries the replies are pointedly, that the export is of a very few years' standing, and that the increase has been so immense, as to have occasioned the establishment of a great number of new factories, many of which have been built within the last two years.—These answers having been obtained, en‑ quiry is next made what becomes of this twist when exported? The reply is, that it is manufactured in various parts of the continent of Europe, into goods of different descriptions.—It is natural to enquire further, what are the kind of goods they make from the British twist? in answer it appears, that in the infancy of the business, they only attempted the more simple articles, such as nankeens, &c., but that *now* they have made such progress in the art of manufacture, as to rival us in many more complex articles, which they can dye, bleach, print, and finish, equal to the British manufacturers.

" It is asked why they do not spin warp for themselves; and we gather in reply to this question, that numerous factories have been established upon the continent, but that their produce is as yet of so inferior a nature and quality, that it cannot be used as warp, but answers very well for the purpose of weft, so long as they can obtain a supply of British warp; but that it would be totally useless, and the spinning concerns abroad become *ruinous to the proprietors*, unless they could depend upon warps from Great Britain.

" One more question occurs upon the general ground of candid enquiry—which is, what is the comparative situation of those countries where these manufactures have been established, *now*, and ten years ago, before this exportation took place. The answer from every quarter is, that the necessaries of life are much cheaper there than in this country, the taxes very small, and wages trifling; the foreign manu‑ facturer has many advantages over us, and consequently that commerce has advanced with rapid strides amongst them, and that the constant subject of their conversation, is their ability to undersell the British manufacturers in consequence of these local advantages.

" From these premises (which it is presumed are neither ex‑ aggerated, nor in any way mis-stated) it may be gathered, that the subject *is very important to this country*, and a just dread be enter‑ tained that, for the sake of a temporary advantage to a few individuals, we may be furnishing our rivals with weapons which they will use to the destruction of our own manufactures, and that by so doing (so long as they cannot proceed without our more perfect spinning) we enable them to establish factories for their own future supply, and therefore, that the exporters from this country will, in a very few years, be the means of removing the cotton manufacture to the continent of Europe, to the utter ruin of our own trade; in which general overthrow, the spinners themselves must necessarily be included, as it cannot be expected that taxes will materially decrease in this country, nor that wages can ever be lower than at present—the reverse is much more probable, whenever we enjoy the blessings of a secure peace.

" The political calculator will have no hesitation in asserting, that the more operations a material undergoes before it is sold, the greater will be the profit to the country at large, and the community be benefited in proportion to the number of hands employed : therefore, that 100lbs. of cotton, when spun, warped, woven, bleached, dyed, printed, and finished, will leave a much greater sum of money in the country for labour and profit, than an equal quantity, if exported as soon as it has undergone the operation of spinning only. This truth is so evident, that no sophistry in the world can overthrow it : this, happily, has been the case with the cotton trade of Great Britain, to its very great emolument and prosperity ; the manufacturer and spinner have flourished hand in hand, and to our honour in every point of view, we have been manufacturers for three quarters of the globe—having prospered so well under the old arrangement, we surely should not adopt a ' new order of things,' without duly weighing the consequences.

" Were I to be asked for my candid opinion what mode would be most likely to transplant our manufacture into other parts, I should not recommend the immediate establishment of factories, even though they were to be supported by a royal treasury ; neither should I be so much alarmed as many persons are, at the emigration of ingenious mechanics ; but permit the free exportation of the best twist, and you at once remove all the obstacles to the establishment of an infant manufacture ; as from the introduction of such excellent materials, people unacquainted with weaving, find no difficulty in learning that very essential operation, which may be considered as the corner-stone of the whole fabric. It is surely a great inconsistency to prohibit the exportation of machinery under severe penalties, and at the same time to permit the unlimited sale of the produce of such machinery, to the very persons of whom we are so jealous in the former instance.

" In a moral point of view, it is very far from being desirable to become merely spinners for the rest of Europe, as every thinking person must lament the depravity that may be traced to these *seminaries of vice :* the health of the rising generation is certainly very materially injured by the daily, and frequently nocturnal confinement of children, to whom exercise and a liberal allowance of time for relaxation, are absolutely necessary. *Where is there a respectable and thinking parent that will put his child apprentice to a servitude so destructive both of health and morals ! ! !* These facts deserve consideration, especially where it relates to spinning for foreign markets; thereby taking from our own poor the more healthy occupations of weaving, bleaching, dying, and numerous other branches of manufacture, which require manly exertion, and are productive of health and independence; treasures unattainable by those emaciated wretches who work day and night, to the disgrace of the country, which has too long permitted such slavery to exist, though laudably alive to the more trifling sufferings of the African negroes, whose toil ceases at sun-set.

"I have been respectably informed, that to these causes may be attributed the very great number of diseased limbs, with which the Manchester Infirmary has been crowded of late years, as well as the prevalence of a most fatal and malignant fever, from which some factories are seldom entirely free. It would be an act of great injustice to the respectable proprietors of a many buildings, were it not stated to their honour, that they take every possible pains to prevent these evils, and to render the situation of the children as comfortable and healthy, as they can be under such confinement; but with every caution, the serious evils before stated do exist, and are likely to increase, if we, by continuing the free exportation of twist, make ourselves general spinners for the rest of Europe.

"*April,* 1800."   "SPECTATOR."

Although very few of the papers addressed to the public at that time, pro and con on this subject, have fallen into my hands, I am sorry the limits I must prescribe to myself in this narrative, do not permit me to record those that are before me. As they would exhibit, *in embryo*, the outlines of all that mal-metaphysical genius by which the Foreign Anglo Junto, in Manchester, of late years,* have been enabled to mature *a sovereign controul over our ships, colonies, and commerce,* far greater than they could then contemplate. And by perseverance (with two exceptions) have carried every measure the cabinets of *their mother countries* could wish, with the greatest applause!—But this junto, fearing that John Bull, when sobered by reflection, would take second thoughts, and retrace his steps to prevent;

* With the aid of Liverpool, their port, and cabinet ministers for its representatives, having their Liverpool office at the elbow of the cabinet itself!

if possible, such an event, they have recorded the strongest anathemas against our *stupid forefathers*, who had so long debarred them from *their* metaphysical reciprocity, (all on one side.) Yea, even our great pilot, Mr Pitt, must not escape without a *lash!* but they had instructed their late representative to administer it in the most gentle manner, and if possible, in the shape of a compliment ; and their instructions could not have been placed in better hands! for the Right Hon. Gentleman, in the execution of his duty, approaches his victim with great awe!— I *do not wonder at this!* He compared Mr Pitt to the greatest of all luminaries—the sun ! (applause.) But, adds the Right Hon. Gentleman, as the sun itself has sometimes spots upon it, so, of course, the copy of that great prototype could not be supposed to be free from blemish, and the only dark spot in his administration, was his obstinately supporting the absurd restrictions of his predecessors, without paying any regard to the new lights that were now enlightening the country!—(great applause, and justly merited.)—For never was a disagreeable task, (as this must have been to the Right Hon. Gentleman) so well performed. It was very important to the reciprocity party, that *this cut*, should not only be given, but that it should be such a *home stroke*, as to prevent the name of that old-fashioned statesman being again mentioned during these discussions ; and to the best of my recollection, this *lash*, surrounded as it was with such a complimentary *halo!*—fully answered the end intended.

On the corn-bill question, and the export of machinery, the two exceptions before-mentioned, in which the junto have not yet been able to give more than one half of what their mother countries were anxious to obtain, some explanation is required.— The obstacles they have hitherto met with in the former, being as well known to every one as myself, requires no further remark from me. But as to the latter, from having kept a *steady eye* on the proceedings of this junto from the first, perhaps I may be able to dive a little deeper into their secrets than mere superficial observers may have done. But before I proceed further, that I may be clearly understood, I will explain what I mean by the term *Foreign Anglo Junto.* By the former, which constitutes the legislative part of this junto, I mean every sovereign state in Europe—some part of Asia, and the United States of America ; from whence very clever men have long sat themselves down in Manchester, for the purpose of *carrying off our cotton trade to the states from whence they came.* The late panic, the deplorable state of our operatives, *particularly in Ireland*—the general scarcity of money, *even up to his Majesty's exchequer itself*—with many et ceteras, are the best evidences how far they have succeeded. And had it not been for the successful efforts of the writer of this narrative, by introducing the new system of manufacture, that has prolonged their stay with us for awhile, till they have sent off a sufficient quantity of this sort of machinery, and the most skilful hands, to teach them how to work it ; these clever men would, long ago, have left us nothing in this trade worth keeping, unless we are anxious to retain those empty honours, for which our liberality has made us so notorious ; that we are at this day the laughing-stock of all the sovereign states I have enumerated, and in the highest degree, by the foreign part of this junto itself, when spending their evenings together, and cracking their jokes, over *their smuggled wine, segars,* &c.

As these bold assertions are easily made, and amount to nothing unless supported by corresponding facts, I must (before I come to the anglo part of this junto) endeavour to point out some of those facts on which I have made these bold assertions.

For although all I can say on this head, is as well known to every person in trade in Manchester as to myself, and to many much better, yet, as none of them *dare speak out!* and as those persons to whom Lord Chesterfield & Locke give advice how to act on extraordinary occasions, must be ignorant of the working and detail of this traffic for the last twenty-seven years, for their information, and as a guide to the historian, I will record some particulars of what I allude to.

In the first place, I lay down this principle, that from the day a cotton mill is built and filled with machinery, the whole becomes national property ; every cargo of cotton after once dispersed amongst these mills, the same, no part of which ought, or can legally be used, or disposed of afterwards, without it is done with an eye—yea, and with a comprehensive eye too, to national interest and advantage. For if the individual who builds the mill or purchases the cotton, fails to make his payments good, the deficiency is made up at the loss of other individuals in the same national copartnership.

Before the foreign part of this junto sat down in Manchester, these losses, whether they arose from a total wreck of any of these mills, or from a rich house losing a great part of its capital by a sudden fall in the price of cotton, * or from an over supply

* Witness the scenes that took place among the greatest spinning concerns in the trade in 1825-6. From the 1st Jan. 1825, to Midsummer, every mill was at full work, supplying themselves weekly with cotton until it had nearly trebled in price. The home trade, as usual went quietly on, by goods advancing in proportion to cotton, while most of the great shippers of twist had, in *their* usual way, made contracts in Dec. 1824, with all *their* great spinners, for 2 to 5000 lbs weekly, for three to five months to come, at very bare prices, even as cotton *then* stood ; hence, in less than two months, these spinners had to pay as much for their cotton, as they got for their yarns, and if their contracts run for three to five months, as some of them did a great deal more.

With these weekly supplies, and the great stores they have been very particular in keeping up on the continent, ever since *we gave* of yarns beyond the demand ; all these apparent losses did not reduce the amount of wealth in the nation ; on the contrary, though it may appear anomalous, I believe they were often the means of increasing it. For if the produce of these mills for a few months (during those *little panics* that often occurred) were obliged to be sold for a little more or a little less than the spinner had paid for the *raw cotton ;* these jobs were *all* purchased by the great manufacturers in the United Kingdom, thereby obliging them to employ more hands to work them up, and by this additional demand for their labour, their wages generally advanced.—Or when these stocks were too great for the manufacturers, the surplus was bought up by the great capitalists in Manchester and the neighbouring towns, (who laid them up, even for

them such an alarm in the session of 1817 ! the foreign part of this junto on making their calculations, as to when *such and such* spinners would be *obliged* to sell in order to meet their payments, found themselves sufficiently independent to summons a diet, in which they unanimously resolved not to purchase any of the high priced yarns produced by the great advance in cotton, knowing there would be a fine harvest for them *by and by,* when the period arrived that these payments *must* be made.

In the mean while they lay on their oars, amusing themselves in the way I have before observed and when any of the parties had pressing orders to procure supplies for particular concerns abroad, the junto managed to keep them out of the market, by serving them with part of their supplies coming in weekly, from the contracts before-mentioned, or by an order on their stores abroad, on better terms than they could procure those articles in the market. In this way they lay by, till August and Sept. following, (firmly abiding by what they had told every spinner from the first, viz. that they would not purchase until yarns came down again to their old price) by which time all the warehouses in Manchester, in which this article of traffic, (as deadly in its results as so many tons of Congreve's rockets, if sent to our enemy could possibly be) is usually kept were all full, and large empty rooms in every quarter of the town, as temporary stores, were also filled with the overflowing surplus ; the prime cost of this immense stock would amount to millions of our money ! and though one half of its amount was never realised by the sale of it, yet, this was not *a tythe of the loss* it has otherwise occasioned to our empire at large !

years, in some instances,) by which they not only realised to themselves great fortunes, but at the same time, keeping the raw material up to such a reasonable price, as not materially to affect the price of manufactured goods in the market.

But since the foreign part of this junto have been allowed to sit down in Manchester, and take the helm of this trade into *their own hands*, all these over-plus stocks have been purchased by them for an " old song," and sent off to their mother countries! Yet these are only trifles, compared with the advantages they have had in what may be called their regular traffic. It is well known that at all times during the last twenty-seven years, there has always been too much spinning for the regular demand, even when trade was apparently going well, and many great spinners professing to spin solely for the home trade, would at times be so much over-stocked, as to induce them to clear it off with a great sacrifice, if they would do it (under the rose) so as not to reduce the current price for the future in the home trade, or injure their credit in the cotton-market. These foreigners, with their bank-notes, (especially since they got their loans in London) have been very convenient for this purpose, who, by clubbing their purses together, and agreeing in what portions to divide this spoil ; no quantity was too great for them, at 20 or 30 per cent. under the market price!—the spinner can at any time go to them with confidence, as they never expose names.—Yet it sometimes happens, when another spinner, in the regular course of his business, calls upon them to make a bargain, the foreigner will take one of these job invoices, double down the head of it, so as to cover the name and place from whence this sacrifice came; by these means, and a mutual understanding amongst themselves, they are very soon enabled to establish these job-prices, as the regular price in the market, so far as the supply of their mother countries require.

Now, this mode of clearing off the surplus yarns from our market, may appear pretty fair in the eyes of the spinner, the cotton-broker, (who having lost his cent. per cent. as a merchant adventurer, is now glad of his 10s per cent.) and those interested in the dock dues in Liverpool. And if the loss to the nation had ended here, I should not have taken the trouble to notice them as matters of much importance; but, I think I can shew, that if these yarns had been bought up with exchequer bills, and *burnt* on the next common, this national loss would have been trifling compared with what they afterwards occasioned to us. For after following them through the sovereign States before mentioned, (where they have given employment to perhaps millions of those, who, in the contest have been *deadly rivals* to our operatives in every branch, from the winding, &c., to the finish of all goods, made wholly or in part, from this *raw material*.) We again meet with them in every part of the world, in deadly array against us; but in such new shapes and features, that no one can recognize them as an old acquaintance.—For in their transmigrations through those states, they have been transformed into every description of necessary clothing and fancy dress; and having been fabricated and finished, under the circumstances I have mentioned, *i. e.*, 25 per cent. on the raw material in their favour, to start with, and the labour upon them at one-third of what our hands ought to have, as the minimum of their wages, if they were to be allowed the common necessaries and comforts of life.

But, that the wise men of the age, whom Lord Chesterfield and Locke call to their duty on great emergencies, may understand what is meant by that deadly foreign competition that has brought on our empire such an *alarming crisis,* I will endeavour to

shew them how it has been effected. And that I may
be clearly understood, I will take a cotton-mill, of
moderate size, which, by working the hands *seventy-
two to eighty-two hours per week*, produces 6,000lbs.
of No. 40's twist, the prime cost of which, (leaving
the wear of machinery out of the calculation,) is
1s. 1d. per lb.; the spinner sells 4,000lbs. to Blackburn, at 1s. 3d., and the other 2,000, (under the
rose) to Elberfeldt, at 1s. per lb. I will also take
another mill, the same size, which produces the weft
at about 2d. per lb. lower, which that spinner sells
to the same people, at prices in the same proportion,
from which I will endeavour to illustrate the fact I
am driving at, by an estimate of the

First cost of a Piece of Calico, **28** *yards long.*

IN BLACKBURN.				IN ELBERFELDT.			
lb. oz.	£.	s.	d.	lb. oz.	£.	s.	d.
2 4 of Twist, at 15d......0		2	9¾	2 4 of Twist, at 1s........0		2	3
2 12 of Weft, at 13d........0		2	11¾	2 12 of Weft, at 10d........0		2	3½
Paid for weaving, one part in money, and the other, more or less, as the wages ebb and flow, out of the poors' rate—non-payment of rent, and shop-bills the weaver is not able to dis-charge; all of which is the same as money, in a national point of view 0		6	0	Paid for weaving, in money, on which the weaver can live without poors'-rate, pay his rent, shop-bills, &c........ 0		2	0
Other expences, including the master's profit, say...... 0		1	0	Other expences, say...... 0		1	0
	£0	12	9½		£0	7	6½

This calculation is made on a common article,
but if we go regularly up to the finest jacconot, mull,
or book-muslin, and the finest cotton cambric and
lace, (not a yard of any of which fabrics could they
make without *our yarns,)* as well as every description of dimities, quiltings, nankeens, &c., with all
kinds of fancy-goods made wholly of cotton, or mixed with silk, linen, or wool, we shall find every thing
in the same proportion against us!

Thus abundantly assorted, this rivalry that *we have created*, has long met us in every foreign market; when, notwithstanding many local advantages we possess, our merchants, to get rid of their adventures, have, for a series of years, been obliged to sacrifice **20** *to* **40** *per cent. on millions of this sort of property every year!*—until the greater portion of them were ruined!! Others, who had something left, retired, and lodged what they had saved out of this general wreck, in the funds, foreign loans, and in their bankers' hands, ready for any other adventure, or *scheme* that might offer itself. And, here the same genius that had spread his nets so widely a century ago, to catch the merchants of that day, (who had experienced similar reverses, occasioned by the export of wool and woollen yarns,) awoke, as it were, from a trance! and the history of 1824-5 will long record a pretty fair counter-part of the scenes that took place at the former period.

Notwithstanding this shipwreck amongst nearly all our old merchant adventurers, many of them having considerable establishments abroad, with partners or confidential servants in them, and some property left, and others, who had got their certificates, equally at liberty to seek their future livelihood; though they all, as they got out, had resolved to send out no more adventures in *this line* on their *own account;* yet it is very natural that they should wish to retain these establishments, and keep up their old connections. For this purpose, they either personally, or by their agents, visited the manufacturing districts, as usual; only that they said they could *not purchase!* but as they had establishments abroad, they called to solicit consignments. When, by holding out strong inducements to manufacturers, who having no other vent for their heavy stocks of goods, they were *obliged* to comply; and as the merchants engaged to advance two-thirds of the amount at the market-price of the day, in money, or an acceptance at six months; this gave a considerable revival to trade for years, and an immense business has been done in this way.

Those who were aware of the *deadly competition* these *new merchant* adventurers had to contend with, have always said these consignments would never realize more than these advances; and I was lately in company with a first-rate accountant, who has been employed in winding up some of the most extensive concerns in Lancashire, Yorkshire, &c., (who, *unaware of what they had to contend against*, had thus taken the field against such a *deadly enemy*,) and he tells me, that so far from any balance turning up in favour of the estates of these shippers, (of which he did not recollect one instance!) in most of them balances of 2 to £10,000 have been proved against these estates by the consignees!! The foreign junto in Manchester have *upset and crippled* many great spinning concerns in the same way, viz. by saying to a spinner, when over-stocked, and must raise money to meet the acceptances, by which he had purchased his cotton, "we cannot buy, but if you will consign it to us, we will send it to our house in St. Petersburgh, Hambro', Leipsic, &c., and return a faithful account of sales, which no doubt will pay you well; meanwhile, we will advance you one-half, or two-thirds." —The result of which I have already stated!!!

The United States having been admitted, by the junto in Manchester, to the same privileges as any of the most favoured nations.—It is well known they have been anxious for many years to come in for a part of the spoils of our country, while we remain in our *liberal mood!* And out of many instances that have come to my knowledge, I will state two facts, as specimens of what we are doing for them daily :—In addition to that of sending them plans, models, and machinery complete, or in parts, with

the choicest of our mechanics, in order to make them
more independent of such favours in future.—
Especially, as they are daily *in fear*, that John Bull,
when *goaded too deeply*, in self-defence, will, some
day, suddenly, in one of his pranks, cast off his
liberal mood, and return to his *old, stupid, stingy*,
and restrictive mood! under which, on a moment's
reflection, (the names of *Pitt* and *Nelson* being his
monitors,) he may recollect, that heretofore, *no one
could approach him with impunity*! ! !

The former of the two facts I am going to record,
was very ungracious to my feelings when I heard it.
The reader will recollect the extreme caution with
which I took out my patents, and my motives for
being so—I must also call his recollection to the plan,
the pains, and expence I was at, in introducing this
system to the trade, in Glasgow. Happening
to be in that city, in January, 1818, and while
breakfasting with one of their merchants, who
is also a spinner and exporter of cotton-yarns, in
conversing on this subject, this gentleman told me,
he was at that time shipping to the United States,
cotton warps on the weaver's beam, already dressed
in the patent machines, and drawn into the reed and
healds, ready for the hand or power-loom, which
looms, as well as every other part of (what I have
hitherto a right to call) my machinery for the new
system, had been sent over to them long before the
dates of my patents had run out. And to shew
them (hard learners, I fancy) the practical mode of
working these simple things, these beams, &c., were
sent to them in this working state.

The second fact I have to record, is of such
every-day occurrence, that it can only be useful to
those unacquainted with the trade, by shewing them
the basis on which the cotton-manufactures of the
United States are rising so rapidly, as our rivals in
the western hemisphere.

The clever men who represent the United States in the Manchester Sovereign Junto, are great importers of cotton, for the sale of which they have large establishments in Manchester, that gives them regular intercourse with the great spinners, many of whom make up a part of their water or throstle-twist, (as these articles are termed in the trade) into calico-warps for the home trade, chiefly for the circle of Blackburn, and the western parts of Yorkshire.

But the various panics during the last twenty-seven years, have so pressed down the masters at those times, (long before there were any power-looms to lay the blame upon) that they had neither money nor credit left, by which they could purchase these warps from the spinners. In this dilemma, the latter, when the open credit or acceptance, on which he had bought his cotton, was coming due, and his credit with his banker at full stretch, had no alternative, save that of stating his case to the cotton-merchant, or his commission-agent, from whom he had made such purchase. When these gentlemen, as a special accommodation to their friend, would always (under the rose) relieve the spinner, by taking this surplus stock (whether in the bundle or in the warp) off his hands, at two-thirds or three-fourths of the price the spinner was then getting from the manufacturers before-mentioned. As to payments, if it was an open credit, they would place the amount to his credit in cash—if an acceptance, they would give him some of their foreign bills nearly due, (which I shall again have occasion to notice) to enable him to to meet it in London.

Although I shall stagger the belief of persons unacquainted with the workings of this great trade; yet it is a fact, that has universally been complained of by the richest manufacturers in the trade, for more than twenty-seven years, that none of them, even with bank-notes in their hands, could purchase these surplus stocks of yarn at less than 15 to 20 per cent. higher than what these foreigners were always able to buy them at! because the spinner could not be certain he was doing it *under the rose ;* for although he might have confidence in a pledge of secrecy from the master, yet the book-keeper, who posts the invoices into the ledger, is sometimes known to blab a secret over his glass in the evening.

These cotton-merchants, for want of weavers, &c., in the United States, until the sovereign junto, in Manchester, got the repeal of our old acts, prohibiting these mechanics from going abroad, could only partake of a small share of these favours, compared with what their brethren (in the junto) from the continent had long enjoyed without a rival of any consequence. But on the repeal of these acts, with the shoals of these weavers, &c., they have since sent over, (to the heart's delight of their brethren from the continent, to whom the genius and industry of these artizans had always proved themselves successful rivals in their Hans Towns,) they have, in order to facilitate the transfer of *their share* of *our cotton-trade,* sent out a proportionate quantity of the raw material along with them. And as their own spinning was too much in its infancy to produce a *good warp,* except in very low numbers, these calico-warps were of the *first importance to them,* even if there had been a duty of 50 per cent. ad valorem on a fair price to the spinner ; considering the high protecting duty they, in *their* reciprocity lay on our piece-goods. But when, by the blab of an Englishman, a book-keeper in a great Anglo-American house, I was told, that in 1826, they were sending out these warps in large quantities at 10d. per lb., bought in the way I have before stated—while no English manufacturer could buy them under 14d. to 15d. !—My wonder is not that these rivals get on so fast, but rather that they do not get on much more rapidly than we have yet heard of; for by being supplied with these warps from us, they can use their yarns for the weft, while they learn their hands to spin the former; therefore, if they do not become serious rivals, and that very soon, they have only themselves to blame; for it is not in the power of John Bull to do more than he is now in the habit of doing for them daily.

I must further record the regular practice of these clever foreigners, not only of evading our stamp tax on bills of exchange, but, at the same time, so managing this tax, as to *receive* from it a very great revenue to themselves! In the detail of which I shall more fully explain my reasons for calling them the sovereign part of the Manchester junto, than any of their transactions I have hitherto related; and that I may be clearly understood, I will relate from my own experience, how rare it was to see a bill without a stamp, before we came under the control of this foreign junto.

From the year 1788, few people have been better acquainted with the Manchester trade, in all its details, than myself; during which time, I have given circulation to more than a million and a half in sterling money, which I received in exchange for the *real* manufactures of our country; and by far the greatest part of this business was done with foreigners, from Hambro', Frankfort, Leipsic, Moscow, Brussels, Vienna, Milan, Bayonne, Paris, &c.; as well as with some parts of the United States.— And though the bulk of it was done directly with the merchants who came over to purchase, yet I had occasional orders from Moscow, Paris, &c., for certain goods as they came up from the bleachers, that might continue for four or five months; in some cases giving two months' credit before I saw a bill for them; yet, to the best of my recollection, from **1794 to 1807, no bill ever passed through my hands** without being on an English stamp; nor till after the peace of 1815, when the loans to Russia, Prussia, &c., &c., were granted, bills without stamps were rarely seen in our market.

But when the *bits* of paper they cut off these *great loans*, were sent to the junto in Manchester, to purchase the raw material for their mother countries, these pretty things enabled them to clear the market, even at more ruinous prices to the spinner than heretofore—the bits of paper being *so good*, the latter could not resist them, in exchange for the surplus stock of his yarns, especially as it enabled him (under the rose) to keep up his price for what he could sell to the home manufacturer, from whom *alone*, those spinners who *had*, or *have* realised independent fortunes are indebted!—*many* of which, these little scraps of paper have sent *clear out of the country;* while all that remains to many others, is reduced to the value of " old bricks, pieces of wood, and bent iron." For if their mills can do nothing better than work 70 to 80 hours per week, as many of them have been *obliged* to do for some time past, in spinning the warps for the foreign loom, at barely prime cost, (leaving jobs out of the question,) and this to continue only for a few years longer, while they learn to spin their own ; what value can any person put upon such property, beyond that of the above quotation ? It is true, I am making these remarks at a period when there has been a long depression in the price of cotton yarn ; but viewing it as a national traffic, I fearlessly assert, that if we were to make a profit and loss account of the *whole* that has been done in it from 1794, to this day, the balance, on the side of loss, shall not only exceed the profit, but exceed it in a sum that would stagger belief ! but,

To return to these *little* papers that have sent such *great* fortunes from *this country ;* whether they had stamps upon them, or not, though I saw a few of them, I do not recollect ; but when *they* were run out, the junto hit upon another plan of filling the market with a sort of bills that has enabled them, *ever since*, to create a circulating medium, by which a great portion of the trade in Manchester has been carried on *without any stamps at all ! ! !* It has not yet come to my knowledge, how, or where these bills are manufactured. If they say they receive them in remittance for business already done, I can only answer —*fudge*, as to by far the greater part of them. The most probable conjecture is that they have them drawn at St. Petersburgh, Hambro', New York, and every place from whence they come, on their bankers and correspondents in this country, and sent in parcels, in order to *save postage !!!* Or whether they get over reams of foreign paper, with foreign ink, if necessary, and manufacture these bills themselves, (in the sanctum sanctorum of the counting-houses of the *Dons,* and the bed-rooms in the *cheap* lodgings of the other parts of this sovereign junto,) at dates corresponding with the arrival of the packets ; all of which appears to me quite practicable—and I know of no check against this mode, save their honour ! And if I may judge from many facts that have come to my knowledge, when the interest of *our revenue* has been at stake I fear *their honour !* will hardly prove strong enough to resist such a temptation.

However, leaving these conjectures for others to ruminate upon, the fact is, that while the Bank of England and the Country Bankers are contending for the privilege of supplying the trade with the circulating medium, this junto are quietly running away with the best part of this bone of contention, by daily issuing their unstamped bills in payment for every purchase they make, or, I should rather say, they did so some time ago, (until the credit of this new manufacture was sufficiently established,) for they now find it more to their interest to carry these bills to the Branch or other bankers, and exchange them for bank notes, at three or four per cent., and make their payments with these notes, for which they *always* charge six per cent. interest! and the saving of this two per cent is so dear to them, that I am told you might as well ask them for one of their teeth, as for one of these bills, although the contract was made for a bill at three months. Yet, as those bills which are discounted by Country Bankers and other monied men, are again sent into the market, there is always plenty of them in circulation in every branch of trade..

The law obliges the purchaser to pay for the stamp on which he draws the bill for payment. But a custom was introduced into Manchester, more than twenty years ago, by a few Jewish houses, when trade was bad, that when these houses drew a bill, they charged the receiver with the stamp—which custom spread wider every year, until the period before-mentioned, when it almost became general ; but still the tax was paid by one of them.

But these sovereigns, true to their system of reci-procity, when they have to make a payment, select out of their stores such bills as come near the amount, and though no stamp has been used, they have established the custom of deducting from what they have to pay, *such sum as it would have cost them* if they had been *obliged* to draw it *on an English stamp!* and so rigidly I am told do they enforce this *direct tax,* that *their subjects* must either conform to it, or lose their connection altogether ; which to any business, so long as the *town and trade of Manchester* remain under their *present rulers,* would be equally bad as to be outlawed or excommunicated from the trade altogether ! The consequences of which, I shall hereafter have occasion to explain, when I come to record the *crude examples*, the Anglo or *ex-cculive* part of this junto have made on myself, and some others, (thereby frightening the whole trade into silent submission,) for attempting to draw the veil that has hitherto screened their mal-proceedings from the eyes of their country.

From the above direct tax upon his Majesty's *former* liege subjects, with several deductions formerly unknown in the trade, which they now take off, before they make their payments, it is believed they raised more money than the whole foreign part of this junto spend in this country altogether, including their rents, taxes, carriages, horses, servants, wives, daughters, &c. ! ! !

I hope the shoals of English, Irish, and Scotch lords and commoners, with all *their et cetera*, who reside in Rome, Naples, Paris, Brussels, &c. &c. in numbers equal to these sovereigns in Manchester, have some similar mode of taxing those countries, to support themselves without sending for the gold of this country to pay their expences ! Otherwise, I fear, reciprocity, under this head, will, in the end be found to be like the other reciprocity this junto has imposed upon us, viz.—*all on one side!*

When in the course of my narrative, I have had occasion to state that the exporters of cotton yarns not only spoke of it as exporting so many bales or cotton manufacture, but until 1816 they absolutely entered the bulk of it at the custom-house, either under this name or that of British cottons. In alluding to which, many of my readers may wonder why I have always done it with so much asperity of language, and have so repeatedly recorded my protest against such a *prostitution* of the word ! I have always witnessed the most urgent necessity thus to remonstrate against such a practice, but especially since the fatal convoy granted to the Manchester junto in the autumn of 1810 or 11, for the purpose of protecting a fleet laden with this traffic. The circumstances that led to this fatal occurrence were briefly these :—

Prior to that period, notwithstanding the continental system for prohibiting our piece goods, great shipments, along with cotton yarns, had been made to the Baltic, chiefly under some sort of license obtained by the merchants from the authorities of France, Prussia, Russia, &c. Whether it first emanates from a deep stratagem of Buonaparte, or from the junto in Manchester, in order to bankrupt our shippers of piece-goods, and thereby get rid of our competition in their free towns at once—with these questions I have nothing to do—but so it was, that during the year 1809, and up to near Midsummer, 1810, a great trade in piece-goods was carried on to the north of Europe under these licenses. But when the great spring fleet of 1810 arrived at their destined ports, lo! and behold! these licenses all turned out (I do not recollect an exception) to be what they called assimilated papers, or in other words forgeries! of course all these merchant-men, as they successively arrived at the ports from Hambro' to St Petersburgh, were seized as contraband! and a general confiscation of the *piece-goods part*, of their cargoes, took place, which were all burned I suppose!! The news of this seizure gave a great shock to our trade, and as few ships went out to that quarter for some time after, the manufacturers on the continent, (amongst which are our great rivals in hosiery, the Saxons,) began to suffer very much for want of the raw material of cotton yarns.

If I recollect right, Buonaparte and the King of Prussia were at Erfurth about that time, planning how to prevent another piece of our goods entering their States, when a deputation from these manufacturers waited upon them to state their necessities which, on being understood, and the mode of relief pointed out, these sovereigns granted them a real license to import what they wanted into Lubec, and perhaps some other ports in that neighbourhood.

Meanwhile, the junto in Manchester, from whom I suppose the deputation had their instructions before they waited on these sovereigns, though they knew of the great opening this license would give, for clearing off the vast stock of twist that had accumulated since the former shipment, kept every thing secret from the spinners, until they had secured, not only all they had on hand, but all their mills could produce, till the time of shipping took place, at 15 to 25 per cent. under the prices the home trade of Lancashire, Glasgow, and the hosiers in Nottingham were then paying for these yarns!

Having thus accumulated a stock of cotton yarns, with samples, patterns, drawings, parts of machinery, and a hundred little et ceteras *under the rose*, (such as their mother countries were in want of,) sufficient to load a large fleet; the junto then applied to our Privy Council for Trade to grant them a convoy to the Baltic; but they were refused, on account of the lateness of the season. And no argument would avail, until they pleaded the *distress of our weavers, manufacturers, &c.*, and the almost impossibility of their existing through the winter, *if something was not done for them*—and on their showing to their Lordships the immense tonnage of *British manufactures* this fleet would take out, and promising to bring back hemp, &c., they at last made such an impression on the feelings of their Lordships, as to gain their point; and a convoy consisting of *two eighty gun ships*, with the usual proportion of smaller vessels, was accordingly granted.

After landing this vast shipment of *British manufactures* as they called it, which in fact was only the *raw material for manufacture* and re-loading their merchantmen with hemp, &c. the convoy re-

turned. When to the extreme regret of their Lordships who granted it, as well as the nation at large,
while off the coast of Holstein, the two eighty gun
ships, with I don't recollect how many of the smaller
vessels, foundered, and with their crews, *all went to
the bottom!!!* owing to the tempests which generally prevailed at that season of the year. To have
avoided such a risk was the reason why their Lordships were so reluctant in granting that convoy.
But had the Anglo part of this junto who solicited
it, been so candid as to have told their Lordships,
as every *true* friend to his country would have done,
that what they were sending out was cotton yarns
only, an article which the *men spinsters* who produce it, have never yet, either in the Manchester
Directory, or on the sign-boards over their warehouse doors, *dared* to call a manufacture! *They
know* they would not have been listened to! or,
even if they had not *prostituted* the name of the poor
starving weavers to obtain their ends, they a'so knew
full well, they would not have got that convoy!
And those valuable ships and men would not have
been sacrificed to serve the purpose of that *vile,
deadly, traffic!!* For it must appear clear to every one,
that instead of serving those poor weavers as *they*
pretended, it was the very means of depriving half
of them the year following, of any work at all, and
reducing the wages of the other half to the lowest
starvation price; at the same time driving the
neighbourhood of Nottingham (in the hosiery line,)
into open rebellion!! and creating Luddites in
abundance, in every district in the trade!!!
    The above is recorded for the purpose of shew-
ing the consequences of *not* calling things by *their
proper names.*
    If the measures contemplated in 1817 had been
carried into effect, the foreign part of this junto
would have been sent to their respective homes soon

after; when the anglo part of it, by again uniting the English spindle with the shuttles of the three Kingdoms in *one common interest*, would have been *much richer* men than they are this day. No panic would have happened, or even if there had been some re-action from over production, this would soon have righted itself without any loss to the nation. The master manufacturers in the circuits round Dublin, Belfast, Glasgow, Carlisle, Blackburn, Nottingham, &c., would not have been driven so frequently, on their return from market, to the necessity of reducing the wages of the weavers, in order to make their future goods to come in at the current price of the day ; and, if possible, one, two, or three-pence per piece over, *as a profit to themselves.* For although they knew, as well as those who have so often blamed them, that this mode of proceeding was so baneful in its results, by reducing the value of every piece of cotton goods in the world, then made, beginning with those these masters had on hand, unsold ; and going up to the great depots of the Manchester and Scotch warehouses in London, with those of wholesale drapers, and merchants at home and abroad, and only ending with the remnants of pieces in the smallest drapers' shops, amounting in the whole to many millions sterling ! at every period when these deductions occur, all of which must be marked down, as the retail draper terms it, to *these reductions* of wages, however great might be the loss ! thereby ruining in every branch all those of small property in a very short time ; and by a regular succession of these reductions, the greatest capitalists that have remained in every branch of this trade !—yea, the princely fortunes the loyal town of Blackburn was so celebrated for, before this foreign junto sat down in Manchester, are many of them gone, and others much reduced in this general wreck ! yet, as I before observed, although the

masters foresaw the evils this system of lowering
the wages would produce, they had no choice left ;
as they must either go on in this way, or give up
their manufacture altogether. But notwithstanding the low price at which the masters in Blackburn could make a piece of calico, after they had
reduced the wages of the weaver, *below the bread
and water level*, still they must have given it up
entirely in 1826, if it had not been for a very liberal
supply of the raw material, from a source that had
been gradually augmenting in the same ratio that
wages had been declining for the last 27 years, and
at this period had been so organized as to become
a distinct and extensive branch of business, having
its regular travellers through every town, village,
or lonely cottage in the whole circle of this trade.

Until the year 1800, the weavers as a body
were as faithful, moral, and trust-worthy, as any
corporate body amongst his Majesty's subjects ; *
and before the curse of modern political economists,
and liberal *(meaning retrograde)* march of mind
were known, they wore their armorial bearings of
merit—an escutcheon of which is placed at the head
of their Address to the Public, which I have re-
printed in page 73, with as few stains upon their
coat-armour as any individual or corporate body
on whom these marks of Royal favour have ever
been bestowed.

* The good old custom that had existed ever since Great
Britain became a commercial country, was not only continued
but spread wider every year with the increase of our manufactures
and commerce. Up to the time I am speaking of, every father of a
family whose daughters could not get married without having the name
of spinster tacked to that of Miss So-and-so, no matter however wealthy
such family might be, even a rich rector, county magistrate, or merchant.
These gentlemen when placing their sons, always preferred fixing them
in the family of one of these weavers, for a few years, to teach him how
to fabricate a piece of fustian, and hundreds of other articles. Afterwards he thought himself very fortunate if he could place him in some

Having been a weaver myself for seven years, while in my teens, and being intimately acquainted with their principles and habits at that period, and up to the time I speak of, I can pledge myself that their former character, as a body, is faithfully recorded. And though while labouring under the greatest distress that ever befel any body of people on the face of the earth, some of them may have had recourse to measures for keeping themselves in existence that apparently might justify the junto, in stamping upon these poor weavers a character corresponding with the deep-rooted hatred they have long borne towards them, merely for continuing to fabricate articles, which, in competition, were so injurious to the fabrics of their mother countries. And although this junto have prevailed upon government to transport a million of these poor wretches into the woods of Upper Canada, *if means could be found!* as a just punishment for their past crimes, or, in plain English, from a fear of what *is to come!* yet, notwithstanding they have been branded with so much infamy, and are now remaining under sentence of transpor-

---

manufacturing house, at the common premium of £500. besides finding his son with clothes, washing, &c. for the period agreed upon; and whilst the son boarded and lodged in the family of the weaver, when the father and mother paid him a visit, they were not ashamed to sit down with the family, to a homely though wholesome dinner at twelve o'clock. But since these clever men sat down in Manchester, and our manufactures in consequence have become a losing trade, all such fathers place their sons in the law, or some other profession, until the supply has exceeded the demand in these professions in a ratio pretty similar to that of the poor weaver, now lying under sentence of transportation, because the junto have run away with his bread, and he grumbles at the loss of it. As to that of the law, there are hundreds of young attorneys, many of whom I know, or sometimes hear of, who, if these clever men were sent home, as they ought to be, and this trade was again restored to its legitimate rights, would be glad to give up this profession, and go into that of manufacturing, agreeably to the original intention of their fathers before they sent them to school.

tation, when the *twenty millions* can be spared to ship them off, it is a question not easily solved, whether there *is*, or *is not*, any guilt in transactions such as I am going to relate.

I will suppose the children of an *honest weaver* to rise in a morning with empty bellies, and that their mother has not a drop of milk, a morsel of bread, oat-meal, or a potato in the house, by which she can soothe their cries, with an infant at her breast, run dry for want of necessary nourishment the preceding day! In this forlorn state, if the mother should put a few cops, or a few hanks of cotton yarns in her lap, and (under the rose) run to some neighbour and sell them for half their value to purchase a little oatmeal, with which, though she has no fire, yet, by mixing it with a little salt and cold water, she is immediately enabled to serve each with their portions, not forgetting one for the father. Humble as this fare may appear to many, yet, the most sumptuous breakfast the citizens of London, Dublin, or Edinbro', can set before their families and friends, is not partaken of with half the epicurean enjoyment these little brats feel while devouring their meal.

Here we come to the puzzling question, viz.— Can a man, belonging to a corporate body, who is entitled to court-armour, allow and partake of a breakfast so provided, without forfeiting his claims to that "*honour and honesty*" for which the body he belongs to became entitled to such a mark of court favour or not? As I do not pretend to take either side of this question, I will pass it by, suggesting another, viz.—Where is there a father possessed of conjugal and paternal feelings, enjoying a coat of arms to himself, or as a freeman in some corporate body entitled to such honours, (if similarly situated with the poor weaver I have described, a true sample of thousands at various times,) that can lay his hand on his heart and say he would have done otherwise? Now having done my duty in recording the origin and foundation of this modern branch of business, I will leave these questions to be answered by the political economists of the day, and return to my subject, in order that I may inform the Lockes and Chesterfields of our day, (the trade know them too well but dare not speak,) of a few particulars as to the workings of these clever men, that when added to those already stated, will, I feel pretty confident, lead these *legitimate rulers of our country* to inquire whether all, or any, of the numerous charges I have recorded against the mal-administration of the Manchester Sovereign Junto! are well founded or not.

After the great fall in the price of cotton in 1818, the shock it gave to our manufacturers gradually subsided in the course of the following year; and the re-action in favor of our weavers was greatly assisted by an error *these clever men* fell into in Dec. and Jan. 1818-19, arising from a *fear* lest the measures they had concocted to stop our proceedings to prohibit the export of cotton yarns, might prove as abortive, as those they had been trying for the four years preceding. Under this impression, they made larger contracts than usual in the months I have named, for yarns at the market price of the day,—for instance, No. 40's at 2s 4d per lb., (to follow large stocks just sent off at 3s) with all other numbers in proportion. Hence, long before these contracts were spun and delivered, the home trade, by a still further reduction in cotton, was fully supplied with this article at 20d per lb., and as the same feeling which I call *fear* amongst the clever men in Manchester, had in its travels worked itself into DESPAIR in the minds of the merchants and manufacturers of Astracan, Moscow, St. Petersburgh, and, though perhaps in a less degree, in the nearer provinces of

Europe. These mother countries, alarmed at the
news, that the great source of their wealth, by which,
if continued, they might safely calculate on subduing
our possessions in the east, was going to be cut off!
they, with the aids of their commercial banks, well
filled with the *money of our capitalists in London*,
who durst no longer trust it in the hands of the
declining manufacturers and merchants of our country, sent to their agents in Manchester unlimited
orders to contract for all they could procure in the
autumn of 1819 and spring of 1820, which period,
in many instances, was a partial exception to the
general rule of job-prices before-mentioned. Again,
while these contracts were filling the stores of the
great depots on the continent with stocks in some
instances sufficient for many years' consumption, the
home trade was regularly supplied with the number
before-mentioned at 16d per lb., thereby enabling
the masters in the United Kingdom to give full
employ to their weavers, on a raw material daily
coming from the mills at the price last mentioned;
while the masters on the continent had to work up
their vast stocks, laid in at 3s, 2s 4d, and 20d; for
though these clever men were constantly supplying
the foreign stores with all the surplus yarns in the
market in the way I have before explained, yet,
owing to the great bulk they had laid in at high
prices under their panic of fear, they never could
reduce their calculations, as to the prime cost of a
piece, so as to meet us in the markets of Leipsic,
Frankfort, &c., or in the celebrated depots of the
Rhenish West India Commercial Company in St.
Domingo, expressly established for the purpose of
driving our *piece-goods trade* out of the markets in
the western world.

It was peculiarly fortunate for our country, that
this state of things should happen at the time the
country was placed in such a ferment, by the state

trial of the late queen ; for notwithstanding *every effort* the emissaries of discord resorted to, in order to raise large riotous mob-meetings amongst the weavers, to make her cause the cause of the public, not one of them would budge from his loom, and could I recollect the *proud* and droll answers by which they excused themselves, they would be very amusing. But had this unfortunate affair happened a few years sooner, or in the latter part of 1825, or the spring of 1826, when the foreign looms were filled with *cheap yarns*, and the home looms with yarns at nearly double the price of the former, trifling as the subject I am speaking upon may appear to some people, yet, it is my decided opinion, that the parched empty bellies of these weavers at those times, would have been exactly the sort of fuel these emissaries were seeking for, in order to gratify some petty party feeling of revenge, *reckless* of the consequences that might follow.

To illustrate the subject I promised to return to, respecting the supply of yarns from the new branch of business before-mentioned, and the great service it rendered to our weavers on a particular occasion, I will take the year 1826, and Blackburn, Bolton, Bury, and the neighbouring towns and villages, as the places where the facts I am going to relate were of daily occurrence ; but to be clearly understood, I must first premise that during the period I have been speaking of, while the foreign looms were working up their high-priced yarns, the masters in these districts, in order to relieve their poors' rate, and to prevent their operatives from returning to their former wretched state, held public meetings for the purpose of fixing amongst themselves a minimum price of wages, in which they were unanimous ; and they advertised accordingly in all the public papers in the district, to which the names of the masters were attached, and the trade went on steadily up to

the autumn of 1825, when the home looms and all
the stocks in the masters' hands were filled with
high-priced yarns. But, as before observed, the
junto not having purchased any of the high-priced
yarns, and their old stocks being worked up, the
foreign looms were all then filled with the low-priced
yarns produced from the contracts of Dec. 1824, and
the month following, as before related.

It is well known that 'during the panic in the
autumn of 1825, a great portion of that stock which
had filled all the stores in Manchester, were sold to
these foreigners at half their prime cost; and although a great part still remained in the hands of
some of the strong rich spinners, and that by repre-
senting these yarns to Government, and through
Government to the Bank of England, as *cotton manufactured goods*, the latter sent down a large sum
of money to relieve the holders of them for a time,
and if they had been *goods really manufactured*, as
was the case in 1793, and had the manufactures and
commerce of our country been under the *same protection* as they were at that period, these stocks would
have been bought by our merchant adventurers, and
sent off to every point of the compass, during the
time limited by the Bank for repayment. And
though some of the manufacturers might have been
ruined, and others have lost a part of their capitals,
yet the cent. per cent. returns that would have come
back to our merchants, in gold and silver bullion,
with all the other articles of wealth their former
cornu-copias are used to pour into the laps of our
country, the result of such adventures in the second
necessary of life, these would have more than com-
pensated for such losses, in a national point of
view.

Our manufacturers being so battered down and
paralysed by this great panic, which came upon them
at a time when they had been losing money by their

trade, rather than alter their patriotic list of wages, none of them could purchase these yarns, which must be sold to repay the Bank. Hence the fine harvest, I before spoke of, to be reaped by these foreigners, became fully ripe, and the whole of these stores fell into their hands, for much less money than John Bull had paid for the raw cotton ! ! !

The former part of this harvest, (with a certainty of reaping the latter in due time) being safely deposited in their magazines, these clever men thought they had not only secured to themselves every thing valuable in the trade, but that they had so far subdued the country itself, as like conquering heroes they might safely march into the district I have mentioned, and make slaves of its operatives in any way that might conduce to their interest; and being not only furnished with more yarns than their mother countries were in immediate want of, but having the spinners so much *under their control,* as to command from them the future produce of their mills, in warps, cops, or in any state requisite for their new subjects to operate upon, several of these foreign houses, as the reconnoitering vanguard of the sovereign body, marched into the towns and places before named, (and as no one *durst* do otherwise,) they were received in the way that Buonaparte always said he was received by the inhabitants (Moscow excepted) when he entered the cities and towns of the countries he had conquered, and their first measure was to engage and give a commission to some master (whom the panic had run down) to give out work for them to the weavers in their neighbourhood, many of the latter at that time having no work at all. They promised these masters they would regularly supply them with the materials for the weavers, on the following *conditions,* which will be best understood when given as regards a piece of common calico.

If I recollect right, the patriotic list of wages
for this article was 6s., but the agent was on no account to give more than 5s. 6d.! and if the regular
masters came down to this price, then this agent was
immediately to go sixpence lower! and so on *ad in-
finitum.* In this way business went on for some
time, before the patriotic masters would depart from
the standard of prices they had mutually agreed to
support. However, as these clever men got large
weekly supplies of calicos, &c., into their warehouses in Manchester, made from the yarns that had
fallen into their hands in the way before mentioned,
with a further saving of *sixpence per piece* in the
weaving, they were enabled to sell these goods to the
great printers in the trade, at such low prices, as
not only compelled the old masters to break down
their mutual minimum list of wages, but to start
and run the sixpenny-down race, understood by the
instructions given by these clever men to their agents
when they entered the field.

During the period of this *sixpenny-down race,*
which began in the latter end of 1825, and continued
up to the spring of 1826, the wages were reduced to
nearly one third of the patriotic list!—and many
of this veteran band were broken down in every heat;
and if patiently working 16 hours to the day, under
the greatest privations that ever befel such a body of
people, can entitle the operatives, in this arduous
struggle, to the commiseration and sympathy of
their country, none were ever more deserving than
these poor weavers. This feeling was not only produced, but acted upon, and that in the only two
ways the wisest of men could possibly suggest,
namely, immediate relief to those in distress, and a
remedy suggested, that would not only remove the
cause, but prevent any more of these ruinous *sixpenny-down races!* whether an attempt to renew them

might emanate from *these clever men*, or from any other quarter; for while large funds were subscribed in London, and regularly distributed amongst those who were *dying from hunger!* some gentlemen in Bolton and the neighbourhood, well acquainted with all I have related, on being consulted in a committee, (selected from the intelligent men amongst the masters and weavers) who often assembled under these extraordinary circumstances, advised them to make their case known to Government, and humbly request the sanction of ministers to a law they would petition for in the ensuing sessions, by which these masters and men might be allowed to regulate their own trade in future, in such manner as they could mutually agree upon, without having their patriotic plans upset with impunity by these foreign intruders, who care as little about the amount of our poor-rate, as they do for what may become of a people perishing under so degrading a system.

The reply the operative part of this committee gave to this advice, was in language of the most *abject despair!* They said, that during the last 25 years, they had raised by their penny-a-week subscriptions, at sundry times, no less than £1,500., which had been expended in various attempts to place their trade under the pale of government protection, but without the slightest success;—that door being so guarded by the anglo-part of the junto, so often-named; and having no hopes of passing their *Argus eye*, in any further attempts, they had determined for some time past, to petition no more!

In this hopeless state, one of these gentlemen volunteered to state their case to a certain board, formerly called *our* Board of Trade, and so long as it protected the interest of the internal manufactures of *our* country, it was properly so called; but lately, especially since the peace of 1815, and the establishment of the *Anglo-Foreign* Chamber, in

Manchester, it has literally become the board of
trade for the purpose of *raising* and *protecting* the
manufactures and commerce of *every foreign state !*
at the *expence* and on the *ruins* of our own! I state
these facts coolly and advisedly, and am ready to
prove what I have thus recorded.

However, this committee very gratefully accepted of the kind offer of this gentleman ; and giving
him authority to address the board on their behalf,
(as a drowning man would catch at a straw,) a correspondence ensued, which being published in the
papers at the time, requires no further comment from
me, only, that the result (as was expected) left these
intruders in quiet possession of the district they had
invaded ; and had it not been for the masters, or
more than three-fourths of them, when filling the
looms of their weavers with yarns to fabricate upon,
mixing up with those they got in the usual way from
the spinner, a considerable portion of the yarns they
got from the stores created in the new branch of
business before-mentioned, (to which these intruders
contributed pretty freely) and at *half the price* that
even these cheap buyers could procure them at, they
might have kept possession to this day. But with
the aid of these *very cheap yarns*, and by keeping
neck and neck with their rivals, our brave heroes,
with the cordial assistance of their celebrated Amazons,
(the *Lancashire witches,)* all inspired with that enthu-
siastic zeal, with which they have so often joined in
their favourite chorus,—" *Britons never shall be
slaves !*"—their bellies at the time being girt up like
the greyhound, with the bone, blood, and bottom of
the first Arabian that ever entered for the celebrated
stakes of *their* Lord Lieutenant (the Derby), they
run the latter heats of that *sixpenny-down race* in
such style, as to enable their masters, in the end, to
supply the printers with calicoes in abundance, at
2s. to 4s. 9d. per piece! thereby under-selling their

rivals so decidedly, as to drive them back again to their head quarters in Manchester ; from whence, another such a pull, "and a pull altogether," if the agriculturist and those who dislike heavy poor-rates, will lend us their hand, these clever men will soon be removed to the places from whence they came ! and instead of their being able to take our cotton trade along with them, those ingenious hands they have sent abroad to assist in planting its different branches in every state from whence they came, will be glad to return to their native country, to partake in the happiness she will *unquestionably enjoy*, when once she has learned to be *honest* and *true* to herself, before she shews *so much liberality* to others ! ! !

There is something more that I could wish to have recorded while on this subject, if I could have come at the bottom of it. During this rapid rundown of wages, the weavers, on grumbling at such heavy reductions, were told by *some* masters that the power-looms were the *cause* of all this ; and unless *they* could get *rid of them*, their trade was gone for ever ; and it is well known, that *some of them* went so far as to encourage and stimulate the weavers, in *direct* terms, to commit that riotous destruction of property which then took place, threatening to upset the country at the same time !

It is also well known, that these power-looms were the only obstacle that prevented these clever men from fully accomplishing the object for which they were first set down in Manchester ; or, at least, the principal part of it, namely, that which Mr Hume calls the "important branch" of this trade, (see page 51,) which, as this Hon. Gentleman says, would ere this have left the country, but for these *power-looms!* And when we consider how its *superior fabrics* have reduced the demand, and run down the value of all the goods they make from the yarns they get from us *in every part of the world;* and when we

consider the time it will take them, and the expence
they must be at, (notwithstanding the facilities the
anglo-part of the junto is constantly procuring
for them,) before they can establish *this system* in
their mother countries, so as to be able to rival us
with any success, it is very natural to suppose these
clever men would have *rejoiced* to have seen them all
destroyed! and as *they* were *then* employing many
weavers in and near Blackburn, and had *commissioned*
certain *masters* to serve those weavers with materials
and take in their work—*if* it was *any* of *these masters*
who prompted *their weavers* to the proceedings before mentioned, (which is a point too delicate for
me to ascertain,) a suspicion attaches itself to these
circumstances that I have never been able to get over!
but having pointed out the grounds of my suspicion,
I hope those who have paid for the damage done at
that time, will sift this matter to the bottom.

Although I have frequently complimented the
foreign part of this junto with the character of *very*
clever men ; and although I had before detected them
in a serious error they committed under the panic
of fear in 1818-19, by over stocking their mother
countries with high-priced yarns, yet, as this might
proceed from instructions they received from abroad,
written under impressions that our government was
going to do what any of *their governments*, if similarly situated, would do in the time it takes me to
scribble one of these pages. With these considerations
in their favour, I could hardly deduct the word *very*
from the character I have given them ; but since the
period I am speaking of, in which they must have
acted without any instructions, I am at a loss what
to think of them ; yet, if I was pressed to give my
judgment, I should say, that for their gross ignorance,
—bad policy,—want of tact in entering upon,—and
in their bad mode of conducting the campaign I
have just described, they ought to be recalled by

their sovereigns who sent them, and impeached for the highest *political economical* crimes ! and that a confiscation of *every frank* this junto can call their own, would not be more than a just punishment for the irreparable injury *their* sixpenny-down race has inflicted on all their mother countries, from the Pillars of Hercules to Kamschatka, and from the Straights of Babelmandel to the most northern cape.

If these men had been faithful to their trust, and had possessed the talent I had given them credit for, they would, on having secured from *us* such immense magazines of the raw material for carrying on the commercial war against *us*, on the advantageous terms before-mentioned, have pursued an opposite course ; for as all the piece-goods made from this raw material, when fabricated and finished, whether in Blackburn, Elberfeldt, or elsewhere, promiscuously find their way into every fair or market in the world, in spite of heavy duties,—prohibitions,—political obstructions in transit,—or any other obstacle that man can devise ; when they run their heads together in a competition that must ruin the weaker side. If these men had pursued an opposite course, and sacrificed a trifle by raising the price of weaving 6d per piece in those districts, while their mother countries were stocking their fairs and filling the foreign markets with goods made on the calculation before given, there would have been something like good generalship in this mode of managing their trust ; but, painful as the reflection must now be to their feelings, the effects that have resulted from such a Quixotic expedition, will be seriously felt by their mother countries for many years. Ask the finance minister to the king of the Netherlands, who, to encourage their manufacturers to compete with us in the East and West Indies, the Levant, South America, &c., guaranteed to them 4½ per cent. profit on all their shipments, in case they could do no better; ask the thirty odd German sovereigns who gave their names to the Rhenish West India Company, established at Elberfeldt for the same purpose, and I suppose with the same guarantee; ask them how they like the returns that have been laid before them in the year 1827, and what sums they have had to pay for such guarantees! chiefly occasioned by that *sixpenny-down race*, and I query if the confiscation I spoke of would amount to sufficient to repay such demands.

The fact is, that while this race was running, it not only brought to its aid the full force of that new branch of business I have described, but it ran every thing that constitutes an item in the calculation of the cost of a piece of goods, down to the lowest level hitherto known; and notwithstanding such efforts had been made to *cry down* and *destroy* every thing connected with the new system of manufacture, all of which (under the rose) emanated from the junto, who saw they could never "drive this important branch," as Mr Hume calls it, out of our country, if this system was allowed to remain!—yet, like a life-boat, that will weather any storm, this system not only survived this *double attack*, but it poured out of its inexhaustible cornu-copia, that fabric which has set all foreign competition at defiance, in such increased quantity, and run down in price in the same ratio with those produced by that celebrated race, that by taking the goods of the latter under *its protecting wing*, and allowing *its name* to be stamped upon them as occasion might require, (for since we allowed these foreigners to sit down amongst us, they have taught us not to be so nice about these little points as we formerly were,) a bulk was formed which had nothing to fear.

When the whole of these fabrics, after having gone through the various operations of the bleachers, dyers, printers, &c., were *shipped* off together, under a thousand different names and styles, and under the protection of the British flag, were placed in the great marts of trade all over the world, with the assurance of a regular supply from the same magical source, to replace these goods as they might be sold off, John Bull bids defiance to all foreign competition ! and it is our own fault if ever we *hear of* it again.

As a friend to my country, I feel great pleasure in thus being able to record the vantage-ground on which our trade stood at the commencement of the year 1827 ; and though as the inventor of the new system of manufacture, I had sunk a fortune to enable our country to take this strong ground, (without which our " ships, colonies, and commerce" would, ere this time, *unquestionably* have left us) yet, I feel a sort of pleasure, and a sort of *pride*, in thinking that through my humble efforts *alone !* during which, I have had to contend against every difficulty, —every obstacle,—every opprobrium of disgrace that the junto could heap on the heads of myself and my family, *without the slightest foundation in fact*, in order to compel me to let go my hold, and allow them quietly to carry away that important branch of our trade that Mr Hume so well described. I say that when I reflect upon this, and can thus record the success that has crowned my efforts almost beyond my most sanguine expectations, (the pledge given me by the trade being *still* unredeemed) I feel such a mixture of pleasurable pride, compared to which the loss of my fortune would, to my feelings, weigh like a feather in the scale. Were it not that owing to the wicked conspiracy which I shall feel it my duty to record ere I close this narrative this junto resorted to, to effect their purpose,—there are certain figures in certain books, that my certificate does not erase from my mind, which are a great draw-back upon the pleasures I am describing.

As a friend to our wooden walls, I also feel a great pleasure in being the means of preserving to our country that "important branch of trade" that will, as heretofore, prove a better nursery for seamen for these wooden walls, than the junto wish to give us in lieu of the former, or I should say, have given us, to a wonderful extent, considering the comparative short time they have had the control of our affairs in their hand ; for, according to the scale of time Madame de Stael has laid down, it is scarcely a moment! She says something to this effect— "that what may be called an age with individuals, is only a moment with a nation." Now, though they have not been in power for more than 28 years, which is not a moment, according to this scale, (in my opinion very wisely laid down) yet they have made such good use of the latter part of this time,— say not more than seven-eighths of a moment, as to give us a fair specimen of what they will do, if we allow them to rule us only for the other eighth part. The basis of their plan is, that the United States, in their own bottoms, shall carry and lay down the raw cotton, in Liverpool ; and after it has run through their mills in Lancashire, Yorkshire, &c., in the way before recorded, and found its way into Hull, they have their Baltic, Hambro', &c., vessels ready to carry it to their mother countries in every direction, and this is all the commerce they allow to us!!!— And as the Americans must be paid for their cotton, and as this payment can only come back through the same channel in which this traffic has run through our country, so as to suit the interest and convenience of themselves, they broke down our old navigation laws, in order that the Baltic ships, which come to Hull for this traffic, may bring in their timber: the bills drawn upon which, are very useful in paying for their cotton, as well as giving a cargo to their vessels. But their grand object for these two purposes, has been that of opening our markets for their corn, and though like Buonaparte, (of whom they are the true prototype,) when he set his mind upon the Peninsula of Spain, they have to a certain extent succeeded, so far as to get some bills on Mark-lane, (the *great object* for which they have struggled so hard,) to pay their brother Jonathan for his cotton, freight, &c., as the former did in getting some part of the Mexican dollars to pay his troops ;—yet I shall be much mistaken, if this junto, ere long, do not as much repent their having taken John Bull by the horns, in meddling with *his corn laws*, as ever Buonaparte did that of setting his mind on those dollars,—especially as in all their memorials and petitions, they have gone up to government under the cloak of a name to which they have not the *shadow of a title*, viz. as the *manufacturers* of Lancashire, &c. !—for, excepting a few, whom they have so far under their control, as that when they lay a parchment or paper before them, they are sure of their signature, I do not believe they have had one voluntary, real manufacturer's name on their list. I have taken some pains and been at some expence to ascertain the sentiments of this class of gentlemen, but have not met with one that would not prefer to buy his corn from a farmer in Norfolk, though he might pay a little more for it, because his money would find its way back again into Manchester, for muslins, prints, &c. &c. &c., at prices that would do him some good, rather than from any part of the Continent, which will not take a piece from him at any thing like a price, by which he can save himself from loss; as their governments, by their heavy duties, or rather prohibitions, have taken good care that such an exchange can very rarely be made.

While speaking of the pleasure I felt in having to record the triumphant position of our trade, from which emanates the life and vigour of our wooden walls, I was insensibly led into the above remarks; and if what I have said should expedite the happy deliverance we all wish for, I will record this as a pleasure to come, and proceed to dilate on another pleasure which I hardly know how to describe. This pleasure arises from having been the humble means of giving a practical illustration of the few lines from an ancient writer, which I have placed in the front of this narrative; and as they so fully accord with what I have already said, as well as with what I shall very soon feel it my duty to say again, I will here re-state them:—" *It is a manifest instance of the great national advantages in trade this nation enjoys, that it hath not been ruined, long ago, by the consequences of our own ill-management!*"

In the same essay from which I have borrowed these lines, the writer frequently quotes from another of the name of GEE, who, " in his discourse on trade, (page 186,) computes that we have one million of people supposed to be out of work;" to which the writer of the essay adds in page 139, " If 100,000 of the above million of unemployed poor are *woollen-manufacturers*, though I imagine they must be much more, in the present declining condition of this trade," &c. what a striking coincidence this is to the present period! out of a comparatively small population, a million of people out of employ, and for what cause! !—not that the power-looms had thrown them out of work, no !—there were none at that time, on which those *bad managers* could then ease their own shoulders of the blame, which, like the present period, lay somewhere else. These, and many other writers in those times, instead of recommending emigration, to get rid of the unemployed, said, " the labour of these individuals makes the *riches* of the *whole.*"—Hence, they fearlessly told their King and their country where the blame lay; and by drawing aside the veil that had screened the junto of that day, while they had occasioned so much distress, and by convincing government, that if a transportation must take place, it would be *more just* to send away those that had been the cause, rather than to transport the innocent million, who had been deprived of bread from no fault of their own!!—Thus when the eyes of Government were opened by this plain matter of fact mode of reasoning, our Lockes and Chesterfields sent the foreign part of that junto to the Low Countries from whence they came, and the anglo part to the right-about ; and when the reins of government fell into *their hands*, the protecting restrictions which followed, and raised us to that pinnacle on which we *lately stood,* are sufficient proofs that those bold writers did not labour in vain.

If the Chesterfields and Lockes of *our day*, will procure us a hearing in the proper quarter, in such a way as that those in the trade who agree with me, may venture publicly to express their opinions without the risk of losing their *credit* and *business*, by offending the anglo-part of this powerful junto, should they still act under the principles on which they conspired to do against any such offenders, it would so far strengthen our hands, that in one "*pull altogether*" we could remove that veil which the special pleadings of the rhetorical, sophistical, mal-metaphysical logicians of the liberal political economists of the day, all argued from briefs drawn up by this junto, without which jargon they long ago confessed in confidence, (as they supposed) they had not a leg to stand upon ; yet, with these aids, they have hitherto kept the veil I speak of over the eyes of government ! However, when this is removed, we yet have it in our power any day to return to the same healthy state of our trade that I have before described ; a few years longer, as we are going on, will be very dangerous, *i. e.* so far as any profit from it goes. France, by the aids we are daily *giving*

her, will be the first power to become independent
of our fine twist, from which they make their warps
of cambric and fine muslins, with fancy goods of all
kinds, and *lace*. I have it from the first authority
in France, that the most sanguine persons in those
departments where their spinning and manufactures
are carried on, that if we should prohibit the export
of our cotton yarns in less than three or four
years from this time, (Nov. 1827) we should ruin their
manufactures in these articles, and also throw
them very far back in many others. But, notwithstanding such consequences would inevitably
be the result of such a measure, were it not for
the obligation *they* have imposed upon us, by the
liberal manner that government met the president of
our Board of Trade two and three years ago, whom
our foreign-anglo junto had sent over to lay *our*
reciprocity at their feet, in exchange for their wine,
brandy, *manufactured* silk, linen, &c.! and by the
handsome manner in which *they* condescended to
accept of this boon!! if we are not too fast bound
by such obligations, I should be tempted to do it
without delay. We have seen bills read two or three
times in both houses of parliament the same day,
the necessity for which was always occasioned by the
effects of the *cause* which forms the Alpha and Omega
of this narrative; and surely if this *cause*, always
pressing on for new measures, can be so easily removed
to the benefit of every *subject* in the British empire,
giving at the same time full employment to the peasantry in Ireland, and such wages as will enable
them to become good customers to their *bakers and
butchers*, and leave them no time for debating whether
if M. P. were added to the name of O'Connel, Shiel,
and a few such like persons, who have been bred to
the profession of talking, would fill *their* bellies,
clothe their backs, and make their cabins into
comfortable cottages or not! Let us only turn our

helm, and run our 1000lb. bales of twist into Ireland to be fabricated, instead of Russia ; and the hands and mind of Pat will be so engaged in the various operations this manufacture will impose upon him, that his answers to those who may ask his aid on the M. P. question, will be as laconic and decisive as those of the Lancashire weavers before-mentioned respecting, the affairs of the late Queen ; and as to Great Britain,—distribute the other bales amongst her weavers, &c., from the Land's End to John O'Groats ; point to them their coat of arms, and with the means in their hands, by which they can wear them with honour ; your Overseers of the Poor will only have the infant and the aged under their care ; your prisons will almost become untenanted ; and when the weaver looks up to the motto in his coat armour, and finds the *means in his own hands* by which he can feed and clothe his wife and children, as well as his aged father or mother ; so situated, his *honour*, when he finds his legitimate rights are restored to him, will be a sufficient protection to your game. Hence, I say, that if the *cause* which has led to such rapid legislation, can be so easily removed, why not give it the same expedition ?

With regard to the bad management of which I spoke so freely a little while past, I will endeavour to shew the source from whence this bad management proceeded ; and as in desperate cases, it is sometimes necessary to probe the wound so deep, as to give pain to the limb from which the whole body becomes diseased, before you can proceed to a radical cure ; such is my respect for this patient, that has engrossed all my attention for the last twenty-seven years, and my fortune into the bargain, that to save her life, I must resort to the same means ; for, having my fears that the cure will not be a radical one, unless I first probe the wound to the bottom, I feel it absolutely necessary to proceed in my own way, even though I

may give a little temporary pain to a few of my best
friends. Individually, with one exception, I have
no personal enemy ; and amongst the few who may
feel a little of this temporary pain, there is not one,
if he knew my heart and my motives, that would
raise this exception into the plural number. It is
against the junto—the "*body without a soul*," that I
contend ; and so far as my best and dearest relation,
or friend, is found amongst them, as a part of that
body, I spare him not !—while as an individual,
when detached from this junto, he may command
the best services of my *hand* and my *heart*.

Hitherto I have chiefly narrated on the workings
of the foreign, or legislative part of this sovereign
junto ; but now, however reluctant it may be to my
feelings, I am obliged, with the probe in my hand, to
approach the anglo, or executive part of it ; whom,
from the numerous facts that have come to my knowledge, and from my own experience, I fearlessly
charge as the prompters behind the veil ; with depriving our *loom*, our *sail*, and our *plough* of any
assistance (during the seven-eighths of the moment
they have been in power) from that Board of Trade,
which those, whom Locke and Chesterfield allude to,
had established to *raise* and *protect* the "ships, colonies, and commerce," of our country. Yea, truth and
facts compel me to go further, and to charge them
with turning *all* the influence of that powerful machine to raise and protect the loom, the sail, and the
plough of our rivals, while *they* establish *their* "ships,
colonies, and commerce," reckless of the ruin such
measures were daily bringing upon us ! ! !   Here,
and here only, lies the source of that " bad management," which would have " ruined our country long
ago," if the new system of manufactures, so often
mentioned, had not come to maturity just at the very
nick of time, so as to *catch her in her fall !* and had
I the command of language possessed by our immor-

tal Johnson, I could not find words to express the
pleasure I feel at being the humble individual that
has saved such a country as ours, and as it were,
even in spite of herelf.

But to return from these sallies of *empty* pleasures
that have so often drawn me from my subject. As the
two declarations I have filed against the junto are
of very serious import, and as, in imitation of declarations in other quarters, I have not been sparing
of hard words, if the facts already related do not
sufficiently warrant me in making them, I am now
arrived at that stage in my narrative, where I can
add a few more that will bear me out, not only in
the spirit, but even to the very letter of my charges.
And here I come to a pause—not for the want of
what Buonaparte would call the material requisite
to enter upon such a campaign, but from the super-
abundance of facts that have been accumulating for
the last twenty-seven years, I am pausing where to
begin :—for though my wish is to be as brief as
possible, yet, that the historian may fully comprehend the origin, as well as the progress of this liberal
system, as they call it, the workings of which have
placed our country in such jeopardy, I am obliged
to go back to the period where I first set out, and
enlarge a little on the state of things at that time ;
which, had I foreseen that my Narrative would have
swelled itself into a Book, which I now find that it
will do, in spite of my best efforts to have kept it
within the compass of a pamphlet, as I first intended, I should have stated in their proper place.

The hand-bills, given out by the weavers in 1799,
re-printed in page 73, and the following pages, will
shew what led to the public meetings in Manchester, in the spring following ; and that their
masters were not deaf to the calls of that *then* respectable part of the body corporate, the *main* of the
three national props I have so often mentioned,

deprived of which, the other two could not support the nation as an independent one, even if she was relieved from the load of her debt!

Up to that period there had been a Chamber of Commerce in Manchester, I suppose ever since it had been known as a manufacturing town, the members of which were composed of the great oaks of the forest that had rendered our wooden walls so *strong* for centuries past, that *none* could meet them with impunity!—they were the *manufacturing merchants*, (for all those great merchants were manufacturers with scarcely an exception) whose rich assorted bales, containing the second necessaries of life, that when sent off by themselves, or by the merchants of London, Bristol, Liverpool, or Hull, as adventures to the fairs of Balikesri in Natolia, Tifflis in Persia, Bucharia, on the borders of China, with the aid of land carriage, and a hundred other marts in the interior of Asia, which formed the cream of our trade to the Levant: shipments were also made to every other mart in the four quarters of the globe, to which the union jack could approach with these bales; and the cent. per cent. returns that came in the materials from which guineas and shillings were coined, gave these manufacturing merchants a sort of princely rank in the country, that with the authentic information they were constantly receiving from every quarter, and their high character for *honour* and *integrity*, rendered them fit persons to form such a chamber as I am speaking of;—a memorial from whom, when presented to the Lords of the Privy Council for Trade, had *hitherto* never failed to meet with the most satisfactory attention.

Having mentioned those old oaks of the forest, though I shall be digressing from what I was going to relate, I will here state my reasons for having named those marts in the interior of Asia, from whence such rich returns were poured upon our little island.

My reasons for so doing are simply to call the attention of the reader to perhaps the richest markets in the world for our Manchester goods, *really manufactured* and finished, believing they are but little known or thought of by the trade or the country in general. It is well known that ever since the gold and silver of Peru, Mexico, &c., found its way into Europe, a very considerable portion of those precious metals have continued their migration eastward, to purchase the rich manufactures of Turkey, Persia, Hindostan, China, &c., as well as their teas, indigo, and various other articles for the consumption of Europe and her colonies in the western world. Now, as Bolton, Blackburn, and the whole circuit round Manchester, along with Norwich, Exeter, Lincoln, &c., were celebrated for their stuffs and various fabrics, especially since the laws of Elizabeth, before-mentioned, furnished them with the raw material to fabricate upon, and as Manchester was the mart for the disposal of these goods, prior to the introduction of cotton to much extent when the fustians and the hundred other articles made from cotton, or cotton mixed with their former materials, were so far introduced as to become an important part in the catalogue of their shipments: their fustians in particular at Bucharia, in the north of China, to which their former fabrics, either by a distinct Company, or by a branch of the Turkey Company, established in that town for the express purpose of disposing of our manufactures, had introduced them, became so acceptable and so useful as to establish a fashion and dress amongst the inhabitants of the northern parts of these empires, who, with the wealth they have been known to possess for thousands of years, were made doubly rich by the gold and silver before-mentioned, that will enable them to support those fashions that, like " the laws of the Medes and Persians, alter not." But it is to the trade of the

north of China that I wish to call the attention of
the readers, and particularly in the article of fustians,
the old staple, by which these manufacturing merchants were raised to their princely rank; and though
a considerable portion of the fustians that supplied
this mart for ages past were sent up the Black Sea,
or over land from Smyrna, by the Turkey Company,
yet, another portion found its way in modern times
through Leipsic to Moscow, and down the Volga to
the Caspian Sea, creating in its transit through
Russia a strong desire in its own merchants to get
full possession of this lucrative trade; and before the
period I am speaking of, these Russian merchants
became the principal purchasers of this article in the
Manchester market, for the market alluded to.

But though our Turkey Company deeply felt
the loss of this branch, yet for some time, as far as
Manchester was interested, no harm appeared from
these fustians having changed their usual route.—
Now, much as I have complained of what our country
has suffered, by allowing our yarns to be exported,
the loss we have sustained, by our liberal system not
allowing us to watch the workings of those clever
men, is far more serious! for while calling themselves merchants, come here to purchase these goods;
they had amongst them their best and most ingenious mechanics brought here, for the purpose of carrying away by piece-meal, this branch of trade altogether; and when I have narrated their proceedings
and success, I think our stupidity and folly, in
suffering such things, will appear even greater than
that which has called for this narrative.

The Chinese, who excel in the manufacture of
their porcelain and other things, have their mart at
Canton, where merchants from all parts of the world
may purchase what they want; but under no pretence can any one see the process of such fabrica-
tions, or purchase any part of them in an unfinished

state—*they are wise!* I suspect, the Hindoos, though
under the sovereignty of a foreign power, have a sort
of sanctum-sanctorum, in which their rich articles
are fabricated and finished, as I never conversed with
a gentleman (and I have conversed with many) who
had been long in that country, who was *at all* acquainted with any of these things—*hence they are
wise!!* Our old staple trade in Yorkshire has its
halls, where merchants from all parts can make their
purchases of every article they want, in its finished
state; and though the seller may treat his customer
with a dinner and a bed, I suppose he does not, or
at least *did* not, shew him through his works, in
order to teach him how to make those goods for his
future wants, without the trouble and expence of
coming to his hall again; or, if he wanted a recipe
for dyeing, or any part of his goods in any stage he
saw them in, in order that he might finish them
off abroad, &c.; the finishing manufacturer, I suppose, does none of these things—if so, *he is wise
also!!!* Yet, there must have been a time when such
things were common in this trade, or those men whom
Locke and Chesterfield speak of, would have had *no
occasion* to have surrounded it with such *wise*
protections.

While these fustians were sent to the marts I have
mentioned by the Turkey Company, or by the princely
manufacturing merchants in Manchester to Leipsic,
to meet those eastern merchants, who came in the
style I spoke of in the former part of this narrative,
all was safe at home. But when the Russian merchants saw the source of this trade *quite unprotected*,
they brought over their most ingenious mechanics,
and, under the garb of merchants, they sent them out
into the trade to buy pieces from the little makers,
in the grey, as they came from the loom, as our merchants had always done, and getting them cut by our
fustian-cutters; and, like ferrets, by following them

through every stage to their final finish, in a few years they became practically acquainted with every minutiæ of the latter processes of this leading branch of the cotton trade, that, as before observed, had raised so many families to that *honourable* independence, as to qualify the heads of them to become fit members of the Chamber of Commerce I was speaking of. But from that day, (1800) every one of those oaks of the forest, that *stuck* to the trade of their fathers, that through ages had descended to them as an inheritance, have been levelled to the ground! and their old faithful servant, the Turkey Company, has been brought to lick the dust along-side of them, by the sovereign control of this mighty junto!! On the ruins of the former, these Russian *mechanical merchants* have risen, so as to establish in Moscow, a chartered company, to vend these fustians in the north of China, which, two or three years ago consisted of forty members, who are called the Millionists, of whom I shall have a little more to say by and by.

To an English feeling, there was something very galling in their mode of sacrificing the latter, our old faithful servant, the Turkey Company!—but to the legislative part of this junto, who planned it, I must give them credit for good generalship. Its great and unpardonable crime was that of sending the fustian and other *finished* manufactures through the north of Turkey and Persia, to the great mart I am speaking of, which came in contact with what they call *their* fabrics; and though they had rendered it very feeble and weak, yet as it was found occasionally trespassing upon them in its old way, and particularly when it was bringing in the incomparable fabrics produced by our new system of manufactures; and foreseeing that if this was permitted much longer, this company would rise like a giant refreshed, and their tonnage on their Volga would be reduced in proportion; it was, therefore, very prudent in them to despatch it altogether.

I must also give the mother country of these clever men from Russia, great credit (since against my will I am become a politician) for another very prudent measure she has lately resorted to; for though this old servant of ours was laid in his tomb, yet there is a sort of inherent genius in our merchants and seamen, that if our country produces any article for which there is a demand in any part of the globe, we have only to consign it to *their care*, and it is sure to find its way to the mart where it is wanted, through every difficulty that sea or land may present. Therefore, though this old servant was defunct, yet these geniuses, with these goods consigned to their care, found their way through the north of Persia to that favourite mart before mentioned; and to put a stop to such intrusions from John Bull in future, I give Russia great credit for the wisdom of her policy in taking the western part of the north of Persia under her own maternal care! And such is my respect for the Emperor of Persia, that if by any means I could send a whisper of advice, so as to reach his ear, it would be to caution him, *on no account*, to suffer any of our traders to pass through the remaining part of his dominions to that forbidden mart; and, at the same time, to give every assurance to the great Autocrat that he is doing so; or the southern parts of that ancient empire, will very soon fall under the same maternal care !!!

We had another old staunch friend, that for ages, may truly be said to have been the most faithful of our *commercial allies*, viz.; the Grand Sultan. He, as well as the Shah of Persia, has frequently been caught in the *very fact*, not only of permitting our fabrics into his extensive dominions for the use of his own subjects, but also of wilfully allowing a transit through his dominions to the same forbid-

den mart, to the great injury of the subjects of the
Czar!—for which offence his days are numbered!—
And if the sovereign junto in Manchester, (with the
aid of their seaport, a cabinet minister for its representative, with his office at the elbow of our Privy
Council for Trade, ready behind the veil to prompt
our government to any measure the junto may desire,) should retain their power so long as to complete their moment of time, (according to Madame
de Stael's scale) the Czar will say to our old faithful
commercial ally, as Buonaparte said to the King of
Portugal, who against every remonstrance, still per-
severed in allowing us to trade in and through his
dominions, " the House of Braganza has ceased to
reign ;" and for the *very same crimes* which the Porte
has continued to commit, even after the Company,
of which he had been so long at the head, had been
laid low the great Autocrat of all the Russias will
say—" the House of Omer has ceased to reign."

The Cabinet of Russia is composed of very clever
practical men, some of whom were on the raft, and
were consulted when the treaty of Tilsit was concluded, in which the Danes and Portuguese were to
be sacrificed for the same crimes Persia and Turkey
are now suffering ; and having the true interest of
their country at heart, they retained in their minds
such parts of Buonaparte's continental system as
might hereafter be useful to their country. When,
at the treaty of Vienna, and that of Paris in 1815,
they reduced them to a practical effect ; for by their
flattering address, and the sanction of some of the
leading members of the Manchester junto (from whom
alone our ministers could take advice) who were frequently in close confab with them (the Russians) at
the latter place, they so managed as to secure by
negociation, what Buonaparte had failed to accomplish for the continent by the sword.

From an official document I have in my possession, and from facts that occurred on the return of
the members of our Manchester junto, and many
other corroborating circumstances, I am fully persuaded that satisfactory *(under the rose)* pledges were
then and *there* given to our rivals, on which *our* reciprocity has since been founded, and which have since
been carried to such a ruinous extent. However,
one fact is certain, that ever since this treaty of Paris,
every thing that had contributed to our former
greatness has been thrown open to all the world
that chose to come over, when our liberality would
allow them to carry away such parts of any thing we
possessed, as might contribute to make every state
in the four quarters of the globe as great as ourselves!
for I suppose the most liberal of *our* liberals never
intended we should go further ; and, considering
the various political opinions the French Revolution
gave rise to, and the vast number of what we may
call clever men, such as Paine, Robespierre, and
thousands who have been strong advocates for
" *liberty and equality*," a better plan could not have
been devised to give this fine *theoretical system* a fair
trial on the *great broad scale*, than that I have just
recorded as a guide to the historian ; nor can a stronger
proof of the disinterested motives of John Bull, when
mixed in the affairs of the continent, be produced,
than that he *alone* would be at the *sole* expence of
such a trial. But, like all the other experiments
that have so often been tried on a smaller scale to
introduce this system, to our sorrow we find it won't
do !—it won't work at all ! ! for instead of each state
being content with its *fair share*, in the third part
of a moment, (according to the scale before laid
down) we find a general scramble for all the good
things John Bull had spread before them in such
profusion takes place, when, of course, the strongest
always ran away with the greatest share and *equality*,

—the main and only prop in this system, was, in every sense of the word, gone in less than a moment! If we may presume that nations are like individuals, of whom it is very rare to find one that will say he has enough, Russia, the strongest in this scramble, having got *by far* the greatest share of these spoils, seems determined to use them in such a way, that ere long she will be able, with *ease*, to accomplish what the great Napoleon so much wished for, viz.—the conquest of our India possessions; and when once *she is able*, where is *our* security? Buonaparte was very candid and open in telling the world why he took Holland, Hambro', Prussia, Italy, Naples, &c., under his paternal care and protection, viz.—that he might be able to shut out our piece-goods and commerce, (except the traffic in cotton yarns) and thereby so far cripple us, as that we might not be able to impede his ulterior views in the east. And though Russia is not so candid, yet, when we see her so carefully following his steps, by shutting us out of the trade of, and transit through, Persia, and leading us into such a broil with our old faithful commercial ally, the Porte, that however we may come out, in all probability it will leave us deprived of any trade or transit in his dominions. These facts, in my mind, speak as clearly the ulterior views of the Czar, as the candid language of the great Napoleon; of whom, if we do not cripple the great Autocrat by withholding the means, (which emanate from us in the way I shall by and by explain) he will very soon become a true prototype, and place us in greater jeopardy than ever we were in by the open hostility of the late Emperor of the French.

As we are daily supplying Russia with the means, and as she now shows a willingness to use them in such a way as may tend to strengthen and extend her dominions, while I am on political topics, to which circumstances, connected with the subject of my narrative have unavoidably drawn me, I will, for the sake of argument, suppose, that ere long she either subdues Turkey, or clips her wings in some way similar to what she has done those of Persia; so that she can safely trust them both, while she turns her views to the east, not only from following her, but also with keeping a sufficient guard, so as to prevent any of our traders from passing through those countries to her forbidden marts in the east. Thus leaving every thing behind her safe, when her commanding officers arrive at the longitude parallel to the head of the Ganges, their boundary officers, whose duty it is to guard the frontier, so as to prevent our traders from approaching their forbidden marts in the north of China will, as in duty bound, have to complain that the English traders are constantly forwarding all sorts of cotton goods to those marts, to the great prejudice and injury of the fabrics sent there by the chartered Millionists of Moscow. These complaints will, of course, be forwarded to the Cabinet of St. Petersburgh, the practical, clever men I have before mentioned, who, after the most mature deliberation, must pronounce to their sovereign, that as they have found us guilty of the same crimes for which Persia and Turkey have suffered, the interest of their country requires them to adjudge the same punishment; when, notwithstanding the personal regard he may feel for the hospitality and favours we shewed him when he visited us, and the loans of money, raw materials, skilful artists, machines, plans, drawings, with the numerous etcetera we have sent him since his return, on the breaking up of that national machine our wise forefathers had so judiciously put together. Yet, when the recorder of that cabinet waits upon the Czar for his signature to the death-warrant, he will find himself reduced to this alternative, either of submitting to the bowstring, or of declaring,—the crown of Great Britain, over Hindostan, has ceased to reign !—But my great fear for the permanent safety of our India posses- sions, under the circumstances I have just described, arises from another cause, which is rapidly in- creasing; and unless the Directors of that Company can put some check upon it, a very great proportion of its numerous inhabitants will unquestionably be reduced to the greatest poverty and distress; in which case, from sheer hunger, such as I before mentioned, they will be ready to give their physical strength to Russia, or any other power that will promise to restore to them their former means of earning their bread.

Until lately, the different provinces, as they suc- cessively came under our rule, always found the be- nefit of such change, and of course became contented and happy. In the first place, we purchased their rich manufactures of cotton, silk, &c., to an immense extent, for the markets of Europe and her colonies in the western world, sending none of our own, ex- cept such as they did not make ; and by the aid of our shipping, carried another portion to all the marts in the Eastern Archipelago, where, for want of shipping, they might not have found their way ; hence, we made them *rich.* In the second place, they found that protection for their persons and property under our regulations and laws, which they had heretofore been unacquainted with, therefore, they became *peaceable* and happy, the *only* foundation on which they could afterwards be made *godly.* I am not acquainted with their present condition ; but when I hear of large cargoes of cotton twist, that will rob their spinsters of their former employ, and of British manufactures, in all the variety that Manchester and Glasgow can furnish, that are sent into the ports of Calcutta, Madras, and Bombay, reversing the order in which things stood ever since those ingenious and industrious people fell under our

protection, and consider, that after having nearly
deserted them as purchasers for the consumption of
Europe, &c., we are, by these cargoes, dividing with
them a share of their home consumption; I feel for
the thousands that must, by this change, be reduced
to a situation, that I fear will be worse than their
predecessors ever knew; this, as regards the vital
interest of that vast population, is the growing evil
I spoke of. And if our India possessions are worth
keeping, should these brief remarks meet the eye of
any of its Directors, I assure them, they are worthy
of their most serious consideration! especially, as
the movements of the leviathan of the north are re-
gulated by the same motives, and to accomplish the
same ends as those that Napoleon were, in the celebrated movements he made *eastward*, when he took
the kingdoms before mentioned under his paternal
care.

These conclusions are not hastily drawn up to
fit the circumstances of the times, except so far as
to shew the *main spring* from whence *alone* these
hostile movements in the east have emanated.—
They are drawn from the practical experience of
thirty-four years, in the working of which, my interest was so deeply involved, that, seeing dark
clouds approaching—in self-defence, I was led to all
the public efforts I have hitherto taken, and *always in
time*, to have averted the evils that were approaching
(and but for the junto would have succeeded) that, like
so many hurricanes, while breaking down the old oaks
of the forest have, with their fall, laid so many of
us, the younger saplings, level with the ground along
with them !

Hence, as my predictions hitherto, with respect
to a certain cause, if suffered to go on, would produce certain effects, have always proved true to the
very letter; and being still in time, I will again sound
my trumpet of woe! to the *east ! !*—if her sovereigns

here do not protect her in time, by clipping the fins
of that great leviathan in the north! and having
sounded this alarm, I will return to her mechanical
merchants in Manchester, from whom I have been
drawn by a long digression.

I left these clever men about the year 1800,
when they were just becoming so far practically
acquainted with the minutiæ of the intricate different branches of the fustian trade, that by living in
lodgings at a small expence, plodding industry, in
seeking out and picking up pieces in the grey from
needy makers at some under-the-rose price; ferreting out fustian-cutters that might be short of work,
who, as a temporary thing, would cut them at a low
price, rather than their journeymen or women should
be without work for a few days; and on the same
plan, going through the singers, dyers, and finishers,
until they were finally packed up ready for their
voyage to the east; (savings, which the old merchants would have refused with disdain!) by which
means they were enabled to under-sell our merchants
in every market in which these goods came in contact. But these clever men did not stop here; for
having learned their trade, they found they could
get many of these operations, such as dyeing and
finishing, done in their own country, where the
labour was still lower than the lowest they could get
here. They had also another very strong induce-
ment to this latter course, viz.—that by dyeing and
finishing these goods at home, they could stamp them
with their imperial crest, and have the honour of
sending them to the borders of China as *their own
fabrics!* And by steadily pursuing the course John
Bull had so *liberally* laid open to them, from 1800
to the peace of 1815; passing laws in the mean time,
(for there was no anglo junto there to hinder them)
that not a piece of our goods should enter their dominions, either dyed, printed, or with any thing

like finish upon them, for fear they should interfere with their imperial stamp:—they, with the grey fabrics *we* had furnished them with, (which, instead of leaving a profit to the individuals who supplied them, had been done at a great average loss,) by that time had succeeded in breaking down all our merchants who stuck to their trade in those quarters.— These merchants, of course, fell in succession ; and, as a natural consequence, the makers of grey fustians, cutters, singers, dyers, finishers, &c., who had immense expensive establishments depending on them for work, were in succession thrown upon the market, where there were none to purchase their goods in the grey, or to employ the other branches, save these mechanical merchants.

Hence, in the face of a growing market in the north of China, that to this day can only be supplied from Manchester and its neighbourhood, all the *laborious* industry, practical ingenuity, and skill of its operatives, with the very expensive establishments before mentioned, fell into the hands of these clever men, at any price they chose to give them for such parts as they wanted ! And as each of those forty Millionists, who form the chartered company I spoke of, had each their mechanical merchant in Manchester, of course, a strife would take place amongst themselves, as to which of them could enable the house they represented, to realise the greatest profit, when these goods again met together in the mart above mentioned.

Though I spoke of little manufacturers as supplying the merchants with these fustians in the grey, there were also many rich and extensive concerns in Oldham, Warrington, the High Peak, in Derbyshire, and many other districts, who had large warehouses in Manchester, in which these grey goods were stored and piled up, (in a way similar to bales of cotton in Liverpool,) ready for the old oaks of the forest, such

as Marsh, Reeves, and Co., Entwisles and Sturtevant,
and scores of similar rank to purchase from, as their
orders through the Turkey Company, or the Leipsic
Channel, before mentioned, might require. But,
alas! most of them were gone, by the returns of
their former adventures having only realised half
their prime cost, instead of their former cent. per
cent. The remainder, whose extreme wealth had
enabled them to stand a succession of these losses,
and something handsome left, seeing, that if they
continued, their all would soon follow, withdrew
from the contest, and left these mechanical merchants in full and quiet possession of this wealthy
field—a field, when properly understood and managed, under the protection of such men as Locke
and Chesterfield speak of, that will produce to its
country *one hundred times more wealth*, than the
same number of souls, and the same breadth in
square miles can do, in any other country on the
face of the globe ; in short, this was the field that
formed the *chief* amongst other pledges, that Mr
Pitt gave as security for the loans that he took.—
However, as it is now under the control of others, I
must proceed to record the mode in which *they* have
managed to cultivate it, since it fell into their hands.

As there were no other customers in the market
for these grey fustians, they were, of course, much
pressed by the holders of these stocks to purchase
them ; when, at last, some of the weaker masters
gave way to the only plan in which they said they
would purchase them, *i. e.*—at such a price per
pound weight, thereby reducing this *celebrated fabric*
to the level of a raw material !—this being submitted
to by a few, it very soon became the standing rule
by which they bought all these goods, and as every
successive purchase must be something lower than
the lot they had bought before, and by every agent
striving to run a farthing lower than the others ; a

farthing-down race for many years has been run by these mechanical merchants against each other, as fatal to the poor weavers and their masters, as the one I have described in the calico trade.

The fustian-cutters, who in seeking out for work, always call where the grey goods are piled for sale, that when a lot is sold, they may know where to follow, to get the cutting of it—they were also successively run down in the same way. And until the skilful men selected from the works of our dyers and finishers, whom these mechanical merchants had sent over to Russia, to teach their people to dye and finish these goods, had put them in the way to do many of them without our dyers and finishers; these also, while they had occasion for them, were run down to such low prices, as would barely cover the expence of their coal, drugs, and wages of their hands, although the latter were run down to the lowest possible level. Hence, in this way, these clever men brought down most of these dyers and finishers, along with the great old manufacturing houses who supplied the trade with the grey fustians during the period I am speaking of, (from 1800 to 1815) to the same level, as those oaks of the forest, under whom, many of them had realised very handsome fortunes, all of which, both the oaks and their branches, would have been *increasing to this day*, had we been under the protection of such managers as Locke and Chesterfield allude to ; and this we should have had, but for the mal-representations of the anglo part of the junto I have so often named.

Notwithstanding the prohibitory laws of Russia prior to the year 1815, I suppose our finished fustians and other goods had occasionally found their way from Leipsic through her dominions to the east ; but as her ministers may be said to have resided for a sufficient time in every district adjoining her frontiers, during the campaigns of 1813-14 and 15, I suppose

they had found out every pass and means by which
such transit had been effected ; for soon after the
peace of 1815, I saw in the public paper a copy of
a treaty between Russia and Prussia, granting special privileges of transit to the latter through the
dominions of the former, but I recollect there were
particular provisos to prevent any thing from us
from participating in any of those privileges ; hence,
she had nothing to fear from us, save what little
might be done through the lingering remains of the
Turkey Company, but, as they knew they had broke
down its merchants, they had little to fear from that
quarter, and the principles on which the chartered
company in Moscow was formed, is a sufficient
guarantee against any thing our merchants (if we
had any) could effect through their old channel of
Leipsic, even if, like eels, they had crept into the
Caspian sea, contrary to the provisos of their transit treaty.

From the time I was in my teens, I was always
given to understand that Russia was the market that
consumed the greatest portion of our fustians, and I
well recollect the fear and alarm that our district
was under, when our government fitted out an
armament about the year 1775 in favour of our old
faithful commercial ally, the Porte, against the rapid
strides the Empress of Russia was then making in a
war going on between those two powers. This alarm
arose from a fear that it would ruin the fustian
trade! and many a report came into our district, in
the high peak of Derbyshire, that the Manchester
trade was going down!! and the ruin of all the
spinsters in the country would certainly follow!!!

From these early impressions, and from every
thing that I could since learn, until a little while
past, I always fancied that the people of Russia
scarcely wore any thing but fustians. However,
about three years ago I was set right upon this

question, on which I had been so long puzzled ; for, being in company (in London) with a gentleman whom I found had long been *practically* acquainted with the trade from Moscow to the (almost unknown) extensive regions in the east. On my expressing such an opinion, he seemed very much surprised, and assured me that so far from this being the case, that out of every fifty pieces we sent from Manchester to Moscow, not more than *one* of them was consumed in the Russian dominions, all the rest were sent to a certain city or town on the north of China, which, to the best of my recollection, he described as nine miles long, one half of which was in Russia, and the other half in China, a certain river forming the boundary, the names of which being of that class that our vulgar tongue dare hardly attempt to utter, for fear that our masticators should be placed in jeopardy. I cannot say that I am sorry I have forgot them, especially as it is of no importance, for as China has only one mart (Canton) on her frontier to the ocean, so I understood from this gentleman, that she has only one mart on the opposite frontier of those vast dominions, where she allows her subjects to trade with Russia, or any other state in the west of Europe.

As the half of this very long town (no matter as to its name) stands on a part of Russia, I do no complain of any regulation she makes to secure every advantage to her own subjects that may arise from the trade that is carried on with it, nor can we blame her for the wise regulations she has shewn in the formation of that company, to whom alone of all her subjects, she grants the privilege of trading with the chinese in that mart. All I am so anxiously driving at, is to shew to the Lockes of my country the extreme *wickedness* (for I can find no other term in my opinion so proper) of suffering the richest district in the

world to be sacrificed in the way that I have just given the rough outline, in order to furnish them with
their principal articles of trade to that mart.

We are all pretty well assured that China contains upwards of 300 millions of people! and when,
as this gentleman told me, they all (of course I understood him to mean chiefly the agricultural and
mechanical class) wore fustian for the upper part of
their shoes—fustian for their lower garments, and
fustian for the upper parts of their dress, if not fustian on their heads, which I think he also mentioned.
What a market for fustians is this! no wonder that
our old Manchester merchants made such princely
fortunes, while through the aid of the Turkey company, they were enabled to supply it, by which they
established the use and fashion of its wear; and however cruel it may be to reflect on the hardship of
having such a trade torn from them in less than Madam De Stael's moment, no one can wonder at the
Russians running away with it the moment we left
it unguarded; or that now she has got it, she takes
such great precautions to keep it. The only wonder
is, why we did not take more care of it, while we
had it!

The chartered company, which in Russia is called
the millionists, is formed in the following manner—
no one is eligible to become a member, unless he is
known to possess a million of rubles beyond all that
he may owe, and a character of honour and integrity
corresponding with such a fortune. Three years ago
it consisted of forty members, and though there are
many barriers from thence, where all traders found
moving towards this sacred mart are very closely examined, for fear John Bull should slip through them
with his fustians, yet as government has full confidence in every member of this company, who, if found
tripping are struck off the list! in addition to the privilege, they grant them to trade with the Chinese,

they also allow them the privilege of a certain seal
upon each of their bales when packed up in Moscow,
that becomes a safe passport through all the barriers
I have spoken of.

Although I have confined myself to the article
of fustians through the whole of the rough sketch I
have just given, yet, in a secondary degree, every
thing that I have said will equally apply to printed calicos and other articles, and would take a page or two
to enumerate, where the same principle of catching
every thing as it comes from our loom, and sending
it off to be dyed, printed, and finished, in their mother country, that they may stamp it as their own
fabrics, runs through their whole proceedings! all,
or the bulk of which they buy by the pound, as a
raw material! And by having these genuine fabrics
as their leading articles, along with which they introduce their own fabrics made from the twist they
had got from us, which answered so well, that they,
a few years ago in the lighter articles, such as calicos
for printing upon, &c., thought they should in future
be independent of us, except in the article of cotton
yarns to make them, under which impression they
had got a ukase, prohibiting our calicos entering their
dominions under any pretence! when lo, and behold!
very soon after they had got this prohibition, their
millionists returned from the frontiers of China, and
their merchants from the north of Persia, under the
greatest trepidation and alarm! saying John Bull
had met them with printed calicos done upon a fabric they called *power-loom calicos*, that had completely
beat them out in those markets!! How, or by what
means John had got into them, no one could tell, but
such was the fact, and unless they could put their
prints in future on a similar fabric, they might as
well stop at home!!!

In this dilemma the millionists, merchants, and
calico-printers held several consultations, the result

of which was a deputation to St Petersburgh to solicit a special ukase that they might be permitted to write to their agents in Manchester to procure them a necessary supply of these power-loom calicos to print upon, until they could make them themselves, for which purpose they had already sent to their mechanical agents in Manchester to procure them the necessary machinery, and skilful hands to teach them how to work this machinery.

As the clever men who compose the cabinet of Russia don't like to go back, and as this application had rather a retrograde appearance, this deputation met with more difficulties than what is usual on such occasions ; for the Court fearing that if they permitted them to import this particular fabric, some others that their own weavers could do as well might come in along with them, and thereby deprive their own looms of so much labour ; for though the cabinet saw the propriety and the necessity of granting this special ukase, yet, before they granted it, the printers had to make out an estimate as to the exact number of pieces they would require, according to the machines and printing tables that were to be appropriated to this purpose. This being done, the ukase was granted with a special proviso, that the number of pieces imported under this ukase should afterwards be compared with what they could shew they-had printed, and for any surplus that might appear, the importers should be accountable. By virtue of this ukase, their mechanical merchants in Manchester are, and for several years past at certain periods, sending over the stipulated quantity which they buy by the pound weight, and their money, since we sent them the loans, is *so good*, that those power-loom manufacturers that make them, who, by the bye, are the very same persons that in time past, when they were spinners only, always sold their surplus stocks to these Russian agents at the job-prices before-mentioned, in order to keep up their price with the home manufacturers, and for the same reasons these periodical orders are, or soon will be, executed on lower terms than they would sell to any of the great printing houses in Lancashire! Hence, these millionists are now *swaggering away* with their power-loom prints and power-loom fustians (for which, under the rose, they are now building large mills in our fustian districts, as they cannot manage them at home, under an idea that their reign here will be permanent) on the borders of China and Persia in such style, that John Bull would not be able to compete with them, were it not that he has *still* a few of those merchants *left*, who ship off his goods on the principle before-mentioned, viz. advancing upon them two-thirds of their value, until returns are made ; and though these fabrics have hitherto been an exception to that general rule where I stated the other third had never come back! if we are to go on in this way, I fear that even these inimitable fabrics will very soon merge into that general rule !

While I am complaining of these grey fustians,. grey calicos, &c. being allowed to be sent off in an unfinished state, I fancy I shall be told that I am arguing against my own principles, for as they are already manufactured, as it is generally called, surely. I cannot object to them being exported as a British manufacture. Now, in order to come at the true definition of this *simple word*, that the want of its true meaning being *properly understood*,. has permitted such distress to come upon our country. I will join issue with my opponents,. if any such should remain, by entering my protest against even these power-loom calicos or fustians, being what our predecessors would have even called a manufacture, and though a little while back if any one to strengthen the opinions he was arguing upon, had by any unguarded slip of the tongue made the least allusion to what

our Lockes and Chesterfields had said upon such subjects, he would only have been answered with a laugh
at his folly for quoting such stupid authorities, yet
I flatter myself the time is not far distant, when the
laugh will be on the other side, if such subjects will
allow of any laughing at all! therefore, anticipating
that such a period is near at hand, I will venture to
give my opinion as to the comprehensive view in
which our forefathers understood the word, and I will
take the manufacture of watches as one instance.
In the town of Prescot we have makers, or what the
junto would call manufacturers of main springs, manufacturers of watch dials, hands, wheels, pinions,
&c., all of which are distinct branches, and yet the
whole only forms *one* manufacture; and so our forefathers understood it when they passed the law that
none of these branches should be exported until they
formed a complete watch. Pin-making has also many
distinct branches, and yet the whole only forms *one*
manufacture; and from what I heard from the lips of
our immortal Pitt a few months before this country
was deprived of that great British pilot, I am confident he understood this word in the same comprehensive view. At the period I speak of, the bleachers
in Lancashire sent up a deputation (Mr Thomas and
Mr Richard Ainsworth) to explain to Mr Pitt, how a
certain duty lately laid upon salt, was likely to be
injurious to their trade, especially as they had nearly
all gone into the chemical mode of bleaching, in
which a considerable portion of salt is consumed.
As I happened to be in London at the time, these
gentlemen called upon me requesting I would accompany them to an interview Col. Stanley had procured
for them with Mr Pitt. A few weeks or months prior
to this, I had made some considerable sales of cambric muslins to a merchant from the Netherlands, in
the grey state, deducting the price of bleaching
from the usual charge, and as, of course, I had

not sent our usual quantity to Mr Richard Ainsworth, our bleacher, I had told him of these sales in the grey as my reason, and that I might give this fact in evidence before Mr Pitt, was their object in requesting me to accompany them. After Col. Stanley, the two gentlemen, and myself, were sat down with the minister, a very close scrutiny into the merits of their case took place, and it was only by the nicest calculations upon fractional parts that they could convince the minister upon two points : first, that from the price of bleachers' drugs in the Netherlands, those bleachers would have an advantage over the Lancashire bleachers, and the second, that if this tax remained, they, the Lancashire bleachers, would have this additional tax to pay out of their own pockets ; however, they at last succeeded, and their request was granted. During the whole of this discussion, I was particularly struck with many of Mr Pitt's remarks, all bearing up to this point, that under any circumstance he would give up every obstacle that lay in the way, rather than that these goods should leave the country before *their manufacture was complete.* ✳

Hence, I contend, that whether in watch-making, woollen-goods-making, or in cotton-goods-making, all must be brought up to their final finish, ready for wear, before the word manufacture can be applied, it is the whole when consolidated into the monosyllable *one* that gives them a just or equitable title to

✳ And though such a thing was not touched upon, I have no doubt Mr Pitt would have granted a bounty on these, or any other articles in the trade, rather than we should be undersold by any other nation in any of the markets abroad.

I am led to make this remark on reflecting on the sophistical genius the junto resorted to, when they got off our former bounties, in order (under the rose) that their mother countries might the better be enabled to cope with us in all such markets in which they could not exclude us.

this term ! and, until they are so consolidated, I shall treat every branch, in whatever stage I find it, under the head of a raw material, or, as the 9th sec. of the Act of the 28th Geo. 3rd calls them, a *" pretended manufacture,"* against the export of which "a penalty of 3s for every pound weight" was imposed, besides " the forfeiture of all ships, waggons, carts, horses, &c., engaged in carrying or conveying the same." This was the act that finally established our protecting system, for the want of which our national vessel had been buffeted amongst rocks and sand-banks for centuries past in *rebellion, revolution,* and *foreign wars ! ! !* and when we look at the cause that has given rise to this narrative, it shews that even when the Captain of a state has got his vessel clear from all rocks and sand-banks, and sailing smoothly along, there is still the same necessity for a skilful pilot to be on the look-out at the helm to prevent her from running upon others equally as dangerous, as there is for the Captain of a ship who may have a crew and valuable cargo committed to his care in a voyage round the globe ; for ere the ink of that final act that carried us on to the victory of Waterloo was scarcely dry, the *seeds* of our former troubles began to vegetate on different and, for want of some one to " look out a head," unprotected ground ! the consequences of which I have pretty fully recorded, and though my opinion for nearly the last 40 years (especially while we lay under the *taunt* of a nation of shopkeepers, with our *guineas,* &c.) as to the *motives* on which certain foreign courts became so hostile, has always been what I have stated, yet, I hardly durst have written them so freely as I have done, with respect to Russia, had it not been for the candid openness of Buonaparte, who let out *such* State secrets without any reserve.

Having, incontrovertibly, (I think) brought the definition of this word (manufacture up to its true meaning, although, for the reasons before-mentioned, the political economist is reduced to his A. B C., yet, as I have fixed these fustians, &c. under the head of raw material, we may learn something worth our notice from those who have preceded us.

The sentiments of our forefathers on such subjects are worthy of note. In several valuable works on trade, written in the 17th century, this question seems to have occupied a good deal of the attention of those writers I before spoke of, amongst whom may be enumerated Sir Josiah Child, Mr Munn, and an ingenious author who published in 1689, under the signature of Philanglus, a work entitled *Britannia Languens*, from which the following passages may be extracted with great propriety, as immediately applicable to the case before me:—In page 23 of his work, he says, "most materials of manufacture are of small value whilst raw and unwrought, at least in comparison of the manufacture, since by manufacture they may be made of five, ten, or twenty times their first value, according to the *workmanship*, which is proved by the woollen, silk, and linen manufacture, and almost infinite others ; wherefore, if a nation hath nationally any materials of manufacture, it is far more advantageous to export them in manufacture, rather than the raw materials, because the manufacture is so much more valuable, and will make a return of five, ten, or twenty times more treasure to the nation than the raw material."

"Besides it is most dangerous to export the materials of manufacture, since it may transfer the manufacture itself into some neighbour nation, and with it the incident riches and populacy ; by which means a neighbour nation may become five, ten, or twenty times richer and stronger than that nation which doth export its materials ; and those innocent materials may return in the shape of *armed men and ships*, to the terror and confusion of an *unwise and lazy people ! ! !*"

As I before observed, if this narrative should meet the eye of any of the sovereigns in Leadenhall-street, I hope they will give such parts of its contents as relate to the safety of their extensive empire, that serious consideration that their importance requires! or perhaps before they are aware, these raw materials of cotton yarns, gray power-loom and hand-loom fustians, and gray power-loom calicoes, &c. will, " in the shape of *armed men*," pay them a visit that may place their dominions in great jeopardy !!—and having thus sounded my second trumpet of woe to the east !!!* I will again return to Manchester, and try if I can bring up such evidence as will bear me out in the declarations I have more than doubly filed against the Anglo-part of this junto, from whom all the evils I have taken such pains and expence in tracing from their source to their final effect, have emanated.

* Just before I sent this sheet to press, *The Morning Herald* of the 8th of March, came to hand, and as to my knowledge, no one in Manchester, is aware that I am writing at all, and as none but myself can have an idea of the sentiments I have so laboriously been dwelling upon, as respects Russia, I was agreeably surprised to find in that paper, the following article, which I here attach to my narrative, as an unquestionable evidence, that the sentiments of the trade are the same as my own on the subject I have narrated upon, under so many different heads.   When the period arrives in which *they dare speak out*, but woe to the man that publicly speaks his mind, while the reign of this junto continues, for though they dare not treat him as Buonaparte treated Palm, the Bookseller, yet they will give him the stab in another quarter, equally as fatal, though in a different way! It is worthy of remark that these nine out of every ten opinions were gathered from individuals, under the rose as I call it !!!

" *Manchester, Tuesday, March 4,* 1828.—No alteration of consequence has been experienced in the market since last week.   The demand for yarns is very considerable, and in goods there has been a great deal done, particularly in steam cloths, prints, and fustians, the latter averaging about from 20d. to 2s. per lb.   The prices of goods generally continue low, which is a subject of complaint with some manufacturers, though it ought not to be, for, if prices advanced, the demand would lessen.   On the whole, things are going on well ; all the hands are steadily employed, which is the surest proof of a fair demand

When I branched off to the east, I was going to
relate the state of things in Manchester, after the
weavers had made such strong appeals to their masters, and that these appeals had not been in vain to
those old oaks of the forest; but, that in their endeavours to procure that protection from government,
which the necessity of their case required, they met
with difficulties that it is now my painful duty to
record.

In the autumn and winter following those strong
appeals of the weaver, the British heart of oak-part
of their old Chamber of Commerce, made several
attempts to memorialise government, by means of
that old faithful organ, on the growing evil in question, but, as some of their members had connected
themselves in partnership with some of those clever
men from Germany that I have so often mentioned,

for their labour. There are great rumours of the probability of a war,
as well as conjectures as to the consequences should one take place.
Most persons are, however, agreed on the impolicy of weakening the
Turkish empire, which serves as a kind of sea-bank against the ambition of Russia. If a war we must have, it would certainly be most
popular, were it intended to cripple the Giant of the North, by rending
from his grasp some of his vassals, and pinning the remainder up in
their deserts. England, as well as the neighbouring Continental States,
will probably, ere many generations are passed, have to lament in tears
and blood, the infatuation which suffered the gathering under one
head of all the regions and people that now constitute the Russian
empire. The young monster is strong, and is still strengthening; his
ferocity is equal to his strength, aud his ambition surpasses both. He,
therefore, of all the "European family," ought to be most observed
and guarded against. Such are the sentiments and opinions of nine
persons in every ten with whom I have conversed on this subject."
The average price these Russians have paid for their power-loom
calicoes to print upon, has never exceeded 4d. per yard, and though, as
to fustians, I am not so well informed, yet, I fancy they do not exceed
10 to 15d. per yard. These are the innocent materials the above old writer
speaks of, which the Russians will sell to the Chinese and Persians, at
five, ten to twenty times what they have paid us for them, from whom
these innocent materials will return upon us in the way above-mentioned.

the Chamber of course became so *divided against
itself*, when, as if it had been seized with convulsions,
it *expired* while struggling with *this very question ! ! !*
Hence, the cotton trade,—that trade which the Chancellor of the Exchequer told me (in the presence of
one of our worthy M. P.'s in 1817) " had by all parties
been acknowledged to have provided the extraordinary part of those means by which this country so
gloriously terminated the long and expensive war,"
has not to this day been able to raise another, by
which its wants and its wishes to the most paternal
of governments can find their way in any official
shape ! of the chamber the junto have established
since they became its sovereigns I shall have occasion
to speak anon.

In March and April following, when the British
part of this Chamber found they could no longer
organise their old instrument, so as to work in its
usual way, they determined to try their strength in
the only way they had left ; hence, they appealed to
the public in the papers of the day, two or three
specimens of which I have re-printed as a record of
the sentiments of the *truly* British party I speak of.
Public meetings were called, at which their sentiments
were embodied in temperate but strong resolutions,
—a committee was formed out of their body, the
names of whom I have given in the commencement
of this narrative, with a brief sketch of their proceedings, to which I will only add, that their
memorial to the Lords of the Privy Council for Trade,
which was forwarded through the same channel, and
in the same way in every respect as the memorials
from their old Chamber were used to be,—for
the reasons I am going to state, these old oaks of the
forest have received no answer to that memorial to
the present day !

At this period commences the reign of the
Foreign-Anglo junto ! when a foreigner of the name of

Rupp (whose name will be found in the following list)
deeply learned in the mal-metaphysical jargon before
alluded to, wrote several articles in the public papers
against the proceeding before-mentioned ; this champion also published two or three letters addressed to
the trade, signed *Mercator* ; the first has not come to
hand, but the second is before me in the form of a
pamphlet of 16 pages, and could I spare room I
would here have re-printed it, that practical men
who have witnessed the workings of this trade for
the last 27 years, might compare this experience
with the plausible theoretical stuff here laid down !
especially as these letters and the other papers he
addressed to the public at that time, formed that
sophistical mal-metaphysical code, from whence all
the briefs of its advocates to this day have been
drawn up.

Under the tactics of this *hero*, with the aid of
several other *Germans*, similarly situated, as partners
in different spinning concerns in the town, he
managed to raise a formidable body to oppose those
very, *very*, old oaks of the forest, who had thus come
forward to seek protection for their winders, their
warpers, their sizers, their heald-yarn makers from
long wool, their heald-knitters, their reed-makers,
their loom-makers, their bobbin-turners, and shuttle-
makers, their weavers, their fustian-cutters, their dressers, their dyers, their bleachers, their tambourers, *
their finishers, their trunk and chest-makers for
packing their goods for shipping, their packers, &c. ;

* And to show that the various branches of which I am here only
giving the outlines, were not confined to the manufacturing districts,
out of several that came to my personal knowledge, I will give one
instance which the present legislators on the Police Laws of the Metropolis are little acquainted with.   This instance shall be the house of
Stirling, Hunter, and Co., factors, in Bow Church Yard, who in executing the orders of the Turkey and other merchants had occasion to
employ not less than three hundred females with the needle, in tambouring cotton goods with coloured silks and worsteds in the various

with which I must include their corn growers, from whom these branches consumed such vast quantities of flour, in size and paste, in many operations, as well as their dry-salters, for drugs used in dyeing, bleaching, printing, &c. All of these with many minor branches, these manufacturing merchants were seeking to protest along with themselves, against the intrusions of that Foreign-Anglo body, amongst whom, (*i. e.* the active members,) not an individual could be found, who was not so blinded by what he *erroneously* fancied would lead to his own interest, as entirely to overlook and leave to their fate, *all* the branches in the above catalogue, on which are consolidated the fundamental strength of our country. While the only objects their opponents could possibly have in view, were, that they might be enabled to realize their fortunes in the half of a moment, reckless of all the other considerations! and to remove the

---

fancies and figures required to *complete* those manufactures, before they could be shipped off. This house on the average of many years prior to the peace of America, remitted to Glasgow and Lancashire, from ninety to one hundred thousand pounds a month, in good bills, (for the rule of that house was never to be drawn upon on goods consigned to them for sale,) collected from those merchants in payment for cotton manufactures alone, the commission on which made them very rich; so much so, that apparently, that old oak of the London forest, —rich in paternal estates, as well as in trade, was so strong, that no storm could ever shake them. Yet for want of the protection I am speaking of at that particular period, this very house, by guaranteeing their sales to the Turkey and other merchants, who successively fell from their returns, being 50 cent. per cent. loss, instead of their old per cent. profit, was obliged to sink under the pressure so occasioned. Thus were upwards of three hundred women and girls thrown out of employ, and driven I fear to seek their living by walking the streets from Bow Church to Temple Bar!—This house formed but a very small part of the whole then going on in the same beneficial way in that great city, and nearly all the others, from the *same cause,* fell to the *same level!*—a level which has driven thousands into crimes that set the best police regulations at defiance!—Give them back their needle work, and then your police laws will be found quite sufficient.

difficulties they then experienced in getting hands
that would work in the tropical heat of their mills,
for 72 to 82 hours per week, while the above healthy
branches remained open to them, it was thought
good policy in these men spinsters, to cut up the
above branches at once, and then these hands would
be reduced to *Hobson's choice!* In the latter of these
objects they have hitherto succeeded, and have a
million to spare, which they have placed under sentence of transportation! and as nothing but the
money is wanting to carry this sentence into execution, the Manchester and Liverpool members, that
form the executive part of this junto, ought in justice
and equity, to pay every farthing of it out of the profits
they realized, (from that legal and honorable trade
they speak of) in the year 1825-6, or up to this day,
even if it should reduce them to the level, the foreign
part of this body will be brought to when they have
remunerated their mother countries for the loss they
occasioned them by their sixpenny-down race.

The Foreign-Anglo sovereign junto being thus
incorporated by these *very* clever men, frequent meetings of its cabinet took place, at which a public
meeting was resolved upon ; when collecting all their
public addresses and letters of *Mercator* together, the
legislative branch concocted out of the most plausible part of them a string of resolutions, and handing
them over to the executive part of their body, sent
them to the meeting, where they got them passed
unanimously ; and as these resolutions embody the
very *quintessence* of *their* liberal system, I will here
reprint them with the whole proceedings of that
meeting, as a guide to the future historian when he
comes to dilate on the eventful period that is now passing over our heads, and also to show the " wise men"
of our day, the foundation of that sophistical jargon
which has brought such distress on our country.

*At a numerous and respectable general Meeting of
Merchants, Manufacturers, Cotton-spinners, and
other persons who disapprove of a duty on the exportation of cotton-twist, convened by public advertisement
in the Manchester Newspapers, and held at the Bull's
Head Inn, in Manchester, on Tuesday the 6th day
of May, 1800, in order to take into consideration the
most effectual means of opposing an application,
intended to be made to Parliament for imposing such
a duty.*

SAMUEL MARSLAND, ESQ. in the Chair.

"RESOLVED UNANIMOUSLY,

" 1. That the mechanical ingenuity and improvements of the
cotton-spinners have enabled the manufacturers of piece-goods in this
country, even under the disadvantage of the increased price of provisions
and high wages, to bear a competition with foreign manufacturers, in
their own markets.

" 2. That a prohibition of or a duty imposed on the exportation
of twist would check and suppress the exercise of those mechanical
talents which have been hitherto so zealously and successfully employed
to the benefit of the manufacturers of piece-goods, and force the manufacturers abroad to invest their property in cotton-mills for the spinning
of yarn for their own consumption, in which undertaking they would
be aided by a multitude of British spinners whose ruin would be produced by the measure contemplated, and who would consequently be
compelled to seek in a foreign country that employment and subsistence
of which they would be deprived in this.

" 3. That the superiority of our manufactures depending not on
manual labour, the price of which is much lower in other countries, but
on our *mechanical improvements ;* if these improvements be once forced
out of this island and established elsewhere, the cotton-trade in general
will be transferred to foreigners, or be limited to the consumption of the
British dominions.

" 4. That an attempt on the part of one class of manufacturers
to interfere with the trade of another class, and to embarrass it with
restrictions and duties is unjust, ungenerous and dangerous. Such an
attempt directed to the spinning of cotton-yarns is the more unjust,
because the capitals engaged in cotton-mills cannot be diverted, as those
of the manufacturers of piece-goods may be, to other trades ; but must
remain invested in buildings and machinery, which, when they cease to
be employed, will be wholly useless and of no value. It is highly
ungenerous, in as much as it proceeds from the very persons whose
trade has been preserved to them by the ingenuity and exertions of the
spinners, whose ruin their measures are calculated to accomplish. It

is dangerous, because if carried into effect it would establish a precedent for a tax on the manufactured goods of this country, and may suggest abroad the policy of a counteracting duty on British piece-goods.

"5. That the exportation of cotton-twist is a legal, fair, and honourable trade, contributing to the employment of a large portion of the national capital and to the maintenance and support of the industrious poor, and causing a great influx of foreign wealth into Great Britain.

"6. That it is the right of every subject (antecedent to any law declaring the contrary) to dispose of the produce of his flock and industry where and in what manner he thinks proper. That in the just expectation of a free and undisturbed enjoyment of this right, many persons have been induced to sink nearly the whole of their capital in buildings and machinery; and that to restrain the spinner in the free disposal of the produce of his manufactory, by a prohibition of or a duty upon the exportation of twist, is a violation of his rights, and an infringement of the freedom of trade.

"7. That the cotton-trade, like every other trade, if unincumbered with duties and vexatious restrictions will always regulate itself in a manner the most beneficial to the general interests; and that any attempt to give it an unnatural direction in order to raise one class of manufacturers on the ruin of another, will fail even of this illiberal and selfish purpose, and lead to consequences very injurious to the community at large.

"8. That this meeting, impressed with a sense of the great injustice and impolicy of laying a tax on or prohibiting the exportation of twist, hold it their duty to oppose any attempt which may be made to effect so dangerous a measure. That for this purpose a petition be presented to the honourable the Commons of Great Britain, praying that no law laying a duty on or prohibiting or restraining the exportation of cotton-twist may be suffered to pass that honourable house.

"9. That the petition now laid before this meeting is approved, and that the same do lie at Spencer's Tavern for signatures.

"10. That a committee be appointed to carry into effect these resolutions, and that such committee consist of the following gentlemen, viz.

JAMES ACKERS, Esq.
RICHARD ARKWRIGHT, Esq.
JOHN ATKINSON, Esq.
THOMAS ATKINSON, Esq.
JOHN BARTON, Esq.
Mr JAMES BARTON.
Mr JOHN BARTON, Shudehill.
JAMES BATEMAN, Esq.
Mr THOMAS BATEMAN.
Mr CHARLES BENNETT.
JONATHAN BEEVER, Esq.
RICHARDSON BORRADAILE, Esq.
Mr GEORGE CRUDEN.
WILLIAM DOUGLAS, Esq.

Mr JAMES McCONNELL.
SAMUEL MARSLAND, Esq.
PETER MARSLAND, Esq.
WILLIAM MITCHELL, Esq.
THOMAS MORT, Esq.
SAMUEL OLDKNOW, Esq.
LAWRENCE PEEL, Esq.
JOSEPH PEEL, Esq.
GEORGE PHILIPS, Esq.
Mr JOHN POOLY, Junr.
Mr THEOPHELUS LEWIS RUPP.
JOHN SIMPSON, Esq.
Mr CHRISTOPHER SMALLEY.
ROBERT SPEAR, Esq.

JOHN DOUGLAS, Esq.
Mr ROBERT DUCK.
Mr JOHN ELLIOTT.
Mr DAVID HOLT.
Mr GEORGE LEE.

WILLIAM STRUTT, Esq.
JOSEPH THACKERAY, Esq.
JOHN WATSON, Esq.
OTTIWELL WOOD, Esq.

" 11. That the committee have the power of adding to their number such other members as they shall think proper.

" 12. That the committee be and are hereby authorized to appoint delegates to attend in London, to oppose the injurious attempts of the piece-manufacturers to lay a tax on or restrain the exportation of twist.

" 13. That this meeting highly approves of the resolutions and proceedings of the merchants, manufacturers, and spinners who called this meeting.

" 14. That books of subscriptions for defraying the expences of opposing any application which may be made to Parliament for laying a duty on or prohibiting or restraining the exportation of cotton-twist do lie at the counting-houses of Messrs Henry and John Barton and Co., Mr William Mitchell, Messrs Baldwin and Cheetham, Mr Richard Clough, and the Holywell Twist company. and at Mr Banck's shop and Spencer's Tavern.

" SAMUEL MARSLAND, CHAIRMAN.

" Mr Marsland having left the chair, the same was taken by Mr Atkinson, and it was resolved that the thanks of this meeting be given to Mr Marsland for his able and upright conduct in the chair.

" JOHN ATKINSON.

" ☞ The Petition now lies at Spencer's Tavern for signatures."

From the high tone, language, and style, the eight resolutions on which they found their counter petition against the manufacturers are drawn up, a stranger would be led to believe that the latter were a set of *over fed* mushrooms *just sprung up*, and that in their public meeting of the 29th April, they had passed some strong arbitrary resolutions, threatening to overturn the former, to whom they were solely indebted for all they enjoyed ; whereas the facts in both cases stood quite the reverse. The manufacturing merchants from the immense wealth they had accumulated from the time of Elizabeth by cent. per cent. returns for goods, fabricated on the yarns produced by ten times as many *happy spinsters* as these men spinsters now employ in *the most miserable slavery!* were the over feeders, by which they had

raised up a few barbers, tinkers, coblers, &c., in
Madam de Stael's moment, that thus, in their purse-
proud attitude, turned round upon *their benefactors*,
who had only come forward to seek protection for
the millions comprised in the branches before-named ;
nor had the latter given any occasion for that high
tone of language from the former. The merchants
had only formed the two following resolutions, on
which they had founded their petition, which they
laid before government, without sending up a deputation to explain its meaning.

Bull's Head Inn, Manchester, 29th April, 1800.
At a numerous and respectable public Meeting of
Merchants, Manufacturers, and others, interested in
the Cotton Manufacturers of the town and neighbour-
hood of Manchester, convened, by advertisement in
the Manchester Newspapers, for the purpose of taking
into consideration the injuries arising from the export-
ation of Cotton Twist:

JOHN KEARSLEY, Esq. in the Chair.
"IT WAS UNANIMOUSLY RESOLVED AS FOLLOWS.

" 1. That the practice of exporting cotton yarns, which continues to encrease in a most extensive degree, is in its consequences
highly injurious to the cotton manufactures of this country, and will,
without suitable regulations, ultimately endanger the existence of trade
in such manufactures.

" 2. That it appears to this meeting the evils before-mentioned
can only be restrained by a duty on the exports of cotton-twist, so as
the cotton goods manufactured in this country, may be brought to
foreign markets on equal terms with goods made in other countries,
from the yarns exported by Great Britain.

" 3. (Two dissentients only.) That a petition to the Honourable the House of Commons, expressive of the sentiments of this meeting, and praying relief, by the means mentioned in the preceding
resolution, be immediately prepared by a committee for the purpose,
consisting of Mr Richardson, Mr Crompton, Mr John Parker, and Mr
James Ollivant.

" 4. That the petition produced by the committee, and now read,
be approved and signed.

" 5. That a subscription be opened to defray incidental expenses.

"6. That a committee be appointed for carrying into effect the resolutions of this meeting; and that such committee be composed of the following gentlemen (five of whom being competent to act,) viz.

Mr RICHARDSON.
Mr PETER CROMPTON.
Mr SILVESTER.
Mr LEIGH PHILIPS.
Mr SAMUEL GARDNER.
Mr JAMES OLLIVANT.
Mr THOMAS SLATER.
Mr ROGER HOLLAND.
Mr WILLIAM LEAF.
Mr JAMES DERBYSHIRE.
Mr THOMAS DARWELL.
Mr RUSHFORTH.
Mr JAMES WARDLE.
Mr ROBERT PARKER.
Mr NATHANIEL GOULD.
Mr JOHN PARKER.
Mr THOMAS POTTER.
Mr JOHN RAILTON.

Mr CHARLES HORSFALL.
Mr BOLD COOKE.
Mr LOCK.
Mr LAWRENCE PEEL.
Mr ROBERT PEEL, Junr.
Mr SAMUEL SMITH.
Mr KEARSLEY.
Mr JAMES HIBBERT.
Mr JOSEPH SEDDON.
Mr THOMAS AINSWORTH.
Mr SAMUEL TAYLOR.
Mr JOHN HEYWOOD.
Mr HENRY FARRINGTON.
Mr WILLIAM STARKEY.
Mr JOHN TETLOW.
Mr THOMAS BELCHER.
Mr JAMES HALL, Son. and
Mr THOMAS SCHOLES.

"Together with such other gentlemen, as the committee may think proper to add to their number.

"JOHN KEARSLEY, CHAIRMAN.

"Mr Kearsley having left the chair, Mr Silvester was requested to take it, and it was unanimously resolved, that the thanks of this meeting be presented to Mr Kearsley, for his impartial conduct in the chair.

"J. SILVESTER, CHAIRMAN.

"The Petition for regulating the Exportation of Cotton Yarns, now lies for signatures at the Bull's Head Inn, in the small room fronting the Market-place.

"Attendance will be given on this business every day (Sundays excepted) from eight in the morning till eight in the evening."

Is there any thing in these resolutions that calls for such a purse-proud farrago of fudge that runs through the whole of their eight resolutions on which the found their counter petition? and yet even with all the strength these *wilful* mal-representations could give to this petition, still they durst not trust it to speak for itself in the usual way when it came before government, for having a sort of foreboding that a scrutiny might take place at the helm when these petitions were laid before the penetrating eye of the great pilot, and conscious of the rotten basis on which

they had founded their case, and that when it came
to be scruitnized by Mr Pitt, it could only be held up
by occasional props from the same *inexhaustible
source!* Under these impressions they passed their
12th resolution, in furtherance of which this delegation had their interview in Downing-street; when the
minister must have placed their cause in great
jeopardy, or they would have had no occasion to
prop it up in language to the following effect :—

These delegates told the Chancellor that the yarns
exported were only an *occasional surplus* that they
happened to have at times on hand, beyond what
the home trade could consume! but, on finding this
statement too equivocal to satisfy such a penetrating
minister, as they were then before, they again drew
out of the *store* before-mentioned such an argument
as the minister could no longer withstand, and this
was by simply adding that this surplus was nothing
but the *refuse quality!* such as the manufacturers in
this country had rejected, as their hands would not
work it!! and being so *trifling* in its amount, they
thought it would be very hard if they were not
allowed to sell it to those who would work it, and it
being admitted that the few goods that could be
fabricated on this trifling surplus would never be
felt in the foreign markets as coming in competition
with ours. The minister, though with some reluc-
tance, permitted them to continue to dispose of those
yarns which our manufacturers threw back upon
their hands, from their being of such bad quality,
as our hands would not work!!!! In this honourable
way these delegates carried their point, to the entire
satisfaction of the legislative part of that junto who
sent them, and the success that attended this mode
of sending up proper persons along with this petition,
led them to pursue the same course with every memorial
the junto have had occasion to send to their office of
trade in London, to explain *their* meaning and parry

off objections, has been followed up to this day, when ever the subject has been of any importance.

Although it is quite unnecessary for me to make another comment on these resolutions, the practical experience of the last 27 years, having sufficiently refuted every thing they have recorded in them that appears in the shape of argument ; yet I cannot pass by the fifth, without calling the attention of my readers, to the pompous style in which they boast of their traffic being a *legal* and *honourable* trade ; if the latter was their real opinion, why, after their interview with Mr Pitt, did they not enter their shipments of refuse yarns (for since that time they could not legally ship any others) in the Custom-house books *as cotton twist ?* the name *they* give it in this resolution. But as I fancy they will be rather *shy* in coming forward to answer this question, I will do it *frankly* and *fairly* for them. Knowing they could no longer legally ship off any more of this article except the refuse before-mentioned, they for the three years following, were *obliged* to be doubly cautious to prevent its name from appearing in the Custom-house books at all, for fear *Mr Pitt should set them down as bad spinners !* and to spur up their genius to make such an article as our weavers could work, would also be *obliged* to withdraw the legal part of that honourable trade altogether, in order to make them better spinners ! ! !

What occurred in a similar way in 1803, is already related, (see page 29 to 33.) I have also a long time ago, recorded the outlines of their ruinous traffic, from that period to 1812, in a pamphlet I published in the latter year, an extract from which, I have reprinted in this narrative, (see page 4 to 9) and the pamphlet itself, I sent to every right honourable and honourable M. P. who formed that honourable house in the session of 1817.

The weavers with the aid of their penny a-week fund, were very active in the session of 1800, and for several years afterwards, when on all *occasions*, their delegates were most courteously received by the right honourable George Rose, then President or Vice-President of the Board of Trade; or from some change that had been made in the formation of this board a few years prior to this period, brought about by the great Mr Burke, Mr Rose might then be considered as the Board itself. And from what occurred in this instance, and many others I have heard of, as well as what I have *seen and experienced*, it has always been my opinion that the practical workings of this Board, have not corresponded with the expectations of those Honourable Gentlemen, who brought about that change in the organization of that powerful machine, a machine, that had taken the toils in successive ages of such men as Locke and Chesterfield speak of put together, before they could get it to work in the masterly style we find it was doing, when it brought out that celebrated act before-mentioned, in the 28 Geo. III, the harvest from which rendered money so plentiful, that as a late Manchester gentleman often remarked, "spade-ace guineas were a groat a-peck, as compared with modern times."

As before observed the weavers' delegation was most courteously received and listened to by the Board of Trade; but the other party were there also, who must be received and listened to in the same manner, and this Board being consolidated into the monosyllable *one*, as it has remained to this day, however clever and impartial this one might be, and the right honourable gentlemen I have named, was unquestionably such a one, yet how is it possible for any *one* to sift to the bottom, and unravel the hidden mysteries of the junto I speak of on the one side, and as opposed to the plain facts stated by the opera-

tives on the other, as they alternately came before
him, so as to come to a right conclusion, as to which
of their measures (diametrically opposed to each
other) were most conducive to the true interest and
strength of the nation. The very external appearance of the former, with their known intelligence,
veiling themselves under the usurped cloak of manufacturing merchants, at once turned the scale of that
powerful machine in their favour. Mr Rose considered the one party as the master manufacturers, and
the other as the weavers employed by them, and
under this erroneous impression, the right honorable
gentleman assured the latter they might depend upon
every assistance he could give them, but expressly
on this condition, (which he followed up in his letters
to their secretary, that have been shewn to me) that
they must leave such questions as that they were then
come upon to be settled by their *masters!*

What a mistake was this as regards this delegation being their 'masters', for so far from this being
the case, even the chairman himself, who presided
at the meeting which passed the resolutions, and
who afterwards became spokesman to that deputation
in London, never employed a weaver at all I believe.
His father had got a little money by doubling cotton
twist for fustian warps for the old princely houses
I spoke of, and the son with this money (whom I do
not charge with guilty motives, as he knew not what
he was doing) thus turned round against their benefactors, and became the *principle* in the *cause*, that
brought such ruinous returns from the east, for the
successive adventures of those old manufacturing
merchants, as either drove them from the trade, or
reduced them to the level before-mentioned, *—dis-
asters that could not possibly have happened from such

* When I speak of the purse-proud executive part of this junto
in embryo, who were then bringing such ruin upon their old benefactors,

growing markets, had it not been for the superior
management of this deputation at that critical moment, by laying open to those countries, such an
abundant supply of the raw material, from which
such goods were made (and shipped as manufactures
for fear Mr Pitt should find them out!) as to supersede altogether the demand for goods manufactured,
aided by the prohibitions the above measures gave
rise to.

My reason for dwelling so long, and giving the
outlines of what occurred at that particular time with
so much minutiæ, is to remove that *erroneous* opinion
that has been entertained by *all parties* from that
period to this day, (including *every one* who has succeeded him in the office Mr Pitt then held) with
regard to Mr Pitt ever encouraging that deadly traffic.
It is true he permitted it to the extent of which I

---

people will of course infer that they were then very rich, but this was
not the case, for with a few exceptions, even their "old bricks, pieces
of wood, and bent iron," were not clearly their own; it was the
apparently inexhaustible wealth of the princely merchants of London,
Bristol, Hull, Liverpool, Norwich, Exeter, Birmingham, Sheffield,
Manchester, Blackburn, Leeds, &c., many of whom furnished them
with the means by which they *appeared* to be rich, and in this way,
all the raw cotton that came to this country for ages up to that
period, had come from Smyrna, Lisbon, St. Domingo, &c., as
remittances in part for goods sent out by all the above merchants, and
were chiefly imported into London and Bristol, from whence they found
their way into Manchester; when the spinners bought them at what
was called six months' credit; but this six months, was in fact, ten
months before the vender could call for his bill, and if the spinners paid
within the two months following it was deemed very respectable payment.
It was the immense capital these princely merchants put into their
hands by such a credit, that made them apparently so rich, and when
we see them using that capital in such a way as to bring certain ruin
upon those who had so placed it in their hands, the unnational and
ungrateful cruelty of such proceedings, can only be equalled by John
Bull's *liberality* when he sends his loans to Russia for the purposes
before-mentioned.

have given a faithful report, until they could spin better twist, but not *one ounce or one day further !* and however, he might be determined in his own mind, not to countenance any thing of the kind, yet, under the circumstances in which he was then placed, with a deputation of several most respectable gentlemen before him, possessing talents for sophistical oratory that would almost pluck a leaf from a tree, introduced and accompanied by one, or perhaps both of their county members ; great as Mr Pitt was, still he was only a man, and no man placed as he was at that time could have doubted, that the true interests of the Manchester trade was not then fairly represented to him by that deputation ; I say under such circumstances, however firm his private opinion might be, I cannot see how he could have done less than have granted them the *little*, *tiny*, privilege they asked, and make the export of this refuse " *legal*," when of course it would become " *honourable !*" It was also true that the refuse twist had for some time before been exported ; for although the vanguard of those foreign clever men had been ferreting for many years in every quarter amongst the spinners, in the manner I stated in page 10, when they waited upon me to get hold of these yarns, yet, there was such a conscious "*patriotic feeling*"✳amongst the spinners as a body, that in very few instances could they purchase that article at all, as no spinner would so far disgrace himself as to be known to encourage so ruinous a traffic ; the only way in which it at last got into their hands, except what was done under the rose, and shipped as manufactures, was by the spinner consigning his surplus stock, (generally the refuse) into the hands of some general dealer, and *winking* at the export, if it should pass off in that

✳ This I had from a very, *very* respectable member whose name they had drawn into their list.

channel. For if they were known to do such a thing, and the facts were brought home to them, the only way in which the spinner could palliate the *shame* and *disgrace* in which this traffic was then looked upon by the trade, was by saying it was *only a little* of his *refuse stock*.

Thus the Manchester trade stood in March, 1800, with its operatives and merchants supplicating their paternal government for protection against a growing evil that threatened their total ruin! They were mutually agreed as to the cause, as well as the remedy; a college of commercial doctors (office of trade) established by those men whom Locke and Chesterfield speak of, was open for them at the helm, to which they were approaching in the way laid out for them by ancient usage. When, lo! and behold!! *Mercator, a German Comet*, rose upon our dark old stupid commercial horizon, who by the brilliancy and lustre of his *intellectual* powers, the *liberal principles* that flashed from the *march* of such an *enlightened mind!* the very first ray of light that emanated from such a compound of *immaculate wisdom*, drove them all into the shades of oblivion!! and by drawing a *veil* between them and their old college, and placing Argus, with his hundred eyes, to see it kept close while they effected their ulterior views, they succeeded in laying the foundation of that Foreign-Anglo junto in Manchester, so often mentioned, the workings of which, so far as affects our loom being already so fully recorded. I will now follow this junto in their fraternal visit to our plough, where we shall find them (flushed with their success against the first of our three supporters) bringing up all their mal-metaphysical forces to pull down the third to the level of the first! when the one that remained (the sail) would soon follow the fate of the other two!!

The general peace in the spring of 1814, not only gave a temporary repose to the great Napoleon in his *empire* of Elba, but it set hundreds of thousands of his conscripts at liberty to return to their homes, where millions went to work on their loom, their sail, and their plough, in all the mother countries from whence those clever men had been deputed to Manchester for the purpose before-mentioned. At this sudden change, when the favourable account of a few of the executive part of this junto, who had gone over to superintend the negociations that concluded that peace were reported to the body, viz. that they had prevailed on our ministers not only to admit in their discussions with foreign powers of the unbending hardships of the restrictions our old Board of Trade had established as the laws of our country, but had also given those foreign ministers a strong assurance that these obstacles to *their* free trade should be rescinded as soon as our ministers could remove the prejudices those restrictions had given rise to in our manufacturing districts.

With these prospects before them, the junto were quite satisfied, and came to the following conclusions, namely, that in order that a great *liberal, reciprocal* trade might be carried on with the continent, and that there might be no jarring competition in future, each party should confine themselves to that branch of manufacture in which their countries most excelled. Great Britain from its immense capital in mills, machinery, coal, &c., with 70 to 80,000 hands, that had been drilled into such discipline, as to tend these machines for 72 to 82 hours per week! —was to have the *manufacture* of spinning, by which a score or two of these men-spinsters in all probability could not fail to make great fortunes!!! But as to the other branches requiring millions of operatives, which must all be done by hand labour, the low price at which these operatives could live, as compared with this country, at once gave the drudgery of this part of the trade, with all the ships, colonies, and commerce, that might arise from it to the continent!!! And to shew the legislative part of this junto, and the trade at large, that this arrangement should be acted upon, two of the executive members who had just returned from the continent as above-mentioned, who before they went over, had made extensive arrangements, the one in Blackburn, for the manufacture of his yarns into calicoes, by the hand-weavers, and the other by building a large mill in Manchester, for the purpose of fabricating his yarns in shirting or printing cloth, for the general trade, in less than two months from such return, gave up both of these schemes at a great loss, and turned their whole attention to spinning for the foreign loom, agreeable to the *free, liberal, reciprocal* division of this trade before-stated.

In this way they went on for eight or nine months, during which time many things occurred which I will pass over at present (leaving them for another opportunity) in order to bring them to the bar of their country, and put them on their trial for meddling with the corn laws of our country in the way they did in February, 1815. Although I kept a steady eye on all their proceedings, I interfered as little as possible with any of their measures ; but one market day about the middle of this month, a posse of these Dons came up to me in the 'Change room, when one of them requested I would lend them my assistance in a particular business they were then very anxious about; on inquiring the nature of that business, I was told by this gentleman who was the active partner of an extensive spinning concern, (every ounce of which, with the produce of several other mills, they exported) the head of which firm was an honourable M. P., that his partner had written down to him to do every thing in his power to get petitions in all the manufacturing towns in the district, against a corn bill, that would certainly pass the house unless its progress could be arrested by numerous petitions; this gent. particularly requested I would get one from Stockport, paying me the compliment that no one could manage it so well. He urged very strongly the advantage it was to our trade, that our ports should be open to foreign corn, otherwise our customers abroad would not be able to remit us in return for our *manufactures*. I told the whole group of them, cotton twist was not a manufacture, and as the continent would take nothing else from us in our line, not a bushel of their corn should ever come into our country (unless by some order of Council in case of great scarcity) if I could prevent it, and they went away to another of our townsmen, on whom this gentleman might be said to have some influence. Before we parted I asked why they did not first begin by a petition from Manchester, to which they replied, they thought it better to get Bolton, Stockport, &c., to set them agoing, and then they would follow, &c. &c.

I watched their proceedings pretty closely for a week or ten days, when being intimately acquainted with the gentleman, who was chairman to the corn bill committee, I sent him the following letter, addressed to the Editor of the *Courier*, inclosed in the letter I addressed to himself, both of which I here insert, as they will shew my sentiments have been always the same on every thing connected with this deadly traffic.

CORN BILL AS CONNECTED WITH THE COTTON TRADE.
To the Editor of the Courier.

SIR,—"I am a manufacturer in the cotton trade, and employ some hundreds of hands ; it is therefore my interest that these hands should have their bread cheap, in order that they may be well fed, at reasonable wages ; and besides this, I consume three sacks of flour every week, in paste for the use of my manufactory ; hence few manufacturers are more directly interested in the question of the corn bill than myself, especially as I have no interest directly or indirectly on the landed or farming side of the question. Thus situated, my neighbours expressed great surprise, when I refused to sign the requisition, to call a meeting in our town, to petition Parliament against the corn bill, telling them at the same time, that it was my decided opinion, that it is for my individual interest, and the trade at large, that the bill should pass, and become a law.

" The object of thus intruding myself on the public, is to give my reasons for differing in opinion with many of my neighbours, who in my opinion, have only taken a superficial or partial view of the question.

" From the immense quantity of common land inclosed of late years, and the great drainings of the wet land, with the modern scientific system of agriculture, I believe if our farmers are properly encouraged, that Great Britain and Ireland will produce corn fully sufficient for the consumption of the United Kingdom, and that if they are assured they shall always have a preference of the home consumption, to which they have as great a right as the silk, linen, and cotton manufacturers have to their exclusive privileges, they will inundate the markets with such quantities as will secure it always at low prices ; but, should I be mistaken in this, and the prices for the next seven years average higher than they would otherwise do if the ports were to remain open to foreign corn, still I contend it is my interest that the farmers of the United Kingdom should have the exclusive privilege of the supply of grain for the home consumption, because if I pay them a higher price for my corn than I could get it for from the Baltic, Belgium, France, or America, yet, the money I pay to our farmers *comes round to me again in the purchase of my piece-goods*, and thereby increases the demand and consequently advances the prices, by which means I am enabled to give my hands full work and much better wages than I could otherwise afford to do, if I distress the farmer at home by giving my money to a foreigner; for if I purchase my corn from the foreigners above named, not one of them can take from me the produce of my looms in return, the laws of their country, either prohibiting them altogether, or by laying on them such import duties that amount to the same, in order to encourage their own manufacturers. What I state as my own case equally applies to *all* my brethren interested in the *piece goods trade* in all its branches.

" But Sir, there is a schism in the cotton trade, or as an honourable Member of Parliament expressed it some years ago, when the House were debating in a committee on the distress of the cotton-weavers, " there must (says the honourable member) be something radically wrong in this cotton trade !" there is something radically wrong in it, and it lies in what I term a schism, and from this party commences all the opposition to the salutary measures of government, when they attempt any regulation in finance or trade. The party which form this schism consists of some large cotton spinners, and a few foreign merchants who export yarns to feed and support the foreign manufacturers, until they can erect cotton mills, and spin for themselves. This class start a petition to Government, to take off the duty from cotton, in order that we may be enabled, as they say, to meet the competition going on on the continent ; now I have it from the best source of information,—a person who has spent many years on the continent, from which he returned last December, who says that we have *no competition there, save what we create ourselves,* and that is by sending them our yarns, we enable them to make those goods they would otherwise buy from us ; now if the duty were taken off the raw cotton, yarns would certainly go to the foreigner 2d. or 3d. per pound lower, but they would not take a pound more from us on this account, nor will they defer spinning their own yarns a day longer ; they will spin as soon as they can, do what we will to prevent it, and the *sooner* we leave them to their own spinning, and the *longer* it will be before they can spin at all. But let us take a view how it will operate with respect to the rivalship in piece-goods,—if the duty is taken off the cotton, the foreigner will have all the advantage of it without paying any other tax in lieu, but the British manufacturer, although he will have the same advantage as far as the duty goes, yet, he has to pay other taxes in lieu of the cotton tax, and of course, as far as this goes, he is further from meeting the foreigner in the fair of Leipsic, &c., than he was before.

" Again, when the question of the Corn Bill is taken up, it is the same party who first started an opposition to it with the same objections, viz. that we cannot compete with the foreigners if we have not bread cheap for our work-people ; now these gentlemen see in their eye only one class of work-people ! that is, the hands employed in their cotton mills, the greatest slaves in the world, and whether the quartern loaf is 6d or 1s, it will not make one farthing difference per lb. in the labour employed in spinning, provided the hands were paid according to the price of the loaf ; therefore, this is not their object, it is only a pretence—bills upon Mark-lane are their real object,—and after having completely ruined the real manufacturers here, by sending our custo-mers abroad the raw material, to make *all sorts* of cotton goods *(stock-ings and cotton-lace included)* for themselves, which, otherwise, they must have had from us, not only for the consumption of the continent, but also for the trade to the colonies, many of which we have now restored to their mother countries ; it seems these gentlemen will not stop till they have ruined the agriculture of this United Kingdom also, rather than the foreign manufacturer should not be able to send them bills on Mark-lane in payment for this raw material. I wonder why the spinners should watch the interest of the foreign loom so carefully, as they always pay them much less for their yarns, when *they* have the lead and control of the market, than the British manufacturer pays when he has a demand for his goods. I will instance the years 1812 and 1813, for by Buonaparte's invasion of Russia, he drew nearly all the cotton weavers employed on *our twist*, from the loom to the field, in his march from the Rhine to Moscow ; the effects of which were (the same that would follow now if we were to withhold our yarns by stopping the export,) that a regular and steady demand grew up for British cotton goods, the wages of weavers, &c. all rose to their old reasonable level, say nearly equal to hands in other trades, their masters did well, and gave the spinners better *prices and profits* for their yarns, than the foreigner ever allowed them, and the quantity consumed at home was nearly equal to the quantity spun, and would be quite so, if the master spinners would only work reasonable hours, and not treat their hands worse than slaves. But from the day peace was made, (mark the change that has taken place in twelve months,) in consequence of these spinners going back to their old traffic! the price of labour has fallen one half, and no demand for piece goods to do the manufacturer any good, even if the weavers, &c. were to work for nothing, every person disappointed, and many ruined. And why is this sudden change? I challenge any person in the trade, or out of trade, to point out any other cause than what I have stated; there is, therefore, as the honourable Member observes, something "radically wrong" somewhere, but it is evident it is not in the price of corn!

"My reason for the above remarks, was the unfair means I have witnessed during the last week in Manchester, that have been resorted to, in order to get signatures to the petition against the corn bill! Pray, are the Legislators to be influenced by the names of boys caught in their dinner hour, in the corner of every street, by a man placed there to say to them, would you like your loaf at 6d. or 1s? The answer is obvious! then the boys are requested to sign their names, which they do, and I saw one add three signatures more, and another two, such of their comrades, I suppose, as they happened to recollect at the time!!

"Indignant at the anti-English motives that have set these petitions agoing, galled at the shameful manner in which they get their sheets filled up with names, and for the reasons before-mentioned, my mind being made up on the subject, as a manufacturer, I conclude in the words of our immortal Johnson, that it is our true interest "*to protect our own land, improved by our own labour;*" therefore, if you can find room for the above remarks in your widely circulated paper, you will oblige your constant reader,

"AN OLD MANUFACTURER.
"*Manchester, Feb. 26, 1815.*"

DEAR SIR,—"I attend the Manchester Exchange two or three days in the week, and, therefore, call myself a Manchester man; the subject of the Corn Bill engrosses the general conversation, and as I do not approve of the prevailing op'nion, I inclose you some remarks, which, if you have no objection, I should esteem it a particular favour, if you could procure their insertion in the *Courier* and any other paper; and also, make what use of them you think proper. If they call forth any reply, I pledge myself to answer. I shall be in town in a few days, and will do myself the honour to call upon you; mean while, I am,

"Dear Sir, your faithful obliged servant,
"*Stockport, Feb. 26, 1815.* "WM. RADCLIFFE.
"P. Milne, Esq. M. P. London."

On receipt of this letter, Mr Milne proceeded to the Treasury and laid it before Mr Lushington, who fully coincided with its contents, and wished immediately to send it to the *Courier*, and copies to some other papers; but Mr Milne desired him to wait a little, until he had shewn it to a friend. Now this friend, another honourable M. P., who shall be nameless, happened to be a spinner and purchaser of cotton twist, of which he was also a great exporter, and of course would not consent to its publication, as there were some objectional points in it. Mr M. returned to Mr L. to inform him of the result. Mr Lushington then requested leave to publish the unobjectionable part of it, but Mr Milne did not consider himself authorised to publish a part only without my approbation. All these particulars Mr M. informed me of in a letter in due course.

Thus, though the veil was very near being drawn so far aside, as that the government and the country might have had *one peep* at their proceedings, yet, the above anecdote will shew there was no mode of escaping the Argus-eye of this most potent sovereign, junto.

Up to this period, though I was aware that my, proceedings from 1802, to prohibit the exportation of cotton twist, could not be agreeable to the foreigners in Manchester, yet, at this time I was under no fear as to any consequences that might follow from having incurred their displeasure. But the conspiracy that now set in amongst the great spinners and exporters of that deadly traffic in Manchester, and three years afterwards, by the importers and dealers in cotton in Liverpool, adding all their strength to the above powerful body, will shew that I was very much mistaken. I was not then aware the junto was so firmly established, but that the true English feeling which I calculated upon, would so far predominate, as to protect me under any emergency that might occur, so long as I was pursuing the interest of my country, even at the risk of my own.

As I am given to understand that every individual who composed the Anglo-part of this conspiracy, have for some time past most *bitterly repented*, that they ever became the executive part of the sovereign junto in such wicked measures, I hope I shall never have occasion to record their proceedings in the latter period I allude, as I shall be compelled to mention great names in a way that may be as unpleasant to their feelings as it will be to my own, if I am driven to that necessity. But, as I can record one of the acts of the former in 1815, without giving any names except those to whom, if the rising generation will look up to, and regulate their movements in business by the examples these names have shewn them, and follow their motions with the attention and precision of well-disposed soldiers while their eyes are fixed on their fugle-man, they will do well, as they cannot have better examples. * I will therefore give the public one specimen of what I have so often alluded to, in which they have always held me up to the trade, as an example (the same as Napoleon did those of the Royal Duke and Palm the bookseller) to any others who might dare to call in question their sovereign control.

Twelve months before I wrote the above letter, which laid the foundation of those persecutions that have surrounded me and my family to this day, the late Mr Brandt and Mr Jones came over to view my

* If contrary to my wish I should be driven to record what I allude, (which can not be avoided unless the veil is "rent in twain,") I must here reserve a point as to one of the names I am going to mention, but still I shall exonerate that name from any thing like blame, in the same way that Mr Pitt and Mr Rose could not be blamed for what they did on the occasions before-mentioned ; for the situations in which they were all placed, under all the circumstances to which I allude, *were precisely the same.*

concern, in which they had so handsomely established me ; they expressed themselves highly pleased with all they saw, I had taken stock for the occasion, and gave them each a copy sheet, in which it appeared the £2,000 they, and the two other friends, had lent me, had accumulated to between 6 and £7,000. They afterwards dined with me, and on returning in the evening, one of their last expressions was that they should consider that day as one of the happiest of their lives.

Although this balance had been considerably reduced the year following by the effects of those measures I have lately recorded, yet, I stood as firm as any house in the trade at the time I wrote the above letters, and my business (with two sons of the age of 27 and 28, regularly brought up to it from their teens to manage in my absence) was doing well, and fast redeeming the loss above-mentioned.

In March, 1815, the Property Tax being either repealed, or going to be repealed, in consequence of vexatious petitions set agoing in Manchester, (in the same way as those I have described against the Corn Bill, but from different motives, *) government was on the look out for some other tax in lieu of some part of it, and a tax on the windows of cotton mills, &c. was proposed for the purpose. Against this tax Stockport, along with all the other towns in the trade, sent up deputations to oppose it, and being *sent for* to a meeting of the mill-owners in the town, and told by them that as I had two sons to manage my business in my absence, they had fixed upon me as one of their deputies, when, after parrying them off as long as I well could, I at last consented.

* The gentlemen who set these petitions agoing, who has since become the editor of the official journal of the sovereign junto, told a friend of mine that *he* set them agoing, and for the express purpose of fixing that tory ministry so fast in their finances, that they would be obliged to resign their places !

While I was in town the distress that had come on the weavers again, put them in motion to find out the cause of such a reverse that had so suddenly returned upon them, and that at the time (just after the peace) when they had always been told their trade would become good and steady. In these movements two or three of them called on my sons, requesting they might be favoured with a few of those pamphlets they had been told I had published in 1812; when my sons without the least hesitation gave them a bundle containing perhaps a score or two. Who they were, or where they came from, my sons could not tell, but they understood them to come from Ashton-under-Lyne or that neighbourhood.

My little snug establishment at that time consisted of just as much spinning machinery as would supply our shuttles with the weft consumed, by about 200 of those hand-looms before-mentioned, which turned me off about 600 pieces of printing cambrics per week, never excelled in quality by any looms put in motion by steam. The other part of my machinery consisted in those necessary for winding, warping, and dressing, with the looms before-mentioned, buying all my twist from the great spinners in the trade, agreeable to the plan agreed upon between Mr Brandt and myself, when they set me agoing in the liberal manner before-mentioned.

At that time I was purchasing nearly all my twist from a rich spinner in Stayley-Bridge, who had long supplied the foreigners largely with cotton twist, but during the celebrated campaigns of 1812-13 and 14, while those foreign weavers were engaged in handling their guns and their swords, instead of working up the twist produced by this great spinner, he, to keep his spindles from rust, until a general peace brought them back to their looms again, employed a great number of the weavers in the neighbourhood these strangers came from.

It afterwards appeared that the object for which these weavers wanted these pamphlets, was to distribute them amongst their masters, one of whom happened to be the gentleman I bought my twist from; for, after my return, on inquiring for the usual supply, I found I was to have no more! and as the former supply became due, I was openly teased for the money which is not customary in the trade, and when I remonstrated, I was told it would become me better to attend to my business and pay my way as I ought to do, rather than *write letters* and send out my emissaries with *pamphlets* to disturb the country about the exportation of cotton twist, &c.! Thus my credit being gone, I was obliged to purchase our weekly supply of twist with the bills that should have paid this gentleman, and another or two, who were equally sh•t up as to credit, and equally pressing for their accounts as they came due, (but not so candid as to their reasons.) Two or three months elapsed before I could pay them off and rid myself of their taunts and exposures whenever they saw they could give me a dun in the hearing of such men as might still be giving me some credit; however, a little after Midsummer I got rid of their duns by paying them off.

At the same time I perceived that a whisper had gone out against me in some of the more refined circles, producing that sort of calm that brought my former bark to a stand in 1807, for my bankers became more nice about the paper they would discount, curtailing little accommodations, with et ceteras, too trifling to mention, only that they all tended to lay me on the shelf again, where, if I wrote any more letters about schism, or exportation of cotton twist, they might not carry any weight with them, as they were only written by *so* and *so*!!! In this forlorn situation they would certainly have run me on shore again, had it not been for Mr Lewis Loyd visiting

Manchester in the beginning of September following, and that I mustered sufficient courage to state the situation I was then placed in to that liberal banker, when he can place confidence in the person who solicits his aid.

Hearing Mr Loyd was in Manchester, I called at the bank and had a private interview with him, I told him there was a conspiracy going on in the trade against me, and that I was not able to stand it unless I could prevail upon him to grant me a little support; and further, that I had cause to suspect, and did suspect, that one or more of the three individuals I would name had spoken to his brother in such a way as to prejudice their house against me, in order to accomplish their diabolical purpose ! and, if I was right in these conjectures, I hoped he would protect me, as I was sure he would agree with me that those whom I should name could have no other object in thus undermining my credit than what I then related to him respecting the letters, pamphlets, &c. before-mentioned. I further implored his protection on the grounds that all I had done, was solely with a view to serve the trade and my country; and knowing that I was right, I thought I was deserving of very different treatment, for as this was the very reverse to what had been so universally promised me from the first, I was convinced it could only emanate from that foreign influence, that I had been at such pains and expence to root out of our trade. When I had given in the three names (the rich spinner was not one of them, as I knew he was only *their* tool) I added, that I had no wish to pry any further into the secret, than in *self defence*, to request he would speak to his brother, and if he found me correct, I should feel confident of their protection.

In reply, Mr Loyd said he would speak to his brother, adding (in a manner that strengthened my

confidence in the success of this application) " that
when people went to work in this way, they did not
always succeed." I promised to call again the next
market day, in the mean time, anticipating the answer I should receive, I examined closely into my
affairs as to the credit I should require to render me
independent of the conspiracy before-mentioned ; and
with the list of various sums to pay off accounts,
and purchase the twist I was in want of in my hands,
I went to the bank, when the brother I spoke of came
up to me, to whom in a whisper, I asked if Mr L.
Loyd had spoken to him on a certain business ? In the
same tone of voice he answered yes, adding how
much will you require ? On shewing him the total
figures, he requested me to go forward and take
whatever I wanted. I then handed my list to the
cashier, who brought me ten or twelve promiscuous
bills, amounting to near £2,000.

Amongst the crowd that were then at the counter,
I noticed a scion of the schism, as I then called a certain
party, who viewed this transaction apparently with
that sort of feeling that we may suppose the great Napoleon would have been under, had some guardian
angel stepped in to the rescue of the Duke d' Enghien,
and Palm, the bookseller, on the eve of those fatal
days on which he thought it *his* interest to send *them*
out of his way.

The estimate as to the amount of credit I should
require was made under the impression that the
cause which required it would soon pass away, and
that the market would open to me again for my
regular supply of warp twist at the usual credit.
But in this I was mistaken, for though I had no
intention of suddenly frightening them again with
letters about schism, or with pamphlets, (which, by
the bye, if I had sinned in the printing of them three
years before, I was innocent as to *that* distribution)
yet, as they *could* not know my thoughts, their own

consciences told them that while the pledge given to me by the trade lay over unredeemed, and I was left at liberty to be *dunning* them for it whenever a favourable opportunity occurred ; hence they saw the strings, by which they held their veil, might be cut asunder any day unless they could lay me on the shelf! when as one of their party told an acquaintance of mine, in language of exultation, that he thought I should not easily find another Brandt, Jones, or any such like persons to set me on my feet again, and he hoped their *legal* and *honorable* trade would no longer be in jeopardy from anything that I might say or write on the subject.

Therefore to effect this desirable purpose, I was proscribed by the spinners, as a body from the customary credits of the trade !—But my bankers remained doubly firm (under the rose, in a way I shall hereafter have occasion to note) for the three following years, when, by taking my sons into partnership, in the winter after the period I have been speaking of, I made such arrangements as if it had purposely been done to set me fully at liberty to bring the great question we were at issue upon fairly and openly before the tribunal of our country. And knowing that I had 999 out of every thousand persons (of course I mean *English, Irish, and Scotch,*) interested in this trade that were on my side of the question, *if they durst speak out,* and none more anxious for the prohibition we were seeking for, than the *hands employed* in the spinning mills of my opponents, as was proved on a particular occasion, with my humble abilities, and nothing to support me but the justice and equity of my cause, I became their herald, their messenger, and their advocate; and after holding consultations, taking my instructions and briefs from the very first men in every branch of the trade, in *holes* and *corners* for fear the 999 subjects should be found conspiring against one of their sovereigns, (who had their spies in every quarter,) I brought up my evidences in the following order :—

The first was, that after calling two or three times at the Treasury, at the request of the trade, I prevailed on Mr Lushington to send out instructions to Hull, and other ports, " that in all their entries, for the future, never to make use of the words British manufactures, or British cottons, but confine their entries to British cotton yarns, and British cotton piece-goods." Thus one main string of the veil, that for twenty years had only shewn the exports in some degree correspondent with the licence Mr Pitt had permitted, was so far removed that their traffic soon after appeared (I suppose) to its full extent.

In one of the above visits, meeting a great bleacher from the neighbourhood of Bolton, by the way, I took him along with me to the Treasury, and when the above order was finally given, I informed him of it, and thus it got whispered to the trade in Bolton, by whom it was thought of such importance, that two gentlemen (both deputy-lieutenants of the county) came over to Stockport, to learn the particulars from myself. When on their return to Bolton, after a private consultation with the heads of the trade, the same gentlemen were deputed to wait on Lord Derby, (as Lord Lieutenant of the county) to take his opinion as to the most certain mode of bringing this question before Parliament, when his Lordship advised them to send memorials to his Royal Highness the Prince Regent, which would be handed over to the Lords of the Privy Council for Trade, who as a matter of course would be obliged to place them, so that the question would be alluded to in the speech from the throne, at the opening of the next Session of Parliament, as one of the divers and important subjects to which his Royal Highness would call the attention of Parliament.

As the whole merit of procuring the numerous memorials that were at that time sent up to the

Prince Regent, have been attributed to me, and to me alone, I have been thus particular in showing *all* I had to do with them, so far as their origin goes.

In the Summer and Autumn of 1816, while these memorials were in preparation, one of the Deputy-Lieutenants before-mentioned, and some Manchester gentlemen, with myself, held several consultations as we occasionally met together in Manchester. At this period the whole country for 50 miles on the manufacturing borders of Manchester was under the greatest alarm from the numerous meetings of weavers respecting radical reform; and while the masters and operatives of Bolton, Preston, Stockport, &c., were signing memorials to their Prince, in the way pointed out by the representative of His Royal Highness in that county, the efforts of nearly all the masters, and some of the weavers in Ashton-under-Lyne and the neighbourhood, to do the same, were unavailing; for, at a meeting convened for the purpose, some very shrewd men amongst the latter said that for the last sixteen years all their petitions to Government had been opposed by * * *, and one or two other members for close boroughs, who were spinners or owners of cotton mills that were supplying the foreign looms, and whose *under-the-rose*-influence had always swayed the Cabinet and Parliament on all questions respecting the cotton trade, in which they could have had *no motives*, save that of their own *individual* interests.

For these reasons, those shrewd industrious operatives, in return for whose ingenuity and labour, as they said, our merchants had been enabled annually to bring so many millions of money into our country, would not consent to any memorial to their Prince, whom they adored, except for the purpose of supplicating his Royal Highness to reform his Parliament, in order to get rid of the influence of three or four of those M. P.'s, who, by their wealth, (which, but for *their* ingenuity and labour they would never have possessed,) had gained such influence as to place them and their country in that wretched state! reckless of every other consideration, save that of adding to it a little more.

These sentiments were highly applauded by a vast majority of the weavers then assembled, and, like wild-fire, they immediately spread over every district in the trade ; when thousands of weavers were assembling in some place or other every week, to get up petitions to their prince *for the purpose before-mentioned.*

While the country was in this alarming state! in the consultations before-mentioned, it was suggested that something must be done to still the rage and madness in which these deluded "people" were then going on. And as we had great confidence in the success that would result from the plan recommended by the Lord Lieutenant of the county, it was agreed that if the subject was introduced, and fully discussed in the public papers, two desirable objects might be accomplished.

In the first place it would shew these deluded men that their masters were not only aware of the extreme distress into which they had so suddenly been driven, but that they were doing every thing in their power to give them a permanent relief, as soon as time and circumstances would admit ; this discussion we hoped would have a tendency to bring them within the bounds of moderation, prescribed to those who petition their Prince, while they are imploring his paternal aid against those who oppress them.

Our second object was that by so doing we should be breaking the ice that for twelve years had been growing very thick under the *shade* of that *veil* I have so often mentioned ; for as we knew we should be opposed by the schismatics, we thought this would be a proper time to join issue with them, and try the question upon its own merits amongst ourselves as the grand jury of the district, before the question came before Parliament.

The Bolton and Manchester Gentlemen fixed upon me as the person to open this discussion, being, as they said, most conversant with the subject. For some time I excused myself on the ground that my limited education had not qualified me for such a task ; but as the state of the country was then so alarming, and as they would have no denial, and as no other means to moderate the proceedings of these deluded operatives could be thought of, I at last consented.

Some remarks then occurred as to the journal in which this discussion should commence ; but as it was well known that the weavers seldom read any other paper than the *Manchester Gazette*, nor would they believe any thing that was not sanctioned and supported by that Paper, it was finally agreed that its Editor should be applied to for that purpose.

This being done by the Manchester gentlemen, the Editor in his reply observed, " that in complying with their request he should offend some of his friends ; but as he had long been convinced that the export of cotton twist was the *only cause* that had brought the weavers into such distress, and the country into such an alarming state, his Paper, at all hazards, should be open for the discussion in question."

A little prior to this, being in London, a friend of mine procured me from the Custom-house at Hull, a return of the twist exported for the first three months after the new entries before-mentioned commenced. On which return we made some calculations, and published them with some arguments that naturally arose out of these calculations, in the *Star* newspaper of the 7th of September. A copy of this article I had given to the gentleman who then put it into the hands of the Editor who promised to insert it in his next Paper, and also to add an article of his own, when he had no doubt they would bring on the discussion we were seeking for, or that such discussion would fail to answer the principal object we had in view.

The two articles accordingly appeared on the 28th of September, 1816 ; and as we could all give our sentiments under an anonymous signature, I found myself supported by such a host, with their plain matter of fact arguments, that though we brought out *all* the strength of the *learned mal-reciprocals* of the day, in four or five weeks they were so completely driven from *this field*, that amongst themselves they confess to this day, they have not a leg left them to stand upon. Even the learned Felix of Liverpool, *(poor Felix)* who was sent up (by express I suppose for he fired the second gun) to protect their dock dues, brokerage, &c. against this tell-tale from Hull, (which said their cotton bags had made a magical transit across the island without leaving any thing for labour, or as Adam Smith says, profits upon labour) was so hampered by these anonymous *unlearned* matter-of-fact tradesmen, that he quitted the field the moment he saw the strength of his opponents in that mode of warfare ! and we never heard of him again, or of those who sent him up on that special occasion, until we found them all entrenched in their office in London, before-mentioned, and under the wings of *their* representative, whose oratorical talents as an advocate, whether in the privy Council, or in the open Senate, the right hon. gentleman could, and did, like old Boreas, blow every *fact* and every *argument* which had no other foundation to stand upon than that of *practical experience* and *practical knowledge* to an immeasurable distance! at which they have remained to this day !! and the

Foreign-Anglo sovereign junto, as I have since felt myself justified in terming that party, (who thus opposed the efforts of the trade, to redeem the pledge they had given to me, so often mentioned in the former part of this narrative,) have made so good a use of this third part of a moment, according to Madam de Stael's scale of time, that with *their* liberal system, *their* free trade, *their* reciprocity, &c. &c. &c. which for a long time has been attended with a loss of half a million a-week to our empire at large, and given such a deadly blow to the ships, colonies, and commerce, of our country, that unless the *broad hints* I have already given in this narrative, which I flatter myself will in some degree open the eyes of those who have the power to make an official inquiry into the facts I have narrated, that if they find me correct, they will bring the trade and the country to act on practical opinions, rather than such as I have spoke of. Or, I fear the mischief already done by the theoretical jargon, that has prevailed since the period I am speaking of, (while practical knowledge, and practical advice has been altogether excluded from having any weight in our country,) will entail upon our country a succession of poverty and distress, the consequences of which no one can foretell, especially while she labours under such a heavy debt, a debt she would carry like a feather on her back, liquidating ten millions per annum, as she goes along, if once she could be prevailed upon to break up this junto, and make a proper use of her own strength. I make this assertion *deliberately*, and most firmly *believe* what I have stated, and if I have not already shewn the course she must pursue to accomplish such a desirable event, to the satisfaction of others, I feel great confidence in hereafter being able to remove their doubts, if such doubts should remain.

"An occasional Reader," "Felix of Liverpool," "An Enemy to Restrictions," and "G. L.," anonymous writers against us, whom we afterwards learned were the very *heads* of the party that have since been the leaders in the Anglo-Foreign junto, being driven from the field by their *practical*, matter-of-*fact* opponents, and "Publicus," their great sophistical champion, sent being after them in the month following; only some of their sharp-shooters remained in the field, who turning the subject into burlesque and ridicule, by a sort of bush fighting, continued the discussion for some time; but they were met by our party with Hudibras and Paddy Whack, as our swords and our shields, with which we gave them such a drubbing, that except a letter they addressed to the "Old-Manufacturer" and "Civis," which, as they said, they wrote from the moon! we heard no more of them; and they will still remember the answer they got from the former, which he addressed to them in the Georgium Sidus; for their flight was so rapid, it was supposed they durst not go into winter quarters until they arrived at that distant planet. *

By this public discussion our first object was fully accomplished; for those alarming meetings in two or three weeks after it commenced, dwindled away to no meetings at all, and the whole district remained quiet until after Parliament had assembled in February, 1817, waiting in anxious expectation for the measures that would be brought forward by Government, in consequence of the memorials that had been presented agreeable to the recommendation of their Lord Lieutenant.

* My friends in Manchester have very often requested me to publish the various articles that were brought forward in that controversy, which was conducted with mutual good temper, but I was not not at liberty. And if the trade come forward to redeem their pledge as I am led to believe they are now ready and willing to do, when any one *dare* lead the way; I do not think it will now be necessary. If my old friends think otherwise, I hereby promise to comply with their request.

But lo ! and behold, though the former most important object was accomplished, this controversy had completely shut the door against any measure that might otherwise have emanated from these memorials. For the party who so early quitted the field, and who afterwards saw all the strength they had left in it so completely cut up, in their panic ran off to their strong citadel in town, in order to repair and strengthen every cord that had hitherto kept their veil over the eyes of Government ; and by reminding ministers of their promises at the treaty of Paris, canvasing and imploring the aid of influential members from the Boroughs of Devonshire and Cornwall ; they managed so effectually as not only to prevent the memorials being alluded to in the speech from the Throne, but to place such obstacles in our way, that it was two to three months after the Session began, before the subject could be even mentioned in the house.

The patience of the starving weavers being exhausted by this delay, they simultaneously made preparations for their blanket expedition ; when on the 17th of March, tens of thousands of these weavers with each a blanket on his back, and a petition in the hand of every tenth man, sallied forth to lay their complaints at the feet of their sovereign, praying his Royal Highness would reform his Parliament, in order to get rid of about four M. P.'s, who so strenuously held fast the four corners of the veil I have so often mentioned ! These facts I fearlessly record as a guide to some future historian, that when he comes to dilate on that eventful period, when in the fourth part of a moment, according to the scale before-mentioned, he will have to speak of the Luddites, the blanket expedition, the great Peterloo meeting in Manchester, the rebellion (as it was called) in Scotland, none of which would have occurred, but for the cause I have taken such pains to unfold. Hence, I conjure the historian never to make use of the words sedition, disaffection to Government, or rebellion, as he glides over this short period, for I assure him there was not amongst them all, a single iota of any thing of the kind.

I have now brought myself to that stage of my narrative, when I should report to the trade what I promised when I first began ; but as those proceedings are so far gone by, as in my judgment, to be of far less interest to the public, than those I have dilated upon from page 70, to the point at which I have now arrived, I shall close this first part of my Narrative, with only selecting a few articles and some brief remarks upon them out of the MS I prepared for the purpose in August 1817, and publish them in order to shew how far my opponents were correct ; when, after their conspiracy had obliged me to remain silent! they exultingly went on in their deadly career, as they had before gone on under their licence they had so honourably got from Mr Pitt, but on different grounds ; the former because it was *so trifling*, and that trifle only the refuse ; the latter when that tell-tale from Hull had cut the main string of their veil, then lo ! and behold " it had become *too great*,—so much property had been embarked in the trade that had so long gone on under the *sanction of government*," &c. &c. that though they all admitted it was an evil ! " it was now too late to stop it ! !" adding, that " if it had been done sooner it would certainly have been a good thing for the country ! ! !" Hence, knowing that I durst not contradict them, they told the Cabinet Ministers and Members of Parliament, who had promised me their support, and were anxiously expecting, and inquiring for me in the session of 1818, " that no part of the trade *had* felt any interest in this question, save myself and a few others (all men of straw) whom I had drawn along with me, and that finding my case hopeless, I had given it up ! when all the rest cared nothing about it ! ! ! These things being since told me by the highest authority, I here note them to shew the vile arts they have all along been obliged to resort to, in order to prop up their tottering cause ; for the fact is, that in every step I have taken, I have only been the messenger and occasional advocate of the trade at large, who have employed me as their agent on every occasion where an opportunity might occur, in which *they* could have a chance to redeem *their* pledge. And though they have many times offered to raise money to pay for my time and expence, and a book was opened in London, in 1817, where many put down five guineas or upwards with their names, 1 always declined to accept of a shilling until the work was finished, that my opponents might not be able to say I was working for pelf.

The first article I select for the above purpose is a list of the memorials that were presented to his Royal Highness the Prince Regent, and also the petitions that were presented to the hon. the House of Commons in the sessions of 1817, in the getting up of which I had no hand, save that of being occasionally consulted on two of them as to the facts on which those documents were grounded ; for except in that of London, where some signatures were given at a public meeting, from whence that document emanated, and to which I might afterwards assist in getting two or three names, I had nothing to do with them, save that as the agent to those who sent them up to hand them to those hon. gentlemen who were to present them, and also as their advocate to explain any point in which those hon. gentlemen might wish for information.

Memorials presented to His Royal Highness the Prince Regent, and by his Royal Highness's commands, were referred to the Privy Council for Trade.

	Master Spinners who signed.	Weavers	Master Manufacturers.	Master bleachers, Printers, Merchants, Dyers, Factors, &c.
1816.—Bolton............ by the Lord Lieutenant of the County.	All but two or three.	About 18,000	All.	All.
Preston......... Ditto.	Ditto.	10,000	All.	Ditto.
Stockport........ by Lord Bulkeley.	10 to 12.	8,000	All.	Ditto.
1817.—City of London by Sir Jas. Shaw, Bart.	—	Nearly All.	Nearly All.	All.
Master Manufacturers in Ashton-under-Lyne, and neighbourhood, } by Sir Oswald Mosley.	The majority.	About 35, who gave employment to 15 to 20,000 Weavers.	—	170 firms.

Petitions to the House of Commons.

1817.—City of London.. by Sir Oswald Mosley...	—	All.	Nearly all.	Nearly all. 170 firms.
Bolton............ by Lord Stanley.........	All but one,	All.	All.	All.
Preston............ by Mr Hornby.........	Nearly all.	All.	All.	All.
Stockport .. .... by Mr Davenport.........	Eight or ten.	All.	All but one.	All.
Dyers, Bleachers, and Printers, in Manchester } by Mr Blackburne......	—	1,900, all in the Town.	—	35, the strongest in trade.
Ashton-under-Lyne...... by Mr Bold	—	All.	All.	—

N.B.—The whole trade of Carlisle having been applied to find out who had instructed Mr Curwen to rise in the House to oppose any investigation into the subject, found it was only *one spinner* that had done it ; and in making this inquiry it was also found, that with the exception of the above *one*, who had been requested by the Manchester spinners to do it, every individual in that city and neighbourhood, interested in the cotton trade, were *urgently anxious* for immediate restrictions on the *export of cotton yarns* ! when this one was compelled to write again to Mr Curwen, who afterwards rose in his place in the house to withdraw his opposition !

London, 4th July, 1817.

*To His Royal Highness the Prince Regent of the
United Kingdom of Great Britain and Ireland,
acting in the name and on behalf of His Majesty.*

*The memorial of the undersigned Merchants, Factors,
Warehousemen, and others in the City of London,
interested in the sale and exportation of cotton piece-
goods,*

" Humbly Sheweth,

" That your memorialists have for many years been engaged in the sale and exportation of cotton piece-goods ; and that the extensive capitals, and the activity, and enterprize of your memorialists, have tended greatly to carry the manufacture of cotton goods, in various parts of the United Kingdom, to an extent surpassing any other manufacture of these Realms.

" That your memorialists are fully persuaded that the preservation and extension of the cotton manufacture is of vital importance to the country, whether it be considered as an object of Revenue and of foreign and domestic commerce, or as an almost inexhaustible resource for every description of labour, ingenuity, and science, and of the greatest benefit to the agriculturist and landowner.

" That the great superiority of our spinning machines, aided by the practical skill and systematic industry of the persons employed in our cotton mills, and the possession of important local advantages, has until recently prevented any foreign state from becoming our rivals in this beneficial trade and manufacture ; nevertheless, foreigners for a considerable time past, with a view to establish themselves in this trade, have been in the habit of purchasing along with our piece-goods, some parcels of our unwrought cotton yarns ; which at first being small, were not considered materially to injure the trade in piece-goods ; but the conclusion of peace in Europe having enabled the continental states to turn their attention to the manufacture of cotton goods, which from the low prices of provisions and labour in some departments, they can do at a cheaper rate than can be done in this country, and their manufacturers being protected by heavy duties upon, or total prohibitions of our goods, their purchases of our yarns, have of late become so great, as to create serious and just alarm to your memorialists for the loss of their export trade.

" That the consequence of the extensive manufacture of cotton goods from British yarns in Russia, Turkey, Germany, France, Switzerland, Belgium, and other countries, is a vast diminution in the demand for our piece-goods from those countries, whereby many merchants and manufacturers have been ruined, and their workmen reduced to such a state of distress, as to threaten the most serious results.

" That your memorialists humbly apprehend that the exportation of our yarns, is contrary to the maxims of sound policy, and a complete

departure from the principle adopted in the wise restrictive laws now
in force, for the protection of our other great staple, the woollen manufacture, and give to other nations all the advantages of our inventions
in machinery without any adequate return.

"That if the exportation of British yarns be suffered to go on,
our valuable trade in cotton piece-goods to the continental states and
their colonies, will be totally lost to the great injury of your memorialists, and the innumerable body of manufacturers, weavers, calico-
printers, dyers, bleachers, embroiderers, finishers, and others depen-
dent on the trade in cotton piece-goods.

"Your memorialists therefore, humbly pray that your Royal
Highness will be graciously pleased to take this matter into your consideration, convinced that in it will be found one of the principal causes
of our commercial distresses, and of the present alarming state of our
population in the manufacturing districts ; and that your Royal Highness will cause such measures to be adopted as will prevent (before it
be too late) the total loss of our trade in cotton piece-goods to the
countries above-mentioned.

"And your memorialists, as in duty bound, will ever pray, &c.

John Mairson, Thomas, and Co.
Rowlandson, Burra, and Co.
James Hunter and Co.
Farr, Corbett, and Edenborough
John and Wm. Cooper
Nunn and Wray
Byrn and Trist
Daniel Haigh and Co.
Helps, Ray, and Co.
Ray and Lewis
Forster, Cole, and Co.
Thompson and Strickland
John and John Wood
Joseph Bulmer, and Co.
Harris and Custance
Francis Ede
Peele, Turner, and Scott
Robert Scott
Frederick Cowper
Wm. Williams
Joseph Bowman
Loyd and Price
John Horrocks and Co.
Zachary Langton and Co.
M. Deacon, Sons, and Ellis
James Deacon
Josiah Wilkinson
Carnsew and Bryson
Richard and Nathaniel Nicholls
W. T. Page
T. Kensett
Charles Gunning

Wm. Mutrie
W. and J. Woodhead
Gillman and Clay
Woollan and Jefferson
Wm. Bowler and Son
James Birkett
Wm. Farrer
John Cowper
J. B. Sharp
Robert Nunn
Marshall and Procter
Richard Baxter
Thomas Bates
Thomas Ainsworth and Co.
William Loyd
Taylor and Barrow
Curteis, Cowper, and Nicholson
John Ansley, Alderman
Stead and Lawson
Moses Whitelock
Henry Eccles
Adam Moffet
Pearse Brothers
Donaldson, Slee, and Mayston
Sangster, Atkinson, and Sangster
Robert Cullen
Robert and James Bathe
Dodgson and Harris
John Taylor
William Skilbeck
Edward Dalby
Benjamin Davis

J. Wilkinson
J. B. Spencer
Sheldon, Cass, and Co.
Isaac Ablett
J. and J. Eccles
William Horne
R. Cunliffe, Jun., and Co.
Bury, Loyds, and Co.
Nunn and James
Brown and Blackburn
Jonathan Croker
Watts and Williams
Taylor and Stephen
George Smith
Hunter, Orr, and Co.
Gardiner and Roberts
John Howell
Moser and Atkinson
Kent and Ridout
Matthew Smith
Thomas Benison
Smith and White
Bradbury, Gratrix, and Teale
Wm. Dickinson
Kenworthy and Ireland
Jos. Sadler
Joseph Gray
John Morley
Miller, Brothers, and Co.
John, William, and Thomas Sutcliffe
Joseph Aspinall
Wm. Williamson
Derby and Davis
Richard Hall and Co.
Gill and Norton
J. H. Midwood
Naylors and Co.
John Gore
Robert Gore
Thomas Gould and Co.
Wood, Martindale, and Fisher
Sculthorpe, Brunt, and Co.
Hole, Wilkinson, and Co.
James Bury and Co.

Brown, Sharpe, and Co.
Watts and Atkinson
Starcy, Wiltshire, and Co.
Thomas Barlow and Co.
Wheelwright and Monkhouse
Muir, Brown, and Co.
Bowman and May
B. Corbett
Storar, Chipchase, and Co.
George Paton
Wm. Staff and Co.
Willock and Clark
Farrer, Wilkinson, and Co.
James Lacy
Francis Todd
William Fell
Stevens and Cramp
Thomas Atkinson and Co.
Strachan and Stubbs
Leighton, Petty, and Co.
W. Geary Salte
John Evans
Henry Petty
John Scarborough
Symonds and Russell
Antrobus Nelson
J. and H. Lainson
Man and Dent
Farren, Robinson, and Co.
Smith, Pattison, and Co.
Locke, Hindley, and Co.
John Paton
John Wilson
Peter Astley and Co.
Turners and Francis
C. Lockyer
Thomas Wilson
Alexander Clugston
Clark, Boyd, and French
William Bradley
John Brander
Price, Postlethwait, and Co.
William Russel."

And about twenty more whose names were not given to me, comprising nine tenths of the manufacturing and wholesale warehousemen and merchants, who were then vending and shipping the cotton manufactures of England and Scotland, to all parts of the globe.

As I have often mentioned memorials and petitions, I give this document as a specimen of their
contents, and the names as a part of those *men of
straw* I was said to have drawn along with me. My
influence so far as my name went had no weight at
all, but as the messenger and advocate of those who
sent me, I confess I had very great influence. For
on explaining my errand to about a dozen of them,
whom I had called together for the purpose; when
they heard that the memorials in Lancashire were
set agoing by the express recommendation of the Lord
Lieutenant of that county, they were delighted
with the prospect thus held out to them, and took
up the business *themselves*, drew up their memorial
to their Prince, and afterwards their petition to the
honourable the House of Commons, to which *they*
got the signatures. For as at least four fifths of the
persons or firms who signed them are, (to this day)
to me perfect strangers, I think the candid reader
will agree with me that the answers my opponents
gave to the anxious inquiries before-mentioned, were
as unfounded, and as *malicious* as all the rest of their
proceedings.

Out of the above names, at the special request of
some of the first Manufacturers, Bleachers, Printers,
and Merchants, in Great Britain, I was enabled to
establish in London, a central Chamber of Manufactures and Commerce, to which branches were afterwards to be formed in Manchester, Glasgow, Carlisle,
and Nottingham. This association being advertised
in the leading papers of London, Manchester, &c.
and that its operations were to commence in February, 1818, the spinners for export, and the exporters
of this deadly traffic, were so seriously alarmed, that
having no other means by which they could stop my
career, they immediately called in the aid of the
cotton brokers in Liverpool, (I speak to the very
letter ; for as regards the cotton trade in any of *its bran-*

ches, that port contains very few men whom we can call merchants) when by their united strength, or rather by the weakness this *ungrateful* and unexpected shock brought upon me, they managed to scotch every measure I, as the advocate for the trade, had so arranged, as to secure the redemption of that pledge so long due to me, if these measures had been simultaneously put in motion. A detail of all the particulars, should I at some future time have occasion to give them, will leave no doubt on any of these important points of which I now give only the outlines. Nor that the party while under that panic, made all haste to establish *their foreign* Chamber of Commerce and Manufactures, exclusively to support their "*legal and honourable trade*," and the fabrics of their mother countries, while they had such an opportunity, that in case my banker should again let me loose, and this central chamber should put itself in motion, *(for which it is quite ready any day)* there might be no room left for *its* Manchester branch.

Although for a time, I must defer many things I have to say as to the workings of the Anglo part of this junto, * yet, I cannot now leave them without

---

* On one of their measures, I want a little more information before I can do proper justice to it, as it has not been in my way to learn how they managed to get a clause into some bill or other by which (they can *and do* legally export *my warping and dressing machinery*, which, in their slow *noiseless* operations, perfect execution of the parts they have to perform, sets all other inventions in the cotton trade at an immeasurable distance ! ! !) with calico-printing machines, &c., while their spinning machinery is still prohibited !—They do it under a license from the President of the Board of Trade, I understand ; but I should be obliged to any one that would inform me of the law by which this discretionary power is given to that board. At the time this question was before Parliament, there was a schism in the Cabinet of the sovereign junto ; the legislative part were for the free export of every thing their mother countries were in want of, but the Anglo-part would only consent to such parts as those I have mentioned ; not a single spindle connected with their "legal and honourable trade," would they suffer to be exported. Hence, owing to this schism, when this Bill was before a select Committee in the upper house, there was a lack

taking the liberty to ask them one plain question, viz. why they took such an *anxious leading* interest in the concocting, and management of that meeting in Manchester, six or eight years ago, respecting country bank notes, especially those of one pound which were then going to be issued at the *repeated*, and *urgent* request of the *Premier* of our country! For it was the strong, violent, mal-metaphysical speeches and resolutions of that tremendous meeting, and *their* influence at the helm afterwards (in which the Premier had *then* lost all controul) that gave the death blow to a circulating medium that had taken the *wisdom* and ACCUMULATING CAPITAL of ages to establish, and at the time was working well for *this* country in the opinion of a great majority. But even if it had been otherwise with those it concerned, I cannot see what *they* had to do with it, especially as they require so *very few* bank notes or sovereigns to forge out the raw material for their traffic in *this country*. ✻

I can clearly see the great advantages the foreign part of their junto would gain by giving the small notes such a deadly blow. First, by throwing the weavers on silk, cotton, and stuffs, in Macclesfield,

---

of evidence to carry it forward, and it would have been lost, I understood, had they not brought forward a *Frenchman*, who, for the last 24 years, has been almost solely employed in supplying France and Belgium from this country with skilful hands, plans, models, patterns, parts of machinery, machines complete, in short, with every thing they were in want of, all of which pay brokerage and tonnage in Liverpool as they go out, as well as raw cotton when it comes in!

In the execution of this arduous duty, this gentleman had learned to speak our language so well as not to be distinguished from a British subject: and though his surname when called before their

✻ I have been led to believe that a celebrated spinnery the Saxon hosiers have in Derbyshire, and another celebrated spinnery the Russians have in Lanark, as well at many others, have for many years so managed those extensive concerns as scarcely to require any thing of the kind, save occasionally *a little small change* once a month, when they balance their accounts with their work people.

206

Blackburn, and Bradford, out of work, (which would of course be the case when their masters were deprived of their usual circulating medium to pay them their wages) it would give more room in every market for the fabrics of their mother countries, and give facility to their reciprocity before-mentioned, in which we are to be the spinners, and the foreigners to do all the rest. And secondly that when they should have occasion to send as much cash (which they can any day raise on *their bills* before-mentioned) in the middle of their 1000lbs. bales of twist, (a mode of conveyance they have often resorted to for various purposes) as will pay for the winding, warping, and weaving of those raw materials in the countries to which they are sending them, these small notes would not do so well as sovereigns! All this I can see clear enough!! But I was quite shocked to see the spinners for export, who scarcely require any thing but small change, so cruel, as not only to lend their own

---

lordships would have told such a tale as would have sent him back unheard; yet, his christian name being a very common surname in North Britain, a certain M. P. brought him before that select Committee as Mr * * * * * * * * *, and the evidence of this gentleman, in favour of the export of machinery, was said to be so conclusive as to cause the repeal of so much of our old laws as to allow the export of those parts above-mentioned; but whether in a separate act, or by a clause in some other, I have yet to learn.

The express that was established about seven years ago as an experiment to see if the mail could be conveyed between London and Manchester in 18 hours, that besides killing so many valuable horses, cost government 6 or £7,000., and gave rise to that unreasonable speed that has since lost the country many valuable lives! was also the work of the *foreign part* of this junto; who, in this case, also became in part the executive, and were seen as the most active in procuring signatures amongst those with whom they had influence! (and who could refuse the request of *their* sovereigns) to a memorial that was sent to the Lords of the Treasury, in behalf of that measure. The *real* legitimate trade of Manchester wanted nothing of the kind. It was only these foreigners who wanted this expedition, that they might get their scraps of the foreign loans, and foreign bills, *in parcels to save postage and stamps!*

aid, but also to call in that of their great carrier and coal master, to assist them in giving that ungrateful and deadly blow ! Ungrateful I call it, as it fell on the weavers, the manufacturers, the capitalists, and bankers, to whom both *themselves* and their *great carrier and coal master*, were *solely* indebted for those means, by which they were enabled to do it so effectually.

One would have thought the former evils I have so profusely placed to the debit of their account, without adding to them the injury they have done to the towns and neighbourhoods in which their foreign mills are placed, by smothering their inhabitants with the magical *smoke and soot* they daily send out, while forging the raw material for this deadly traffic quite sufficient, without going any further! they had already driven tens of thousands of cotton weavers into the manufacture of silks, stuffs, &c. where (until a prohibition of the export of *their* raw material restores to them their legitimate trade) they are glad to get work at any price, and it was cruel to pursue them any further !

And here another striking instance is given of the " extraordinary advantages this country enjoys," as regards its manufactures and commerce. For though this overwhelming mass of low-priced labour, that was thrown on the Spitalfields, Dublin, Norwich, Bradford, and such like trade, for a time threw their old operatives into great disorder and confusion ; yet, the *incomparable* genius the cotton weavers of Paisley, Bolton, Manchester, Stockport, &c. &c. &c. brought along with them into the silk and stuff trades, in a few years, with the aid of some parts of the *new system*, so often mentioned, had so improved those manufactures, as to increase the demand for their fabrics in all parts of the world ; and in a ratio that promised a permanent good trade, not only to the hands heretofore employed in those branches, but also to the tens of thousands, who, (as interlopers) had been driven amongst them by the cause I have stated. Thus, finding there was labour and bread for them all, the two parties amalgamated, and all was working well, so far as the interest of *this country* was concerned, and would have continued so if our manufacture and commerce had been under *British* rule, and *British* protection.

But this state of "prosperity" was not to be endured by the foreign sovereign rulers in Manchester. For knowing their own strength (while they had me in bondage) they simultaneously put all their mal-metaphysical logic in motion, and as it were in a pellmell sort of way, levelling their aim at every link in this chain of "prosperity," with the "liberal march of intellect" they had enlisted into their service, they went to work, and by cutting up the circulating medium, (the very sinews of trade) opening our ports for worsted yarn, and fine woollen yarns, (such as Norwich, &c. manufacture their celebrated crape bombazines, &c. from) to go out, and also, for fabrics of every description to come in, &c. &c. &c., they, in the eighth part of a national moment, gave such a death blow to the old cable on which her ships, colonies, and commerce, had so long ridden triumphant, that had not old England, "by the extraordinary advantage her country enjoys," been in possession of a new patent cable and anchor of twenty times the weight and strength of her former one, (viz. the new system of manufacture, commonly called power-loom weaving,) firmly fixed as the rocks that surround her coast, invented, and brought into practical use, expressly for this very crisis! A crisis that had long been foreseen and foretold, that would come upon us, as certain as the change of the seasons; in which, but for this timely aid, her old vessel, whose union jack had so long kept every other state in awe! would certainly have foundered. And though some parts of her wreck might have been saved, yet, a great part of her valuable cargo called 3, 3½, 4, and 5 per cent. stock, would doubtless have gone to the bottom.

But though the country may be considered as rescued from that total ruin their measures were calculated (I had almost said intended) to bring upon her, yet, by the circulating medium being cut up, the ports open for piece-goods from all parts of the world of every description, and by giving the raw materials of *cotton and wool*, as they come from our magical machines, to be fabricated by European and Asiatic weavers, who can live comfortably on one to four pence per day, like blood hounds, they still pursue the poor million of operatives, in order that they may find no rest until they arrive in the woods of Upper Canada ; * the only means they have left by which they can bring *their* reciprocity to a permanent bearing.

To the two articles I have before given to shew that the trade are all of my opinion if they were at liberty to speak their minds, I will add another public document, that if any thing more is necessary, (though I have plenty of such like in reserve) I think this will be sufficient.

In introducing this article I must premise that as the Chancellor of the Exchequer, had so handsomely volunteered that a committee should be appointed to inquire into the merits of this question, though the session was far advanced at the time, yet, the trade on hearing such *glad tidings*, came out of their holes and corners in such a body, (except Manchester, where *all* were ready, but *no one* durst go first) on the same principle that a *round robin* is on special occasions brought forward, so as that no individual could be supposed to be in fear of losing

"Princes and Lords may flourish or may fade,
A breath can make them, as a breath has made;
But a bold *peasantry,* their country's pride,
When once destroyed can never be supplied."

his credit and business from any thing he might say or do. On this ground the following meeting was called, and though it is advertised as taking place in the sessions room, yet, I was told the crowd was so great before the business could commence, that they were obliged to adjourn to a large opening in the square or market.

Sessions-Room, 16*th May,* 1817.

At a numerous and respectable Meeting of the Master Cotton Spinners, Manufacturers, Landowners, and other Inhabitants of Great and Little Bolton, held pursuant to public notice given by the Boroughreeves and Constables of Great and Little Bolton, in the county of Lancaster,

SAMUEL HOUGHTON, Esq. BOROUGHREEVE, IN THE CHAIR:

" *Resolved,*

" That the exportation of Cotton Yarns, connected with the low price of labour abroad, has enabled the foreign manufacturer to produce Cotton Piece-Goods at so low a rate as to prevent the British manufacturers from bringing the same articles into the market, but by reducing the price of labour so much as to render it impossible for those whom they employ, to acquire the necessaries of life; the consequence of which has been an increase of pauperism beyond all precedent, and an alarming injury to the revenue.

" *Resolved unanimously,*

" That a petition be prepared, founded on the above resolution, signed by the Master Spinners, Manufacturers, Weaves, and other Tradesmen, and be presented to the Honourable the House of Commons, praying that they would take the subject into their serious consideration, and adopt such measures as may, on a full investigation of the facts, be thought most conducive to the interest of the trade of this country.

" *Resolved unanimously,*

" That the Chairman be desired to send the petition to the Members for this county, and to request their support thereto.

" *Resolved unanimously,*

" That copies of these resolutions be transmitted to other Members of the House of Commons, from the Counties of Lancashire, Yorkshire, and Cheshire, and that they be requested to support the same.

" *Resolved unanimously,*

" That a copy of these resolutions be forwarded to Sir OSWALD MOSLEY, Baronet, M. P. and that he be requested to give his support thereto.

" *Resolved unanimously,*

" That these resolutions be printed in hand-bills, and in the Manchester, Blackburn, and one London Newspaper.

Resolved unanimously,

" That the expences incurred by calling this Meeting, and for arrying these resolutions into effect, be paid by the Constables of Great nd Little Bolton.

"SAML. HOUGHTON.

" The thanks of this Meeting were unanimously given to the Chairman, for his impartial conduct in the chair."

" This meeting was attended by five or ten thousand persons composed of master-spinners, manufacturers, bleachers, printers, dyers, deputy lieutenants of the county, landowners, owners of weavers' cottages, shopkeepers, journeymen spinners, weavers, &c., when every resolution passed unanimously, except the first, which was opposed by *only one* master-spinner, and although that gentleman had set all his hands at liberty from work, in order to support him at the meeting, yet, on a shew of hands, *every one* of them put up *their* hands in favour of the *poor weavers ! ! !*   WM. RADCLIFFE."

" N. B.—What is to become of our country if documents like these are to be neglected ? and for no other reason but because it may not suit the fancy or interest of some individuals, (a few of whom unfortunately for the country, have seats in the house,) I hope his Majesty's government will weigh this remark as its importance demands!"

Towards the close of the sessions, it was hinted to me that one or two of my opponents to whom the foreign junto had committed the care of their veil on that trying occasion, were endeavouring to persuade ministers that the trade cared nothing about the export of cotton-twist, save myself, and a few whom I might influence. To meet these insinuations, I enclosed about a dozen papers in a letter to the Chancellor of the Exchequer, one of which was this Bolton hand-bill, with the remarks, and N. B. as now attached to it. The papers were returned to me agreeably to my request, with a handsome letter, and a mutual understanding took place, that certain memorials and petitions, that were moved for and ordered a few days afterwards, should be referred to a committee early in the sessions of 1818.

Since that period I have been obliged to remain silent upon this subject until about twelve months ago, when finding myself at liberty, and wishing to shew the trade that though I had been so long silent,

my principles were still the same, I sent the following letter to the Editor of the *New Times.* It appeared in that Paper on the 3rd of April, 1827, and
as it contains the outlines of the plan, I, as the messenger from the trade, laid before Government ten
years ago, as the remedy I have been devoting my
fortune and the whole of my time for the last twenty
seven years to accomplish, I will here record this
article in a more permanent way than that of a
Newspaper, which, with a note, shall conclude this
first part of my Narrative. And without further
comment I will leave my case to the impartial judgment of my country, perfectly satisfied in my own
mind, that though I have used *very strong language,*
I am still far within the bounds that *truth, equity,*
and *justice* have prescribed to me.

Deep-rooted cancerous diseases sometimes require
deep cuts from the lancet, and strong caustic reme-
dies. And as my country has long suffered most
grievously from a complaint of this kind, that was
and is curable any day, if by the lancet and caustic
I have so freely administered to the continental
sophistical quacks, (who erroneously persuaded a
few of our countrymen it was *their* interest to keep
her in this lingering state) we can once get her
independent of foreign rule and foreign influence, ✽

✽ The influence of this sovereign rule meets us in every quarter
to which we can turn our eyes; for the ink of this line was scarcely dry
when the post brought me a circular letter from the Secretary of the
Pitt Club, in Manchester, (of which I have long been a member) in
which I see a motion is to be made in the committee of management
on the first of May, to dispense with the annual dinner. The official
journal of these foreign sovereigns in Manchester, has long told us that
these Pitt dinners, and our Stockport Wellington Club dinners were very
disagreeable to " the powers that be," as they kept alive unpleasant
recollections. They have hither permitted them with a little official
grumbling, but I fancy they have now given their subjects a broad
hint that such dinners will no longer be considered legal, and that if
they do not voluntarily give them up, measures will be taken to compel
them.

the British empire and her colonies will dance for joy at their sudden recovery to their former healthy state, and those of my countrymen and personal friends to whom I may unavoidably have given a little temporary pain, will give me their hand, and with a friendly shake tell me that I have been *their best friend.*

To the Editor of the New Times.

"Sir,—Many of the readers of your excellent Paper, ten years ago, will, I doubt not, recollect the various articles you then admitted into your columns, on the subject of the export of cotton yarns ; in which articles, the distress that has for a long time prevailed in our manufacturing districts, was plainly and distinctly foretold.

"At that period I might be said to take the lead, and it was my intention, in the session of 1818, to have followed up the question, but circumstances, over which I had no controul, * not only prevented me from doing so, but even from reporting our progress (in the session of 1817) to the trade of London, and the manufacturing districts, who so handsomely supported us at the time (by memorials to his Royal Highness the Prince Regent, and petitions to the Hon. the House of Commons,) in order that, though I was restrained from any further pursuit, yet that some abler hand might be found to go on with the question, from the elevated station to which we had then carried it.

"But although the cause " was scotched, it was not killed." I am now at liberty—and if you will occasionally admit into your columns the remarks that I shall feel it my duty to submit to the public (especially while the emigration question is under consideration,) I feel confident that I shall be able to shew to our country that there is no occasion for the emigration contemplated, and also that it is not in that hopeless and forlorn situation that its general aspect unfor-

---

* This was the Manchester and Liverpool conspiracy before alluded to, in which they had resolved that the firm, in which my name stood at the head, should not have credit for another bag of cotton, if they found me taking *one further step in this business !* On the above being communicated to me by one of the party in February, 1818, (from the particular respect, as he said, that he felt towards me and my family,) I found myself placed in a very awkward situation ; for after the spinners had proscribed us in the market for twist, at a great expence we had been obliged to purchase machinery to spin our own, relying on the unlimited credit we then had for the raw cotton, however, in this dilemma, I was obliged to sit down and be silent ! ! !

I think I made out a pretty strong case with regard to the spinners' conspiracy in 1815 ; but if I am driven to unveil the latter, I shall do it to the very letter with their names.

I have ever since repented I did not at that very nick of time, *again* go to my banker, as I am *sure* he would have set me at liberty to go on with the question. And as this was their last forlorn hope ; on my banker removing it, their "*legal and honourable trade*" would soon have expired ; when instead of Peterloo meetings, rebellions in Scotland, the panic, and the crisis in which our country and her colonies are now placed, the last ten years would have exhibited a higher degree of " wealth, peace, and godliness," than the had ever before enjoyed.

tunately presents. On the contrary, I contend that the resources of the United Kingdom never stood so high and independent of all foreign competition, as regards manufactures and commerce, as at this moment, *provided we are true to ourselves.*

" As my wish is to be as brief as possible, I will, without further remark, come to my subject at once, viz. that it is not from the new system of manufacture commonly called power-loom weaving, having absorbed the labour that would otherwise have been given to the hundreds of thousands who are petitioning to be sent to the woods of Canada (from whence a great part of them would soon be found in the United States, employed on the twist spun and warped ready for the loom by the mills in Lancashire, as is now the case!) No, there is another cause; and the following statement, which I take from the *Manchester Courier* of the 26th October, 1826, will more clearly shew what that cause is, than any arguments I can give.

" 'The following is a summary statement of the exports of Cotton Yarn and Piece-Goods, for the week ending the 21st inst., abridged from the *Manchester Herald* of Thursday last :

Yarn... ....lbs.	1,719,162
Plain Calicoes ....yds.	2,229,214
Printed and dyed do.....................	1,546,832
Cambrics and Muslins....................	482,163
Cords, Velveteens, Jeans, &c............	242,184
Lace, Crape, Gauzes, and Net	481,982
Other descriptions......................	20,352

Total number of yards............ 5,023,057

Lbs. 1,749,162, would make............ 13,995,695 yds."

The calculation as to the number of yards of various descriptions of cotton goods, the above yarns would make, was given me by a manufacturer of long experience.

" It will be recollected that, in October, 1826, a great deal of business was done in Manchester, and many were in hopes that better times were approaching ; but the above exports of one of its best weeks will shew, that three-fourths of those exports were *raw material only,* a great part of which being fine yarn, such as the weavers of Paisley, Glasgow, Preston, Chorley, Bolton, and the circuit round Manchester, are so celebrated for weaving into the finest fabrics, no part of which has the power-loom ever interfered with ; and as it is this class of weavers, *particularly in Scotland,* whose distress presses them into the front ranks of the million who are said to be unemployed, or whose earnings are insufficient for their support, I contend, it is not from any thing the power-loom has done, but because the fine yarns, that ought to have been given out to them to work, are now allowed to be sent abroad, to be fabricated by the million of our rivals ! This, I aver, and *this only,* is the cause of their distress.

" In submitting my views as to the remedy, I will lay before the public the following outline, which was made at the time it bears date. It was not then published, being intended to be submitted to a Committee of the Honourable the House of Commons, had such an opportunity occurred ; and although ten years have passed over (with a loss of, at least, half a million sterling per week to our kingdom and her colonies,) yet I have never seen any reason to alter this plan ; and I am the more confirmed in it, as it has met the approbation of all that I have consulted upon it ; and could I name the individuals, they would be deemed capable of forming a correct opinion on so momentous a subject :

"Feb. 21, 1817.

" When the produce of our *cotton-mills* are exclusively confined to the supply of the looms of the United Kingdom, *they* will form the principal source of wealth to our country; but if the yarns *they* produce are still permitted to be exported, *these mills* will ultimately be the *cause* of its ruin.

"I make these bold assertions, knowing the loss these mills first brought on the country, by supplanting the labour of the whole race of spinsters, from whence, in former times, arose great resources, by the manufacture of various fabrics from the yarns they produced. But this source being for ever lost, it is high time we should make the most of the circumstances in which we are now placed. If, one hundred years ago, Government became alive to the evils of suffering the yarns produced by our spinsters to be exported in an *unmanufactured state,* their employment being healthy, unrestrained, and affording good wages, I think the following statement will shew how much more impolitic it is in us at this time to export the produce of our mills in an *unmanufactured state,* especially as we possess such exclusive advantages in *coal,* machinery, &c., so essential to the production of these yarns. To explain my views more clearly, the following sketch is humbly submitted—

"One hundred and forty-eight hands in one cotton-mill, middle size, turn off in one year 234,000 lbs. of 40's twist, which is generally taken as the average of the whole.

"Suppose 20,000,000 lbs. of cotton-yarns to be exported in one year, the number of hands required to spin it is only 12,649 ; of course this only exports the labour of a small number of hands; and suppose each hand to earn 12s. per week, this only amounts to £6,956 15s. as weekly wages.

"Forty-five years ago, it would have taken 2,368,000 hands to have spun the yarns, either in cotton, worsted, or linen, to have made the clothing the above yarns will make: and if each hand had only earned 2s. per week, this would have given a weekly circulation of £236,800, instead of the £6,956 15s.

"If the above yarns that are supposed to be exported, were woven in the United Kingdom, they would give employment to 153,846 people, besides what would be required afterwards in tambouring, bleaching, printing, dyeing, finishing, &c. &c.; and, as a prohibition to the export of yarns would do away *all* competition on the Continent in similar goods, it is fair to presume, that the weavers, &c. would again be able to earn the wages they did fifteen to twenty years ago, which, on the average, were about four times as much as they have been paid for the last ten months.

"In the present state of the trade, we will suppose 384,616 hands to be employed in the weaving department, reckoning two persons to each loom, and their average earnings to be 2s. 6d. each. This will amount to £45,577. The rapid improvements that would follow the prohibition would, *beyond a doubt,* give to the weavers the wages they earned fifteen to twenty years ago, and, then those now at work would receive each

Week.. £182,308
Instead of the.................................... £45,577

Giving an immediate advantage of £136,731

And to this we may fairly presume, that there would be additional employment for 100,000 more hands in the weaving department, working up part of the surplus yarns hitherto exported, and that they would earn £50,000 per week. This, added to the former advantage, would give a weekly circulation of £136,731 more than we now enjoy.

"To this may be added, far more than the above sum in labour and profits, to the manufacturers, tambourers, dyers, bleachers, printers, &c. ; and last, though not least, our old merchants, such as have stood the storm, would again embark in the trade of shipping cotton goods, the profits of which would raise this country to a higher pitch, in point of wealth, than it ever yet experienced.

"When a law is passed embracing the above principle, then, *and not till then*, shall we know and experience the true meaning of the old patriotic toast—*the plough*—THE LOOM—and *the sail*; or, in other words, agriculture, *manufactures*, and commerce.

"*Sketch humbly submitted for the outlines of a Bill to remedy the evil.*

"From the day of the Royal Assent being given to this Act, all cotton yarns (except not under three-fold cotton thread in the balls,) exported from the United Kingdom, for the first four months, to pay a duty of one farthing per hank of 848 yards—the next four months one halfpenny per hank, and the following four months three farthings per hank; afterwards to be prohibited, on penalties the same as now protect the woollen trade.

"Spinning mills, for the first four months, not to work more than ten hours per day; second four months, nine hours; third four months, eight hours per day; afterwards to regulate the hours of work, as may be deemed proper, by a Committee of Master Spinners, to be appointed by the Act enforcing the above laws.

"It is estimated, that the above duty would raise a fund sufficient to purchase such spinning mills as might be thrown out of work by the loss of the foreign market for their yarns."

"I will only add, that by inserting the above in your widely-circulated paper, you will not only render a great service to the manufacturers and merchants of the United Kingdom, and eventually to all the master spinners *themselves*, but you will also confer an additional obligation on,

"Sir, your faithful obedient servant,

" *March*, 1827.   "WILL. RADCLIFFE.

" N. B.—The writer wishes the greatest publicity to be given to the statements he has now laid before the public, that if he is in error, he may be corrected; but, on the other hand, if he has laid open the *real cause* of that universal distress the country now labours under, and, at the same time, pointed out the only remedy, he flatters himself, that every one interested in bringing back the United Kingdom and her colonies to their former healthy state, will cheerfully lend a helping hand in its accomplishment."

ERRATA.

PAGE.	LINE.	
10	22	for cotton, *read* mule.
14	17	— was, *read* is now.
19	24	— believe, *read* is now believed.
41	18	— shock, *read* stock.
63	5	The asterisk should be placed in the ninth line.
71	19	for its, *read* it.
88		The asterisk should be placed at the end of the tenth line in page 90.
90	20	for would, *read* could.
102	1	— crude, *read* cruel.
164	10	— flock, *read* stock.
169	34	— 4 to 9, *read* 49.